Introduction

"The Rolling Stones are more than just a group – they are a way of life."

It was a comment written by Rolling Stones manager Andrew Loog Oldham which appeared on the back of their first album. At the time he wrote it, this was just typical Oldham hyperbolic gibberish. But it would later become true – so true that the British Establishment tried to break the band.

Within a year of the release of that debut album in 1964, The Rolling Stones were being perceived by the youth of Britain and then the world as representatives of opposition to an old, cruel order – the antidote to a class-bound, authoritarian culture. A flavour of what a formal, starchy and censorious society the Stones' home country was when they first started is provided by an article on them in the *News Of The World* from '64. "The Stones give one the feeling that they really enjoy wallowing in a swilltub of their own repulsiveness," the newspaper declared. And the evidence for this? "They flick ash everywhere." Furthermore, "Charlie Watts, the zombie-eyed drummer, has a habit of dropping cigarette ends in other people's coffee cups – before they've finished drinking."

Of course, that passage represents the more comedic end of what the band – and their generation – were up against. The Stones' articulate guitarist and founder Brian Jones addressed the more serious nature of the injustices then underpinning society when in, early 1967, he talked of "... the basic immoralities which are tolerated in present day society – the war in Vietnam, persecution of homosexuals, illegality of abortion, [prosecution of people for] drug taking ... Our friends are questioning the wisdom of an almost blind acceptance of religion ... The ratio between affluence and reward for work done is all wrong ..." The only thing he left out of that list was freedom of speech, but then he had covered that ground in an October 1966 interview where he had spoken of curtailment of expression by censorious institutions. This, he said, had led to the hounding, both informal and formal, of film-makers, comedians and other artists assumed to have spoken out of turn or obscenely. "The days when men like Lenny Bruce and artist Jim Dine are persecuted are coming to an end," he said. "Young people are measuring opinion with new yardsticks and it must mean greater individual freedom of expression. Pop music will have its part to play in all of this."

Pop music indeed did, and the Stones were one of the most important players. Which is precisely why not long after those interviews, three members of the Stones were facing prison following a concerted attempt by the institutions of Britain to make an example of what were considered to be a bunch of upstarts.

Not that the band ever wrote protest songs *à la* Bob Dylan. Instead, the Stones provided leadership-by-example, becoming a focal point for the grievances of their fans' generation. Their unapologetic refusal to conform to conventions they found stupid or unjust was the kind of thing to instil bravery and determination in the hearts of those who agreed with them and make them stick to their ideological guns. This could be as subliminal as often as it could be conscious on their audience's part but one way or another the Stones helped to change the world. As Jones summed it up in a 1964 interview, "We've become kind of figureheads for all the kids who would like to rebel against authority. We are expressing something they cannot say or do."

None of this of course would matter a jot if The Rolling Stones had been mediocre musicians. Their power and influence came partly from the fact that they created some of the most exciting and innovative records in the history of popular music. So great was their art and so pervasive their cultural and artistic influence, they ultimately came to be considered the very template of a rock band.

Furthermore, that they were the epitome of youthful rebellion did not cause the end of their career when they ceased to be young. Their fans grew up with them, making them the very first rock group to prove that a band did not have to have a limited shelf life but could straddle the decades. Their tours today are the biggest money-spinners in music, testament to the loyalty generated by one of the most magnificent rock back catalogues of all time.

Herein is their story.

Sean Egan, May 2006

THE ROUGH GUIDE TO

The
Rolling Stones

by
Sean Egan

**ROUGH
GUIDES**

www.roughguides.com

Credits

The Rough Guide to The Rolling Stones

Design and layout: Trevor Bounford
Editor: Andrew Heritage
Picture Research: Louise Thomas, Cashou.com
Production: Aimee Hampson
This edition was prepared by Heritage Editorial and bounford.com
for Rough Guides Ltd.

Rough Guides Reference

Series editor: Mark Ellingham
Director: Andrew Lockett
Editors: Peter Buckley, Duncan Clark, Tracy Hopkins,
Sean Mahoney, Matt Milton, Joe Staines, Ruth Tidball

Publishing Information

This first edition published August 2006 by
Rough Guides Ltd, 80 Strand, London WC2R 0RL
345 Hudson St, 4th Floor, New York 10014, USA
Email: mail@roughguides.com

Distributed by the Penguin Group:
Penguin Books Ltd, 80 Strand, London WC2R 0RL
Penguin Putnam, Inc., 375 Hudson Street, NY 10014, USA
Penguin Group (Australia), 250 Camberwell Road, Camberwell, Victoria 3124, Australia
Penguin Books Canada Ltd, 10 Alcorn Avenue, Toronto, Ontario, Canada M4V 1E4
Penguin Group (New Zealand), Cnr Rosedale and Airborne Roads, Albany, Auckland, New Zealand

Printed in Italy by LegoPrint S.p.A

© Rough Guides Ltd. 2006
312 pages; includes index

A catalogue record for this book is available from the British Library

ISBN 13: 978-1-84353-719-9
ISBN 10: 1-84353-719-2

1 3 5 7 9 8 6 4 2

Contents

Contents cont.

ACKNOWLEDGEMENTS

The author would like to gratefully acknowledge the following for providing quotes and/or answers to queries for this book: Geoff Bradford, George Chkiantz, Bill Farley, Dave Hassinger, John Pasche, Roger Savage, Harry Shapiro, Dick Taylor and Pete Townshend.

Grateful Acknowledgements also for quotes used herein to all the books, films, programmes and websites either mentioned in the main text or listed in the Print And Screen section, plus the following sources (with apologies to anybody inadvertently omitted): *Rock On Wood* (Badman, Keith; Rawlings, Terry), *Keith Richards* (Victor Bockris), *The Rolling Stones Chronicle* (Massimo Bonanno), *Faithfull* (Marianne Faithfull), *The Complete Guide to the Music of the Rolling Stones* (James Hector), *Exile On Main Street* (Bill Janovitz), *The Dark Stuff* (Nick Kent), *Keith Richards* (Kris Needs), *Mick & Keith* (Chris Salewicz), *Rebel Knight* (Christopher Sandford).

I'd also like to extend my very grateful thanks to the following Rolling Stones experts who patiently provided help and/or research materials: Felix Aeppli, Alan Clayson, Christian Diemoz, Martin Elliott, Michael Lynch, Ian McPherson, Kevin Maidment, Wendy Ellison Mullen and Chris Menicou.

Picture Credits

Part One: The Life

From the Stones' first publicity shoot, 4 May 1963,
before playing a short gig at Battersea Pleasure Gardens.

Chapter 1:
Early Days

"This is what we like,
being mobbed by people.
This is what we want."

Brian Jones

Early Days
1961–1963

Maybe it was the quite disparate social backgrounds and musical tastes of the individuals who came together to form The Rolling Stones in the early Sixties that has contributed to their sustained invention and longevity. That and, above all, a sheer delight in playing music live. Over 45 years the Stones (as a band) have outlived their contemporaries and competitors and have played to more people than any other group of musicians. How did this extraordinary story start?

A Meeting of Minds

The famous meeting on a train between **Mick Jagger** and **Keith Richards** at Dartford Railway Station in October 1961 effectively marks the beginning of the story of The Rolling Stones. It's a meeting so glowing with poetic resonance that it feels apocryphal, but there is little doubt that it happened.

The paths of these two sons of **Dartford** had bisected before. Both were born in 1943, had lived a street apart when very young, and they had gone to the same primary school. Their paths diverged at the age of eleven. Although Richards later bought a cornet off Jagger when the latter was working on an ice cream trolley, by 1961 they had not met for a long time. Jagger was a middle-class son of a PE teacher and housewife while Richards had working-class origins, growing up in a council house, his father an unskilled practitioner of various trades. In '61, Jagger was a pupil at the **London School Of Economics**. Like Jagger, Richards also took the train to a seat of higher learning each morning, although they didn't normally catch the same train. Richards' place of study was **Sidcup Art College**.

It transpired that the two now had a bit more in common than the fact that they both hailed from the same town 16 miles southeast of London. Richards was intrigued, even amazed, to see that under his arm Jagger was carrying a selection of albums by the likes of **Chuck Berry, Little Walter** and **Muddy Waters**. Coverage of blues and R&B was then sparse indeed, when the BBC still had a monopoly of the radio waves and exercised that monopoly – perhaps understandably – to appeal to the

The Life

Art School Rockers

Keith Richards had no aspirations to be a painter but had opted to go to art school because it was a place in which he could practise his guitar chops while picking up a handy grant from the taxpayer at the same time. Many of his generation had exactly the same idea, and many art school students of the era went on to become famous musicians or singers, Jeff Beck, Eric Burdon, Eric Clapton, John Lennon, Jimmy Page and Pete Townshend among them.

Rockers from art school backgrounds who became famous in the Seventies include David Bowie and Roxy Music's Bryan Ferry. (Ferry – who attended an arts course at Newcastle University – was, in fact, one of the few art-schoolers-turned-pop-stars who started out with a serious interest in his subject.) Bowie and Roxy Music could be said to be artists who actually employed their art studies in their music and public personas, the unashamed artifice and self-consciousness of some of their work suggesting an ingrained concern with imagery which led them to be described in some quarters as 'art-rock'.

With the subsequent decline of the grants system in favour of student loans, British rock will now have to find a new source by which to nurture young talent.

Almost inevitably, Richards joined **Little Boy Blue and the Blue Boys**, a group of Jagger's mates and acquaintances who played R&B informally; Jagger was the vocalist and sometime guitarist. One of those mates and acquaintances was guitarist **Dick Taylor** who, it so happened, was also a student at Sidcup. Taylor noticed a change in the band almost immediately. His words about it bring to mind so many subsequent reviews of Stones records and concerts in which it has been observed that Richards is the engine-house of the Stones' sound: "… you could feel something holding the band together." Similarly, when Taylor also told a journalist, "Keith sounded great – but he wasn't flash," he was succinctly making the point that has been made (sometimes over the course of entire books) that Richards manages to be one of the ultimate guitar gods while not indulging in the masturbatory meanderings of many lead guitarists.

Mick also seems to have appreciated something was in the air, even if subliminally: he began drifting away from the guitar and concentrating on the **harmonica**, an instrument on which his proficiency – several musicians attest – is genuinely significant. It was at the point of Richards' arrival that Jagger's mother, Eva, began to worry. It was then that she felt for the first time that Jagger was thinking of pursuing professionally what had hitherto been merely a hobby. Her misgivings seem from today's perspective, of course, perfectly ludicrous but at the time were perfectly right: the blues was a form of music created from the experience of

lowest common denominator; so, lovers of this type of music existed virtually isolated from each other and, of course a concept like the internet which could point you in the direction of fellow enthusiasts was literally the stuff of science fiction. To encounter another by chance was like meeting a long-lost brother.

What Is Rhythm & Blues?

Though they eventually acquired the title "The Greatest Rock 'n' Roll Band in the World", The Rolling Stones were originally anxious to emphasize that they were a rhythm and blues, not a rock 'n' roll, band. Debate on what rhythm and blues – or R&B – constitutes is practically endless.

R&B was essentially a faster, more exciting and less depressive form of its American black music antecedent, the blues (often referred to as twelve-bar blues), by virttue of it being crossed with 'jump blues', an up-tempo, almost big-band form of the blues, that had jazz influences. Though both the blues and R&B were characterised by 12-bar music progressions, R&B was less repetitive (the blues usually involved the repeat of the first and third lines of each verse), less depressing (not so inclined to laments about love and loss) and more exciting (inclined to breakneck tempos). R&B dispensed with the brass sections of jump blues in favour of a slimmed-down set-up reliant on guitars. Rock 'n' roll was a mixture of black and white forms of music, combining R&B with country music. Though there are obviously overlaps between the genres, Eddie Cochran, Bill Haley and Elvis Presley were 'rock 'n' roll', while Bo Diddley, Jimmy Reed and Muddy Waters were R&B. Chuck Berry is usually considered a rock 'n' roll artist but probably stands squarely between the two brands.

Though rock 'n' roll was very exciting, to some it was diluted: R&B was grittier and less tainted by the whiff of commercial compromise. This feeling began to grow stronger when the first wave of late Fifties rock 'n' roll heroes began to fade and were replaced by less wild-looking and sounding artists like Bobby Darin and Bobby Vee, who managed to squeeze all the grit out of the genre while utilizing a never-changing repertoire of increasingly cheesy-sounding licks and progressions, a stagnant situation which lasted until The Beatles completely rejuvenated rock 'n' roll in the early Sixties.

To add to the confusion, rock 'n' roll – or more often 'rock' – eventually became a term used as an umbrella title for just about all post-Elvis popular music, including R&B. Even more confusingly, the term R&B was hijacked in the Nineties to describe a completely new form of black music which had nothing in common with rhythm and blues, other than that most of its practitioners were black.

Clearly, these definitions are a vexed and never-ending subject for those passionate about it, and reams have been devoted to the issue. However, it so happens that one of the best entries into the debate was made by none other than pre-fame Rolling Stones member Brian Jones in a letter to *Jazz News* published in October 1962:

"It appears there exists in this country a growing confusion as to exactly what form of music the term 'Rhythm & Blues' applies to. There further appears to be a movement here to promote what would be better termed 'Soul Jazz' as Rhythm & Blues. Surely we must accept that R&B is the American city Negro's 'pop' music – nothing more, nothing less.

"Rhythm & Blues can hardly be considered a form of jazz. It is not based on improvisation as is the latter. The impact is, and can only be, emotional. It would be ludicrous if the same type of pseudo-intellectual snobbery that one unfortunately finds contaminating the jazz scene were to be applied to anything as basic and vital as rhythm & blues.

"It must be apparent that Rock 'n' Roll has a far greater affinity for R&B than the latter has for jazz, insofar as Rock is a direct corruption of Rhythm and Blues whereas jazz is Negro music on a different plane, intellectually higher, though emotionally less intense."

being black, American and oppressed. It being clearly the case that nobody would want to hear white, privileged, welfare state English kids playing facsimiles of it rather than the real thing, it was patently obvious that making a living – let alone carving a career - by playing it was an absurd concept. If any of the embryonic Stones had actually sat down and thought about it, especially the very bright Jagger, they would have come to the same conclusion. History, however, is not just made by rational decisions. Something that had nothing to do with logic made the band members persevere with, indeed increase their commitment to, the group. Ultimately, this would lead to some members of the band achieving greater commercial and artistic success than every one of their blues heroes and amassing wealth beyond the dreams of even the most successful graduate of the London School of Economics.

Going Public

By March 1962, the Blue Boys came to the quite staggering realization that there were actually several hundred people in Britain who were into the same kind of music as they. It was in that month that one **Alexis Korner** started a weekly R&B club in the Ealing Club, West London. Richards and Taylor stared in amazement at the advertisement for it that Korner placed in weekly music paper, *Melody Maker*. Jagger was similarly astounded when they showed it to him. Korner's own band **Blues Incorporated** were on the bill, and began packing the punters in. Within a month, the membership list of the club exceeded its physical capacity by a factor of four. People started making what could almost be described as a pilgrimage to Ealing. Part of the reason for this pilgrimage was a club policy to allow the enthusiastic and untried a spot on stage. Amongst those who took advantage of this policy were Eric Burdon (later to become famous as frontman of Newcastle combo The Animals), Paul Pond (who later became Paul Jones, singer with Manfred Mann) and one **Brian Jones** – Elmo Lewis as he was styling himself on the evening in April 1962 when Mick and Keith first clapped eyes on him onstage playing slide guitar in the style of his hero Elmore James, whose skill in that capacity had prompted the *nom de guerre*. Jagger and Richards approached the diminutive but extraordinarily handsome Jones after his performance. When Jones told them of his musical tastes in his upper middle-class accent, it turned out – notwithstanding the R&B-alluding pseudonym – that he was actually more into jazz than Jagger and Richards. The latter started turning him on to the likes of other R&B merchants like **Bo Diddley** and **Jimmy Reed**.

Also more jazz-oriented was one Charlie Watts, a poker-faced but agreeable drummer who could frequently be seen at the club. More boogie woogie-oriented was pianist **Ian Stewart** – universally known as 'Stu' – whose notably lantern-jawed face and gruff-but-lovable persona were also often in attendance. Like Jagger, Watts would sometimes 'sit in'

The Life

with Blues Incorporated. In Jagger's case, this involved singing three songs on Saturdays in the Ealing Club and three at the **Marquee Jazz Club** in Soho, where Korner's band had secured a Thursday night residency. When Jagger's recruitment was actually mentioned in mainstream music magazine *Disc*, the first step had been taken to Jagger becoming one of the world's most famous men. The first steps were also in motion to him becoming the ultimate rock frontman of all: observers have recalled him showing unusual stage extrovertism at this juncture in the way he would shake his head around onstage.

Interestingly, despite Eva Jagger's misgivings about her son beginning to take playing R&B a little too seriously for her liking upon Richards's arrival, Richards himself later stated that it was the arrival into their circle of Jones that led to the impetus to create what he termed "a real band". The first pubic performance by a band billing themselves as **The Rolling Stones** occurred on 12 July, 1962 at the Marquee. The event had come about because Blues Incorporated had been offered the accolade of a BBC radio broadcast on the programme *Jazz Club*. Unfortunately, though the group boasted seven members, the BBC

Jagger fronting Cyril Davies' All-Stars at the Ealing Club, 1962. From left, Dave Stevens, Dick Heckstall-Smith, Alexis Korner, Jack Bruce, MJ and Cyril Davies on mouth harp.

would only agree to pay for six. Korner good-naturedly told Jagger that they would turn down the gig. Jagger insisted they go ahead with it, reasoning that the extra publicity would bring more punters into the clubs for subsequent shows. Jagger has over the years been proven to be a very astute/manipulative (delete as per moral standard) individual and it may be the case that he was aware of just what an opportunity the absence of Blues Incorporated would constitute. Specifically, Jagger got to sing an entire set's worth of songs as The Rolling Stones played the support slot to a band fronted by Long John Baldry. The Stones that momentous night con-

No. 224   Week ending July 7, 1962
Every Thursday, price 6d.

KORNER CANCELS

OWING to a "Jazz Club" broadcast on July 12, Alexis Korner and his Blues Incorporated will not be featured in their weekly session at the Marquee that night.

Instead, their place will be taken by a new rhythm and blues group, Mick Jagger and the Rolling Stones, together with another group headed by Long John Baldry.

The critical moment.

sisted of Jagger on vocals, Richards and Jones (still insisting on being known as Elmo Lewis) on guitars, Dick Taylor on bass, Ian Stewart on piano and future Kinks-member Mick Avory on drums.

The handle of this *ad hoc* group would come to seem a superbly apposite one to the wider world as it became incrementally more well known. '**Rolling**' naturally had a poetic appropriateness for its connection to rock (although a still R&B-purist minded Jagger did say to *Jazz News* at the time, "I hope they don't think

we're a rock 'n' roll outfit"). It also created inevitable endless punning headlines and media slogans centred around the old proverb "A rolling stone gathers no moss", most of them contrived or meaningless but some of them – when applied to the image they acquired of restless young men anxious to kick over the traces – highly appropriate. It also lent itself to chicdom-granting abbreviation: there was something naturally cool-sounding about referring to them as simply "**the Stones**". Later, as the band got older than anyone ever conceived anybody continuing to make rock music would or should (i.e. over thirty), the name was prone to slightly contemptuous punning ("the Strolling Bones", the "Groaning Bones"). All of which makes it remarkable that the name was not borne of inspiration but of what Richards describes as "panic". Brian Jones was on the phone informing *Jazz News* of the first gig and was stumped when asked the name of the band: they hadn't decided on one at this point. Richards says that Brian got the name Rolling Stones from '**Rolling Stone Blues**' by Muddy Waters, a legend that has become accepted as fact. Jagger's friend Dave Godin, however, was there when the name was alighted on, and insists it came from his copy of the Muddy Waters' *Mississippi Blues* EP which did not contain that track but did feature '**Mannish Boy**', which boasts the line "I'm a rollin' stone". (Incidentally, the billing that first evening was "Mick Jagger and the Rolling Stones.")

Ian Stewart was not impressed by the moniker. In a classic example of Stu sarcasm, he harrumphed that the handle was terrible, saying: "It sounded like the name of an Irish show band or something that ought to be playing at the Savoy." Maybe so but, despite that and its *ad hoc* origins, the name stuck forever.

The Stones continued rolling – or rollin': the name was actually rendered with an apostrophe in place of a 'g' in the early days, although not at that first gig – from then on, playing interval spots at the Marquee and a Saturday evening residency at the **Ealing Club**. Some disdained them for their modernism. How quaint it now seems that a group could attract opprobrium on the R&B scene by playing covers by the likes of Chuck Berry and Bo Diddley, whose last big hits and quintessential recordings were then already four or five years in the past. Still, even the supposedly outrageously populist and trendy Stones were horrified when drunks at the Ealing Club would sometimes demand to hear out-and-out rock'n'roll numbers like 'Ready Teddy'.

After Dick Taylor left the band in September 1962 to concentrate on his art course, the group became essentially Mick, Keith, Brian and Ian Stewart, with convenient people

JAZZ AT THE **MARQUEE**
165 OXFORD STREET W 1 (Nr OXFORD CIRCUS)

Friday, January 11th
★ **BILL NILE'S DELTA JAZZMEN**
★ **KANSAS CITY JAZZMEN**
(Members 4/-   Guests 5/-)

Saturday, January 12th
★ **JOE HARRIOTT QUINTET**
★ **DON RENDELL QUINTET**
(Members 6/-   Guests 7/6)

Sunday, January 13th
★ Big Band Night
★ **JOHN WILLIAMS BIG BAND**
★ **PETE SHADE QUARTET**
(Members 4/-   Guests 5/-)

Monday, January 14th
★ Rhythm and Blues Night
★ **BLUES BY SIX**
★ Pete Deuchar's
★ **COUNTRY BLUES**
(Members 4/-   Guests 5/-)

Wednesday, January 16th
★ **HUMPHREY LYTTELTON BAND**
★ **GORDON BAKER OCTET**
(Members 5/-   Guests 6/-)

Thursday, January 17th
★ Rhythm and Blues Night
★ **CYRIL DAVIES' ALL-STARS**
plus the fabulous
★ **VELVETS**
★ **ROLLIN' STONES**
(Members 4/-   Guests 5/-)

The Marquee play bill for 11-17 January, 1962. Note competition and spelling.

drafted in on bass and drums. Jones was the sort-of leader of the group, especially in his own eyes. Though he wasn't the frontman on stage, there was a certain logic to this. As Richards has admitted, Jones was the one who had been most keen to put together a serious ensemble rather than a loose group of kids who assembled for aimless blows. He was also the most physically striking and noticeable of the group. There was also the fact that his well-educated tones conferred on him a certain gravitas, something that came in handy when negotiating with the likes of club owners.

By the latter half of 1962, Jagger, Jones and Richards were living in a two-room London flat together. They took up residence in **Edith Grove**, off the **King's Road** in south-west London. Here, they lived in the sort of squalor that comes so naturally to young men. They also endured the type of hardships that are only bearable to people who imagine themselves to be making sacrifices in pursuit of an attainable target. The only things keeping them from starving were the food parcels despatched from Dartford by Keith's mum, Mick's college grant, cadging food off other residents of their building (they had the middle floor of a three- storey structure) and stealing beer bottles from some teachers resident on the top floor for the pennies their return to their place of purchase obtained. The trio would soon be joined in the flat by a friend, James Phelge. Phelge's name would be made famous by his flatmates when – upon their arrival into the realm of recording artists – they would attri-

bute band-written compositions to '**Nanker, Phelge**'. (The Nanker part was a description of a mildly disgusting band party trick involving pushing up one's nose while pulling down the skin below the eyes.) Phelge received no remuneration for this, but what price your name being granted rock immortality?

The move to the capital for the three-man Stones nucleus was naturally motivated by a deepening of their resolve to make further progress as a band. As someone whom Richards describes as "unemployable", Jones would presumably be of the mind that he had nothing to lose. The ever-cautious Jagger, meanwhile, was hedging his bets, continuing to attend classes at the LSE. Richards was, in a sense, the one making the sacrifice: he had dropped out of art college in pursuit of his muse. "We weren't layabouts," Jones later insisted. "We were so genuinely dedicated to our music that everything we did had to be connected with rhythm and blues." Richards later recalled the consequences of he and Jones being cooped up, penniless, in Edith Grove in the winter of 1962/63. There was nothing to do but sit and play guitar. They studied and imitated the style of, in particular, Jimmy Reed while shivering in overcoats. As Richards later said, "In English bands, you had one hot picker and another one who just strummed. There was no attempt to make a cohesive sound out of the two guitars; it was: 'You're rhythm, you're lead' … it should be seamless … you shouldn't ever hear the joins – like good editing." Thus was born the meshed rhythm guitar sound that has characterized the Stones' sound for all of their career, except the five-year interlude with a conventional lead guitarist that was the Mick Taylor era. Enforced practice seems to have also have resulted in Jones acquiring a skill on the mouth harp. Richards recalled coming back to the flat and seeing an excited Jones coming out to the top of the stairs to tell him he'd figured the instrument out, then proceeding to wailingly demonstrate his new ability.

Getting The Act Together

A line-up of the Stones first entered a recording **studio** in October '62. Jagger, Richards, Jones and Stewart were joined by **Tony Chapman** on drums (there was no bassist) as they laid down 'You Can't Judge A Book By The Cover', 'Soon Forgotten' and 'Close Together', by Bo Diddley, Muddy Waters and Jimmy Reed respectively. The acetate was sent to Neville Skirmshire of EMI with a view to the mighty British recording and manufacturing institution signing the band as artists. It was rejected. "You'll never get anywhere with that singer," sniffed someone at the **Decca** label to Tony Chapman after hearing it, a comment that must rank alongside the (alleged) "guitar-groups-are-on-the-way-out" dismissal of The Beatles by Decca's Dick Rowe in the ranks of utterly unsound record company judgements.

The band persevered, seeking to obtain a permanent bass player. It was Chapman who provided the connection to **Bill Perks**, who would later change his surname to Wyman. He was a quiet individual and at least five years older than all the other Stones except Stewart, who was only two years Wyman's junior. Wyman already had a wife, a son, and a day job. He was less familiar with R&B than the Stones, having been playing more rock 'n' roll-oriented material. Wyman turned up for an audition at the Wetherby Arms pub in Chelsea one snowy Friday in December 1962. He found Mick reasonably pleasant, and Stu friendly. Keith and Brian remained sullen until such time as he gave them cigarettes and bought a round of drinks.

It's a part of Stones mythology that Wyman only obtained the job with the Stones because they were impressed by his **Vox AC-30** amplifier, which was a luxurious contrast to the two battered amps the group had to their name and that, had they not wanted to obtain such an impressive piece of equipment for their set-up, they would not have countenanced the introduction of this sober and mature individual into their young and anarchic stable. This certainly seems to be true about the actual recruitment of Wyman – Wyman has admitted it himself – but from that it has been extrapolated (sometimes by Stones members themselves, at least implicitly) that his services were only retained because of it. This is patent nonsense, as absurd as that other bitchy rock 'n' roll myth that Ringo Starr was not a great drummer. Wyman and **Charlie Watts** would

The Life

later be hailed by many as the greatest rhythm section in rock history. Are we to believe that Watts carried Wyman and covered up his uselessness for three decades to possibly the most merciless audiences of any art form?

Speaking of Watts, after having effectively gifted them Wyman, in early 1963, Chapman found himself nudged aside to make way for the poker-faced stickman when the band decided Chapman wasn't up to their requirements. The Stones were starting their career with the same ruthlessness with which they would maintain it. As Richards once remarked, "... we really didn't care about anybody – just took advantage of everybody." But just as The Beatles' indubitably callous dismissal of their drummer Pete Best a few months previously resulted in their definitive and un-improvable line-up – which is as much about inter-band chemistry, both personal and musical, as it is about technical skill – so the final piece of the jigsaw of The (original) Rolling Stones was put in place by Watts joining the fold. This wasn't merely because Watts was a technically excellent drummer, but also due to him approaching the music from **a lateral angle**, as a consequence of his lack of knowledge about R&B and even rock 'n' roll. As Jagger has said: "... he just played with more of a jazz feel. And that's why The Rolling Stones was a more interesting band than bands like Freddie and The Dreamers, Herman's Hermits, The Searchers or The Hollies... We had a much broader, much deeper musical background."

The date of the **historic** first Rolling Stones gig featuring Jagger, Richards, Jones, Wyman and Watts in the line-up – along with Ian Stewart, of course – is something of a mystery. In his book *Rolling With The Stones*, Wyman cites a performance at the Ealing Jazz Club on 12 January as the gig in question. But as Felix Aeppli, author of *The Rolling Stones, 1962-2002: The Ultimate Guide To The First Forty Years*, points out, "It will probably never be determined which was the first performance by The Rolling Stones to feature both Bill Wyman on bass and Charlie Watts on drums. Bill Wyman contradicts himself on the subject, stating the January 14, 1963 date at the Flamingo in *Stone Alone*, while quoting the January 11, 1963 show at the Ricky Tick Club in *Blues Odyssey* as the first common concert." He adds, "It's funny that Bill has come up with a third date in *Rolling With The Stones.*"

The big **breakthrough** in turning the Stones from just another jobbing band into a small-scale phenomenon – itself usually the prerequisite to being considered sign-worthy by record companies – came when they secured a residency at the **Station Hotel**, Richmond, Surrey, twelve miles outside London. This venue was managed by a tall and larger-than-life figure named **Giorgio Gomelsky**. The Stones made their debut there on 24 February, 1963. Before long, Gomelsky was acting as the band's manager too. Unfortunately for him, this arrangement was a verbal one.

In March 1963, the Stones made another foray into a recording studio when band friend **Glyn Johns** – later to become one of rock's

A posed publicity shot at the Richmond Station Hotel – Gomelsky's Crawdaddy Club, 1963. Ian Stewart top right.

most celebrated producers – offered to oversee a session for them at London's IBC studios. The band laid down a selection of five songs that just about every R&B band in the country had in their repertoire: 'Diddley Daddy', 'Road Runner', 'I Wanna Be Loved', 'Honey What's Wrong' and 'Bright Lights, Big City'. Brian in particular – who Johns recalled very much as the leader of the band – was pleased by the results, and years subsequently still felt it captured something about them that their later commercially-released product did not. Record companies were less overwhelmed. When the acetate was hawked around companies by Johns' boss, George Clewson, it was met with the response that such music was "**too uncommercial**" for the charts.

But the Stones quickly became a sensation at the Station Hotel for their pile-driving R&B – which usually now culminated in a twenty-minute rendition of 'Pretty Thing' or the 'Crawdad' (both were Bo Diddley tunes, and the club was renamed the **Crawdaddy Club** after the latter). However, like all bands who become not merely respected artists but musical and social phenomena, they were also the object of attention because of their image. Pictures of them from the time show young men with hair that wasn't parted, was not slicked back with gel, and which covered their ears. Unremarkable by today's standards, but this was 1963, and although **The Beatles**' mop-tops were beginning to acquire some kind of social respectability – partly because of their charming and endearing public personas – the Stones' hair-length and scruffy demeanours genuinely suggested menace to the majority of the public. **Pete Townshend** conveys a sense of this in comments he made to this author in 2003: "The Rolling Stones, looking like a bunch of reprobate tramps, used to walk past the [art] college on their way up to the Ealing Club to do their concerts and I never had the fucking courage to go and see them play then. It was very much like the Sex Pistols

had arrived. It was really subversive [and] they hadn't quite got their band together but a couple of times I saw them in the streets and it was like seeing Martians."

Enter ALO

Mid-April 1963 saw the Stones gain their first significant **press coverage** with a quite lengthy article in the *Richmond and Twickenham Times*. The article revealed that attendance at the Crawdaddy had gone from 50 to 320 during the Stones' two-month occupancy. Such was the stir they were creating that no less than The Beatles popped in to see their set on 14 April. Admittedly, they had been urged to do so by Gomelsky – who knew they were filming in nearby Teddington and that the club was on their way back to London – but The Beatles were impressed by what they saw. Though The Beatles were then merely the latest chart sensation – with two hits to their name, they were still a year or so away from being the most famous and loved people in the world – their recommendation carried some weight. George Harrison is said to have informed Decca's Dick Rowe that he should sign the group. **Andrew Loog Oldham**, who ensured the formal signing of the band to that label, acknowledges that Rowe had prior knowledge of the group when he contacted him about them. Oldham himself saw the Stones two Sundays after The Beatles had. Though he was alerted to the group by a *Record Mirror* journalist named Peter Jones, Oldham ironically was then working as press

The Management. Andrew Loog Oldham behind shades and desk , with lots of telephones. Jagger looking interested, Easton dramatically cropped.

aide to Beatles manager Brian Epstein, having helped promote their second and third singles. When Oldham saw the Stones, he was bowled over. "When I heard them play I realized that this was what my life was all about and what all the preparation was for," Oldham said. "These people needed me and I needed them and we could finally go somewhere together." He elaborated in his autobiography that the combination of **music and sex** was something he had never encountered in any other group. Oldham determined that he would be this band's manager. Three days later, he was – and unlike Gomelsky's gentleman's pact, this one was on paper. At 19, Oldham was younger than any of the Stones.

However, it wasn't quite as easy as it sounds. Oldham couldn't simply become the Stones' representative because – and this shows just what a restrictive and petty society Britain then was, and why the **free spirit** of the Stones would come to seem a threat to those high up in its hierarchy – in order to be able to manage the Stones he had to be an agent, and in order to be an agent he had to apply to the London County Council for an agent's licence, which was only available to those over 21, with registered offices. Additionally, he had no money. He decided to approach one **Eric Easton**, who though a completely strait-laced figure was an agent, with a proposition that the two go into business together. Easton would provide the capital, Oldham the ideas and the contacts. Easton only grudgingly agreed to give up his weekly TV treat of *Sunday Night At*

The London Palladium to catch a Stones set at the Crawdaddy. When he did so, he smiled at Oldham and said "**All right**". Little did any of the principals know of the epoch-marking nature of Easton's understatedly enunciated decision: within three-and-a-half years, it was a notorious incident involving the Stones' behaviour on an edition of *Sunday Night At The London Palladium* on which they were appearing that would underline the very sociological revolution they were both embodying and causing.

Signing Up

As for to whom to try to sell the Stones, Oldham later said, "You just had to go to the person who turned down The Beatles. It was logical. Dick Rowe should be remembered not as the man who turned down The Beatles but the man who signed The Rolling Stones. He was great. He gave me my head." Indeed, when the Stones did sign with Decca, they actually had a better deal than did The Beatles with EMI, because Oldham and Easton did not sign a standard contract, whereby the record company owned their recordings outright. "We owned the masters, right from the beginning," pointed out Oldham. Oldham and Easton figured that if they contracted recording studios independently, they could then 'lease' the products of such recordings back to the record label, whilst retaining ownership of the master tapes. This lease situation was hugely important. It meant that, unlike any other groups of the era, the Stones could never be told what to record or release by their record company. Even when they were nobodies, they had complete artistic freedom. In addition, the lease deal would – if its benefits had not been rendered moot by business entanglements and settlements with another manager, **Allen Klein**, many years later – have made the Stones as rich as Croesus (i.e. slightly better off than they currently are).

The management agreement that Brian Jones signed with Easton and Oldham on the band's behalf was for three years. The Oldham-Easton deal did not come without some heavy prices. Gomelsky was nudged unceremoniously out of the picture. Additionally, Oldham had reservations about Ian Stewart. Those reservations were clear to Roger Savage who, on 10 May, 1963 engineered the first Rolling Stones studio session to result in a commercially-released record. The tracks chosen for the session were 'Come On', a lesser-known Chuck Berry number, and a cover of Muddy Waters' version of **Willie Dixon**'s 'I Want To Be Loved'.

Despite his interaction with the band at a crucial juncture of their career – albeit a brief one – Savage has not been sought out by many journalists down the years. Speaking to this author, he revealed that there was a certain synchronicity to the way he and Andrew Loog Oldham became interested in the Stones. "I met him at **Olympic** where I was working as a junior engineer," he says. "I read something about this group called The Rolling Stones in some magazine, little tiny article. The maga-

zine was called *Poparound*. It was a real poppy magazine. I can't remember what it said but it was, 'Look out for The Rolling Stones... Playing at...' I was just interested in hearing them so I went down there. I had no intention of doing anything with them, I was interested in seeing what they were like. I went there and I bumped into Andrew. I was very excited when I heard them. I remember a Bo Diddley song they were doing with maracas. They certainly stood out as being **a bit different** to what I heard... I was impressed... There was something about them. I got that feeling as soon as I heard them. A lot to do with their look as well as their sound. So I felt that they were something special... I probably would have approached them if Andrew wasn't there. He was definitely there to do something with them. I remember offering him, 'If you need any help, let me know'. We ended up doing an illicit night session that wasn't official. We arranged to get a demo together to try and get them a contract. I just wanted the chance to record because I was still coming up through the ranks of engineering. I was just dead keen and I was happy just to do it. I didn't have a deal worked out with Andrew – he was a sort of a mate."

Olympic Studios was located in the West End of London and was one of the emerging breeds of relatively rock-oriented independent studios in the capital. Come the late Sixties, and its relocation to Barnes, on the outskirts of London, the Stones virtually lived there, recording some of their greatest music under its roof, but in 1963 they didn't have the

The Life

resources to afford its rates. "I had the keys to Olympic," reveals Savage. "I let them in through the back door when no-one else was there. I'm not sure what time it was. I remember Mick Jagger arriving with a whole lot of books under his arm, so it must have been straight after college. I felt that Brian Jones seemed to be the **dominant** figure. He certainly was the edgy one that was very sort of serious and seemed to be perhaps more in control… I remember Brian Jones being a bit surly, but maybe that's what he was like all the time. He just struck me as being a bit serious and may not have been that happy about what they were playing. There were some other people at the session, not just Andrew and the band but a couple of other people. At that stage of course they hadn't had much experience so they weren't very pushy to me as the engineer so I pretty much did it, and Andrew. There was not a lot of input that I remember from anyone in regard to the recording, except that Andrew wanted me to take the piano down or almost out actually."

Though **Stewart** naturally attended the session as a full member of the group, it would seem that Oldham was forcing him to go through a cruel pretence: Oldham had no intention of allowing him to contribute audibly to the record. Savage: "There wasn't a lot of aggro going on and I wasn't aware of any.. apart from the fact that I felt a bit embarrassed taking the piano out and then the group coming up to the control room, which was on the second floor at Olympic, and then playing it back and nobody saying anything because there was no piano even though Ian Stewart was playing. It was just not even discussed. I don't know whether [Stewart] thought it was me doing it or what but it was the beginning of pushing him out of the group…"

Savage had mixed feelings about the finished '**Come On**': "It's quite simplistic, and particularly I remember that strange bass solo in the middle. It probably might have been better with a piano there… I think on reflection when you listen to the sound it's not the Stones' sound and that's probably why they might not have been happy with the fact that it was what you call a 'clean' pop recording. After that session – which is the only one I did do – they then developed more their characteristic, loose sound. More **dirtier** sound."

'Come On' was released on 7 June, 1963 and would ultimately climb to No.21.

Role Playing

Jagger quit the LSE as did Wyman his day job at around this time. Despite the fact that 'Come On' nudged the **Top Twenty** (Oldham later admitted he bought it into the charts), within weeks it was permanently disowned by the group. Oldham turned up at a gig they were performing and got into a row with them when he was told that the song would no longer be part of the band's live repertoire. Jagger later said of the record, "It really was shit". He is too hard by far on an aggressive and well-played debut.

Oldham's **bewilderment** at the Stones' purism was born of the same commercial zeal which led him to dress the group in matching hound's-tooth jackets for a prestigious appearance on TV pop show *Thank Your Lucky Stars* that his gift of the gab had secured them that July. It was when Stewart learnt that only five of those hound's-tooth creations had been ordered for the appearance that the pianist fully realized what was being done to him. Oldham had decided Stewart's jutting chin was not pop-star material, and six was too many members for a band when, even *sans* Stewart, would still be one over the number that The Beatles had recently set as the ideal for a chart group. Jones attempted to mollify Stewart by saying, "We'll make sure you get a sixth of everything".

The party line amongst the Stones has always been that 'Stu' took the decision stoically or at least philosophically. James Phelge, who was there when he was informed of the decision, recalled that he seemed on the verge of tears. This isn't surprising – Stewart had only recently experienced the **euphoria** of now being a recording artist. Stewart told Philip Norman, "I thought, I can't go back to [workplace] ICI after this. I might as well stay with them and see the world." He became the band's road manager – though one does wonder whether even that gesture was really motivated by the fear of losing Stu's van, in which he transported the group on their exhaustive gigging circuit. Although it's not known whether a new arrangement was later

Chart Positions

There was really no 'official' pop chart in Britain until 1969, when chart TV programme *Top Of The Pops* begin using the chart featured in *Record Retailer* magazine (later renamed *Music Week*) when it began to be compiled by the British Market Research Bureau. Previously the programme had used a chart which aggregated the sales positions of several competing magazine's charts, the most authoritative of which was considered to be that of the *New Musical Express* due to that music weekly's history (it had inaugurated the UK charts), its circulation and the fact that its chart was broadcast on Radio Luxembourg and published in the *Daily Mail*. The UK Sixties chart positions you will see in this book are from the *Record Retailer* simply because it is that chart that was employed by the compilers of the *Guinness Book Of Hit Singles*, now used as the industry's chart bible. Similarly, it is *Billboard* chart positions the reader will find for the band's American statistics, despite a feeling amongst some that the now defunct *Cash Box* provided the more reliable data at the time.

reached, he certainly seems to have had a sixth share during their time with Decca, which lasted up until the end of the Sixties, and he did occasionally appear on their records – although band friends Jack Nitzsche and especially **Nicky Hopkins** ultimately became the Stones' keyboardists of choice, partly because of Stewart's idiosyncrasies (he would refuse to play minor chords, for instance.)

The shoving of Stewart out of the picture

RSG: Ready, Steady, Go! in 1963 was the acme of cool exposure. The boys are still wearing stage outfits, though.

was a brutal decision, and one which nobody would want to be on the receiving end of, but it was also a decision vindicated by history. Up to this point, the Stones' personnel had been neatly divided down the middle between the charismatic, anarchic and morally dubious Jagger, Jones and Richards and the unprepossessing, sober and seemingly upstanding Stewart, Watts and Wyman. While the latter triumvirate were undoubtedly the kind of people you'd trust with your wallet, they were hardly the kind of people to arouse passion, either sexual or socio-political. Though they had no way of knowing this at the time, with the former three now in the majority, it so happened that the path was cleared for the Stones to be not merely a great band but figureheads for a generation increasingly disinclined to 'get what they were given'.

The *Thank Your Lucky Stars* TV appearance prompted letters to newspapers from the type of people who had brought the younger generation to such a state of disenchantment: "It is disgraceful that such **long-haired louts** as these should be allowed to appear on television"; "Your filthy appearance is likely to corrupt teenagers all over the country"; "I have today seen the most disgusting sight I can remember in all my years as a television fan…" If such correspondents were driven to such apoplexy by the Stones in ties and hounds-tooth jackets, one can only wonder at their reactions to the sights and sounds that would emanate from the Stones' camp in the years thereafter. The Stones shortly afterwards refused to wear hounds-tooth jackets, or any other stage uniform, or ties, thus becoming the first 'pop' group (using pop group to signify artists trying to get into what was still called the **Hit Parade**) to dress down. Though this hardly constituted barrier-storming stuff, it still had the whiff of a contempt for etiquette that was quite shocking in a society so restrictive that in workplaces, as the late Ian MacDonald has observed, "all males below one's own level [were] addressed by their surnames, as if the whole country was in the army."

However, Keith did go along with another of their manager's dictates: that he drop the 's' from his surname to make it echo that of UK chart idol **Cliff Richard**. Richards re-adopted his 's' in the late Seventies. For continuity purposes, 'Richards' is employed throughout this book. There had been another change in spelling ordered by Oldham: as from their debut single, they were henceforth not **Rollin' but Rolling**. How could they expect people to take them seriously, Oldham reasoned, when they couldn't even be bothered to spell their name properly?

On the strength of their solitary semi-hit, the Stones were signed up to a **package tour** starting at the end of September. Popular at the time but obsolete within a couple of years, package tours consisted of a famous headliner supported by half a dozen or so acts ranging from the semi-famous to the new hopefuls (like the Stones at this point) to absolute nobodies. The Stones found they were on the bill with two rather substantial stars, the

Everly Brothers and the man whose songs they had long featured in their own repertoire, Bo Diddley. Further, **Little Richard** would also later join the tour. The impression amongst the group members that they were suddenly in the big time can only have been strengthened by the fact that a few weeks before this, they were gifted a song by the hottest composers on the block, The Beatles' Lennon & McCartney. Entitled, '**I Wanna Be Your Man**', it would become their second single that November and would plant a seed in Jagger's and Richards' heads that would result in them becoming almost as celebrated a composing team as John and Paul.

It was no doubt partly the cachet – and the attendant publicity – of releasing a song by the hot **Lennon/McCartney** partnership that led to 'I Wanna Be Your Man' climbing as high as No.12. However, it was also the quality of the recording, a recording as blurred and untidy – but attractively so – as 'Come On' had been clean and in-focus. It also boasted a nosebleed-inducing bottleneck guitar break from Brian that made Richards – who later took to damning his deceased colleague's guitar skills with faint praise – comment, "I think Brian made that record, really." The first composition attributed to "Nanker, Phelge" was on the flip, a pretty nifty subterranean semi-instrumental called – mildly daringly – '**Stoned**'. The chord sequence came from Booker T's 'Green Onions'.

It was in fact while they were promoting 'I Wanna Be Your Man' that the Stones farmed out one of the first compositions by any of their members to be recorded by another artist. Appearing on *Thank Your Lucky Stars* again

The first big UK tour; Little Richard would join after the first five dates.

I Wanna Be Your Songwriter

By early September 1963, when Lennon & McCartney wrote – or more precisely finished – 'I Wanna Be Your Man' for the Stones, The Beatles were a huge source of national pride. Though they were yet to make that sensational and unprecedented inroad for a post-Elvis pop act into America, the fact that they had created an indigenous form of rock (a genuinely novel-seeming amalgam of rock 'n' roll, R&B, Brill Building pop and Everly Brothers/girl group harmonies) was already remarkable in itself. What was even more startling is that all of their three singles ('From Me To You' made its chart debut that very month) and half of their album (there was another due in November) were composed by band members. This wasn't actually that unusual for rock acts – Buddy Holly and Chuck Berry had written their own gear – but it was certainly novel for a band from the UK, a nation whose inferiority complex about their relationship to big, rich, glamorous America was deeply ingrained. The idea of a Briton presuming to write a song in an American form of music was thought to be slightly ridiculous. Hence, British artists had thus far sung the product of Americans or of freelance songsmiths. John Lennon and Paul McCartney, however, had recently proved that home-grown product could have as much artistic and – of sole interest to the music industry – commercial impact as the previous option of asking a Tin Pan Alley hack for material, or picking a hit from the American charts and hoping it made it to the shops before someone else got the same idea.

Oldham bumped into Lennon and McCartney when the pair were on their way back from a Variety Club lunch at the Savoy hotel. When he told them that the Stones were having trouble finding material for their second single (Leiber & Stoller's 'Poison Ivy' b/w 'Fortune Teller' were mooted as their second release, good songs but lightweight pop), the pair mentioned they had something that might be suitable for their gritty style. "They were real hustlers then," Jagger later observed. Indeed, some insiders recall McCartney having his eye on the idea of become a Tin Pan Alley freelance songsmith himself when – as seemed inevitable to everybody at the time – his own and his colleagues' stardom began to wane.

When the party got to Studio 51 club in Soho, where the Stones were rehearsing, The Beatles pair explained that the song had a first verse and a chorus. They went into another room to finish it off. To the Stones' amazement, they returned about a quarter of an hour later, job done.

The Stones were hardly of the opinion that the song was a masterpiece (nor The Beatles – it was given to Ringo to sing on their second album) but that a middle eight and second verse could be completed so quickly was a revelation to them. It would be wrong to extrapolate from the light bulbs clicking on over their shaggy heads that they thought they could do it too, but it was certainly one of the things that would shortly lead to the band beginning to make their own transition to self-contained recording artists. Though Brian Jones' girlfriend of the time subsequently recalled the guitarist staying up, pre-fame, to the small hours to try to write songs, it was "Jagger/Richard(s)" that would be the credit to be found in parentheses beneath the song titles on the labels of Rolling Stones records when the composition did not originate elsewhere. Eventually that credit would be the sole one to be discerned, as the group became increasingly self-reliant. Because of both the quality and the zeitgeist-capturing nature of the joint compositions of Jagger & Richards, it was a short step from there to becoming legends.

The Life

on 17 November, they found that **Gene Pitney** was also on the programme. Pitney was played a song called 'My Only Girl'. Its structure was altered and its title changed to 'That Girl Belongs To Yesterday'. He would release it as a single in March 1964 and it would go Top Ten in the UK. However, it was beaten to the stores by two months by 'Will You Be My Lover Tonight' b/w 'It Should Be You', a single by **George Bean**, both sides of which were written by Jagger and Richards. Bean secured his place in history as the first person ever to release a Jagger/Richards song by dint of the fact that he was a friend of Chrissie Shrimpton, Jagger's girlfriend, and therefore happened to be in the right place when Oldham was looking for artists with which to kick-start his planned production career.

Oldham had been adamant that the Stones must write. The money generated when songs were played on the radio was cumulatively astronomical, and easily dwarfed record royalties. However, Oldham didn't think that the profoundly talented sort-of-leader, Brian Jones, was the man to come up with the original material. Explained Oldham, "He was a **split personality**. He wanted both the fame and the adulation but he wanted to be authentic. The end result is that he basically looked down on the pop process and you cannot write down to the public. They will not accept it."

The legend has always been that in order to force Jagger and Richards to overcome their lack of faith in their ability to write songs fit to even share a planet with the classics of their heroes that they played night after night on stage, Oldham locked them in a room and wouldn't let them out until they had come up with something. Oldham explained in *Stoned*, the first volume of his autobiography, that the story was not quite true: he half-jokingly told them he would not bring them any food back from his mother's house if they had not written a song by the time of his return. The result was 'Tell Me', a pretty decent ballad that ended up on their debut album. "I take my hat off to Andrew," Richards later said. "He had no idea, but it was worth a try, and it worked. In that little kitchen Mick and I got hung up about writing songs."

RSG again, but by 1964 the stage outfits had gone. So have the amplifier cables.

Would you let your daughter go with a Rolling Stone?

Chapter 2:
As Good As
The Beatles?

"The Stones would never have been booked, if we'd known ahead of time who they were…Unfortunately these groups encourage an unpleasant element among teenagers"

Hotel manager Myles Craston,
The Ottawa Citizen, 26 April 1965

As Good As The Beatles?
1964-1966

By 1964 the Stones were firmly placed in the public eye, and regularly pilloried in the Press for their suppposedly unpleasant habits, scruffiness and long hair. Nevertheless, they continued to work incredibly hard; over the next two years they would be almsot continually on the road in the US, Australasia and Europe, as well as the UK, whilst cutting some of the most iconic singles of the Sixties.

On Record

In January 1964, a few days into a tour of Britain on which the Stones' fellow headliners were **Spector** girl group The Ronettes, the Stones released an eponymous EP. Extended Play records usually comprised four tracks and were quite common at the time, even having their own chart in the *Record Retailer*, although they also qualified for the singles charts. The Stones were fairly unusual in that – unlike, for example The Beatles and The Animals who usually put out EPs that gathered together previous singles or excerpted albums – they would release EPs comprising material unavailable elsewhere. *The Rolling Stones* consisted of four fine covers, 'You Better Move On', 'Poison Ivy', 'Bye, Bye Johnny' and 'Money'.

Recordings the Stones laid down at Regent Sound Studios in Denmark Street, London in the early weeks of 1964 yielded both their classic debut album and '**Not Fade Away**', the first Stones single to achieve a lasting resonance with the public. These sessions were engineered by Bill Farley. Farley paints a picture of the minimalist conditions from which the Stones somehow wrenched great art: "It was mainly a demo studio, the studio I was in. The equipment wasn't very good. The limited equipment that was in the place, there was no two of you sitting there doing it. I had to do it all. The sound in there was really good – we had all good mikes – but the tape recorders and things, we were just about to update it all. There was no three of four tracks. I don't think [Oldham] ever worried about money... but it was cheap. The idea of the sound – it was like a performance sound. I think that's what he was really trying to get out [of the studio]. When they came in, I'd never really seen any of them before. I was doing about three or four bands a week, so I was doing a lot of blues bands. Some of them were really good. To be honest, it was old. It had all been done. I think the only reason the actual blues thing worked was because they were young, because there was a lot better blues players about than them. They were good for what they were doing but there were people like Alexis Korner and Cyril Davies playing that same sort of stuff but nobody really wanted to buy that." Despite his reservations about them, Farley acknowledges that the Stones were proficient: "They all played really well. What you hear there is a performance. You couldn't do anything with it afterwards. That was it. It was finished. So everything they actually did in the backing was it. So it had to be mixed while you were doing it. You could actually put the solos on afterwards and the vocals on. It stands up quite alright even now when you imagine you did it on that sort of equipment. Everything went really easy. Some of 'em, they came in and did it again. They took it away and had a listen to it and come back and had another go. Doing the same thing: just setting up the same and just having another go. They started in the day time. We used to sit in a café called The Giaconda and they used to go down there for tea. When they was getting a bit famous, there was thousands of kids. I think that's what finished it off because they couldn't really

get round there in the morning. Couldn't get in there. One of 'em bit my younger brother. I sent him out to throw her out, 'cos a little girl came tearing through the door. He caught her and dragged her out – about fourteen, fifteen – and she bit him terrible." Of their personalities, Farley says, "I got on alright with all of them. Brian Jones, he always turned up but he seemed to be in his own little bit. But he was the real one who was into all the blues. He used to sit there like in a bit of a trance. Somehow, they all reckon that he was the top man in the group when it all started but I never really got that idea. To be honest, I can't remember any of them being very loud. Charlie was easygoing. He came in with his new overcoat and put it over his bass drum."

As with all Stones records up until 1967, Andrew Oldham was the officially cited producer. Farley: "Andrew used to pop in now and again and wave his hands about. He never made out to be a producer of any sort. He was there, basically. He couldn't really say much. He wasn't musical enough to change what they were doing."

Richards has averred that the finished debut album was comprised of '**dubs**' – unfinished mixes of the tracks. Farley says he has clean hands on this score: "Once it left me, I never saw it again. I just give them all the mixed ones separately but they put 'em all together. They put the order in. I never set it out as an album. I gave the tape to Andy but I might have give him two or three different takes of it. Everything I gave them was finished one way or another."

Part of the way through the album's sessions, the band laid down their cover of Buddy Holly's 'Not Fade Away'. A Stones legend says that Phil Spector appears on the track playing maracas but Wyman has revealed that – though Spector did attend another session and this resulted in him co-writing with the band the bluesy chugging B-side 'Little By Little' – this story was an Oldham **publicity stunt**. For Oldham, 'Not Fade Away' was almost as big a breakthrough as the first Jagger/Richards composition. It wasn't, of course, that crucial single that would garner publishing royalties for the band's **songwriting** axis every time it was played on the radio or every time its sheet music was bought at a music store (the latter still – quaint as it may seem from this distance – a big part of the income of songwriters at the time). However, the Stones' manager felt that it was a creative breakthrough; he was

The 'All Night Rave' at Alexandra Palace, 26 June 1964, one of a series of major live events where the Stones (despite being drowned out by screaming) established their performing chops.

of the opinion that when Richards sat in a corner and played its chords, that it became the first song the Stones ever 'wrote' – that the way they arranged it was the beginning of the shaping of them as songwriters. It's difficult to see what Oldham is getting at here. It was a pleasant single – and not only soared to No.3 but climbed to No. 48 Stateside, their first American inroad – but despite using acoustic rather than electric guitar and lots of maracas and mouth harp, it was hardly that radical a rework of the original. It was also somewhat poppy for a bunch of supposed R&B purists.

'Not Fade Away' didn't appear on the Stones' eponymous **debut album**, released in April 1964. Nor did their previous two singles. This was the custom in Britain, where it was felt that making fans pay twice for a track was a rip-off, something that gave singles a real 'event' status at the time: stand-alone, state-of-the-union addresses. What did appear on *The Rolling Stones* were twelve tracks of uniform brilliance, even if they only had a hand in writing three. It also boasted a quite remarkable cover, featuring a darkly lit side-on shot of the group from the waists up and nothing else but the Decca logo. It was unprecedented – because it was considered **commercial suicide** – for an artist's name not to be on a record's front cover. This apparent disdain for commercial considerations couldn't help but make The Rolling Stones seem almost to possess the aura of being not like mere mortals. It was Oldham's idea, the first of many that would mark him out as a master strategist.

Oldham might have laughed at the conservatism of Decca – with whom it was constantly a battle to get his ideas to prevail – but at least they let him do it. In America, Oldham's idea was simply desecrated, with **London**, their label there, plastering the band's name in great thick letters on the sleeve and insisting it be given the idiotic, dated-as-it-was-printed title *England's Newest Hitmakers*. They also insisted on a tweaking of the tracks, which included shoving on 'Not Fade Away', the American logic being the reverse of what the British thought: that the album would sell based on the familiarity of their (semi) hit.

A little flavour of the threat that the band were already beginning to be perceived as appeared in the *Melody Maker* the month before the album's release. **Ray Coleman** wrote a piece on the group headlined, 'Would You let Your Sister Go With A Rolling Stone'. Oldham had come up with the phrase 'Would you let your daughter go with a Rolling Stone?' in an interview, though it was tweaked by the *Melody Maker* and then subsequently toned down when it appeared in national newspapers, who rendered it as 'Would you let your daughter marry a Rolling Stone?' Although this was yet another result of Oldham's media manipulation, it without question summed up the unease that many parents might feel about their female offspring being subject to the **sexual attentions** of such people. The same parents would also not be amused by their sons imitating the Stones' manners and appearance – yet this became increasingly prevalent as the band's fame grew.

The album incidentally, in climbing to No.1 in the UK, knocked The Beatles off the top spot: a position the **Fab Four** had held unbroken for nearly a year, as their debut *Please, Please Me* had only been displaced by their second album *With The Beatles* (November 1963). This inevitably intensified automatic-pilot Fleet Street stories about whether the Stones were the successors to The Beatles and whether the Mersey sound was about to be eclipsed by this new London noise. Jagger playfully helped things along with a comment to a reporter that he thought The Beatles would be finished in a couple of years. In fact, The Beatles and the Stones were friendly with each other, at least during the time the former were extant. The empathy they had enjoyed as Britain's only true **pop aristocracy** of the era began to be spoiled a little after The Beatles' split in 1970, when Jagger began, for some reason, making rather bitchy public comments about them.

Teen Dreams

Between September '63 and October '66, the Stones went on nine tours within the UK. Things were now very different to the days at the Ealing or the Crawdaddy clubs where, despite the excitement they generated in the venue, they had been listened to respectfully by a knowledgeable audience. Regardless of their musical style, their chart success had made them the **preserve of teenagers**. Now they were trying to be heard against an ear-splitting wall of female screams. On-stage artistic fulfilment

was out of the question. Before too long, Jones took to abandoning his proper guitar lines and playing the tune of 'Popeye The Sailor Man' – nobody could hear to know the difference. Not that Jones was completely disgusted with the band's new **teen-idol** status. He kept accidentally-on-purpose getting left behind when the Stones were trying to make an escape from their pursuing fans and getting engulfed by adoring female forms. As Richards noted, "He used to really dig being mobbed."

A visit to Switzerland in the second half of April '64 was the group's first overseas trip. June saw the band embarking on their first journey to the USA. It's very difficult for musicians of today to imagine what a big deal it was for UK musos to cross the Atlantic in the 1960s, before cheap air travel, instant global communication and the realization among British musicians that just because America had invented rock 'n' roll didn't mean they should have an inferiority complex about it. (Transatlantic musician's union squabbles also made visits very difficult for a while.) The process of demystification and the demolition of the inferiority complex had started the previous February when a record 73,000,000 watched The Beatles' first performance on the US TV prime-time *Ed Sullivan Show*, a feat followed a few weeks later by the achievement of Beatles records occupying the top five places on the *Billboard* chart. The Stones' three-week tour proved somewhat less triumphant than the Liverpudlians' visit had been. Although they could deal with the fact that their hair length induced incredu-

Watch out USA... here they come!

THE ROLLING STONES

They're great! They're outrageous! They're rebels! They sell!
THEY'RE ENGLAND'S HOTTEST!... BUT HOTTEST GROUP!

THE BEST SELLERS

HOT SINGLE!
NOT FADE AWAY

Over 170,000 LP's sold.

The fliers for the '64 US tours clearly got Oldham's marketing message.

lity wherever they went in the States, appearing on Dean Martin's television show, they were so outraged by their host's **wisecracks** about their appearance – sample: "Their hair is not that long. It's just smaller foreheads and higher eyebrows" – that they seriously considered walking off. Although a couple of shows in California went well, they were greeted with incomprehension and hostility on a mixed bill in San Antonio, Texas (they responded to the booing by Nankering) and were shocked at the **segregation** between blacks and whites in that state.

Another shock awaited them when they made a visit to **Chess Studios** in Chicago. Although they were there to do two days of recording, the visit was as much **pilgrimage** as work, for this was the venue of the recording of countless classic R&B tracks by the likes of Chuck Berry, Bo Diddley and Muddy Waters. While there, they were pleased to meet Berry and Waters, as well as guitarist Buddy Guy and **Willie Dixon,** the latter the composer of many of Muddy Waters' songs. Though many have questioned it, Richards insists that the band were amazed to find Waters – the man who had given them their name and was a legend to them – not laying down some tracks but painting the ceiling of the studio. Whether or not Richards' memory is correct, it is certainly a sad fact that R&B and blues musicians of Waters' stature had lately fallen from grace. The Stones and their R&B-loving compatriots were certainly far more *au fait* with R&B and (especially) the blues, than were black American youngsters, who considered it old man's music.

More unsatisfactory gigs followed, and Mick summed up the tour as "a real drag" while Richards adjudged it "a farce". Today, Americans constitute the Stones' most passionate and loyal fan base but it would be a while before the Stones made a breakthrough comparable to, let alone, exceeding, those of more clean-cut UK contemporaries like Herman's Hermits and The Dave Clark Five. Nonetheless, the Chicago sessions were productive and – proving how quick was the transition from recording to record back then – at the end of the month whose second week it was recorded in, yielded their next UK single, **'It's All Over Now'**. (It was released in the States in July.) A Bobby Womack composition that had already been released Stateside by his group

The Valentinos, the single was the Stones' first chart-topper in their home country.

Coinciding with the US tour incidentally, was the release of the band's second US single, 'Tell Me'. It was the first Stones single anywhere to feature a Jagger/Richards number on the A-side. Despite the "drag" the tour had constituted, it climbed as high as No.24. It was the first of a trio of US-only singles that – unthinkable today – actually gave them a reputation in the States for a short while as **balladeers**, the other two being the wistful 'Time Is On My Side' (which got them into the US Top Ten for the first time at the end of '64) and 'Heart of Stone' (another Jagger/Richards number, 1965).

4 July saw the group stirring up more outrage with their appearance on *Juke Box Jury*, a British TV programme on which a panel – usually composed of people from disparate walks of showbusiness – were asked to review new record releases. The Stones were deemed to be as **obnoxious** as The Beatles had been charming on their appearance on the show six months previously. In truth, the Stones' appearance was tame – there was no swearing, for instance - and the outrageousness amounted to showing their real feelings about a rather staid show that featured no promotional films, or videos as they would later be termed, thus forcing the director to perform the perennially embarrassing task of panning the studio audience for their self-conscious reactions to what was being played.

August saw the release of one of those "terrible pop songs", as Keith has described the

Sharp dressing for The Ed Sullivan Show, but haircuts and attitude sparked controversy.

Jagger/Richards compositions being hawked to other artists in this period. The song was 'As Tears Go By' and the artist given the task of singing it was a new Oldham discovery, **Marianne Faithfull**, a virginal-looking, posh blonde beauty with a convent school education. It reached No.9 in the UK and No.22 Stateside. When his tempestuous relationship with model Chrissie Shrimpton fizzled out at the end of 1966, Faithfull would become Jagger's partner for the rest of the decade. Also in August, came the Stones' second UK EP, *Five*

By Five. Recorded at Chess Studios on the first American tour under the supervision of **Ron Malo** – who had engineered many of the band's favourite Chess records – it featured, amongst four others, a version of Chuck Berry's 'Around And Around' recorded in the presence of the great man himself. There were also two fairly impressive 'Nanker, Phelge' numbers.

Late October saw the band embarking on their second US tour. They made their debut on *The Ed Sullivan Show* on the 25th. The titular strait-laced host was disgusted by what he saw. "I promise you they'll never be back on our show," he fulminated. "Frankly, I didn't see The Rolling Stones until the day before the broadcast. It took me seventeen years to build this show. I'm not going to have it destroyed in a matter of weeks." Once again, the Stones would squeeze in a couple of recording sessions during this US trek, this time at **RCA Victor**'s Hollywood studios, by now aware that the artist-friendly atmospheres, superior technology and knowledgeable and helpful engineers here were better than almost anything they could hope to find in Britain.

Mid-November saw the UK release of 'Little Red Rooster'. It was an utterly **audacious** move to release this Willie Dixon-written 12-bar blues as a single. There was ostensibly nothing that the sweet-toothed taste of teenagers would find attractive about a piece of music that had no chorus and in whose verses every other line was just a repetition of the previous line. Meanwhile, its typically bluesy sexual innuendoes went completely over their heads. Oldham's rationale in releasing it was that it would be good to put out a song that was not likely to make another No.1 but one that instead, though possibly only making Top Five, would remind the Stones fans of their **Delta** chops and appeal to the bottom-line R&B faithful. In fact, it instantly topped the charts.

In truth, though a pleasant and quasi-sensual rendition (with some nice Jones slide guitar and harmonica, though Jagger would mime to the latter instrument's sounds on the TV appearances), it is doubtful it would have got so high in the charts if the artists purveying it were not established already, and were not lusted after by so many of its purchasers.

Much the same can be said about *The Rolling Stones No.2*, the band's sniggeringly titled second album, released in January 1965. As with the first, it mostly comprised songs composed by others. One would imagine that it would be fairly effortless for such a proficient band with their pick of classics to assemble something highly listenable. The results, though, were limp and the only truly remarkable things about the record were to be found on its sleeve. There was once again no artist credit or title but instead a moody group shot. This one had Keith to the foreground – revealing his zits in full close-up, an alarming sight in the days of twelve-inch sleeves. Oldham contributed another weird sleevenote on the back, one which caused questions to be asked in the **House of Lords** for its suggestion that those without sufficient funds to buy the disc should rob a blind man for the necessary cash and give him a kick for good measure. The sleevenote was amended by Decca who unconvincingly said of Oldham: "He is most apologetic."

Down Under

January 1965 saw the Stones travelling to Australia to tour. Though they went down well with the fans – at one point they had four records in the Top Ten – they were surprised by the hostility of the then very conservative

Australian media. Trips to the Far East and their third North American jaunt followed. Around this time, the Stones' third American album, *The Rolling Stones Now!*, appeared. It was one of several US Stones LPs released before **transatlantic standardization** was established, that had no UK counterpart, it being a mixture of UK album tracks, singles and even an alternate version of 'Everybody Needs Somebody To Love' that was a run-through used in error.

Though the year started with a mediocre work, it was 1965 in which the Stones staked their claim to be the second-best band in Britain. Further, such were their artistic breakthroughs in '65, they even kicked off a previously almost unthinkable debate that then continued to rage through the Sixties: who was better – The Beatles or the Stones? This began with the February release of the UK single '**The Last Time**' (the first occasion since 'It's All Over Now' of an identical US and UK single release, albeit at slightly different times). A mid-tempo account of a relationship at breaking point, it features a nagging, circular guitar figure from Jones all the way through. The riff was as close to tedious as it was hypnotic, and the song itself highly reminiscent of a gospel song that Richards admitted was "as old as the hills", but the point was that Mick and Keith could plausibly put it out as a Jagger/Richards song, which they did. The result was that, in topping the UK charts with one of their own songs, they were being spoken of for the first time as heavyweight artists, not highly-skilled copyists.

The fact that the B-side was the menacing 'Play With Fire' was possibly even more significant in this process of gaining of credibility. It was utterly unlike just about anything to be heard in the **mainstream** at the time: a slow number with a harpsichord part, it saw Jagger giving dire warnings to a posh girl trying to slum it with him. It also featured unusual British references. That the track sounds laughable rather than menacing today is not really relevant: at the time, the Stones were setting aflame the conventions of the pop song. From hereon in, all official Stones singles both sides of the Atlantic would feature Jagger/Richards songs on both A- and B-sides until 'Harlem Shuffle' in 1986.

It wasn't only their artistic credibility the Stones were sealing in '65. They underlined their rebel credentials with an incident at a service station in March that saw Mick, Brian and Bill summoned to court in late July on charges of **insulting behaviour** and using obscene language. The group had aimed some verbal insults at the station's forecourt attendant when refused permission to use the lavatories. The attendant had apparently been alarmed by the appearance of Wyman, whom he told the court was a "shaggy haired monster". Upon being told to, "Get off my forecourt", Jones responded with, "Get off my foreskin!" and Nankered the pompous attendant. Another of the comments made to the increasingly apoplectic attendant has been attributed to both Jagger and Jones but whatever its provenance deserves to go down in history as the Stones' manifesto distilled to its metaphorical the young – and in modern history never was there a morality gap so great between the old and young as there was in the Sixties – love the Stones even more: the Stones' generation wanted a society where this kind of incident was considered too trivial to reach court. To illustrate the extent of the heroes/villains public perception of the difference between The Beatles and the Stones, three months after the incident – and a month before it reached court – it was announced that The Beatles were to be made Members of the British Empire.

A Year of Satisfaction

After trying several American studios, the Stones settled for a while on RCA Studios in Hollywood. Their engineer there was **David Hassinger**. With Hassinger, they would record some of their greatest and most iconic songs, including 'The Last Time', '(I Can't Get No) Satisfaction', 'Get Off Of My Cloud' and '19th Nervous Breakdown'.

More sharp dressing for their "We'll piss anywhere" court appearance.

essence: "We'll piss anywhere, man". Various band members then urinated against a nearby wall. It was as the band's own counsel said "a mountain out of a molehill" but it was the kind of thing that nobody could imagine the studiously polite Beatles being involved in and therefore the sort of stuff to make conservative newspaper editors and their disgusted and outraged correspondents fulminate. The ire of their parents was also the type of stuff to make

Hassinger has nothing but fond memories of the band. "I'd heard of the Stones through Jack Nitzsche," he says, referring to a Los Angeles studio arranger and musician. "I had heard not very much about them but they came to a session I was doing with Jack and they were all dressed in white. That's when I was introduced to them and about a month later I started recording them. I didn't know what to make of 'em to begin with but after doing 'The Last

Bad Boys...
... Or Angels?

Though by 1964/65, the Stones' reputations as bad boys was just about sealed, Dave Hassinger recollects a couple of incidents that put a question mark over that status:

"Bill caught the clap one time. I was out in the entrance of RCA studios and I saw this limousine drive up. I knew the girls they were with. He came in and he wanted to know if I had their address. Well they happened to be two girls that were co-presidents of the Phoenix, Arizona fan club of the Stones that had come there. There was always a crowd outside the studio when they recorded. Apparently he caught the clap and he wanted to tell them. He wasn't mad but he wanted to tell them to take care of themselves and I really thought that was great of him.

"We had been eating over at a place called Martoni's, an Italian restaurant about a block away from the recording studios. These two pretty young girls in their late teens asked if they could come in. I said, 'Well, not unless you take your clothes off'. I was joking. They said, 'Oh yeah, sure!' The Stones had gone inside and I took 'em into a small studio and I said, 'Well take your clothes off here' and when I came back they were standing there shivering and naked. I opened the studio and the Stones were running a song down – rehearsing it – and I shoved the two girls in there and they looked over there and ran to get behind a piano. They were like scared stiff. Didn't know what was going on. I got a big kick out of this because of that image that they had, the bad boy image."

Time' I really started understanding more of what they were doing. I had v-neck sweaters on and slacks and I don't think they knew how to take me at the time. Brian said in print that I understood what they wanted and that's the reason they liked recording with me. I think we hit it off pretty well. They worked very hard and they seemed to have a good time doing it. They were just different than American groups in terms of behaviour, attitude. That British sense of **humour**. Kind of a dry **sense of humour**. I've worked with a lot of groups that just were out of control all the time. I've never seen the Stones out of control. When you're working with a British act, if you don't get on the same wavelength with them I think that you'll never be able to get close enough to them to learn what they're about. They were a pleasure to work with. We never got cross at each other. They never told me what they wanted. They just went out and played and apparently I captured it. They never sat down where we had a planning session: 'This album is gonna be this way or that way'." Of course, the official producer of all sessions was still Andrew Loog Oldham. Hassinger recalls him as extremely helpful and attentive but not a producer in the conventional sense.

He continues, "When they showed up to do a session, it was business. They didn't fool around. It was a relaxed atmosphere – there was no pressure or anything like that – but they came to work. They did a little smoking but nothing to get out of hand. In most cases it would be starting at around six or seven in the evening and working 'til four, five in the morning. There were some afternoon sessions but they never came in like at nine in the morning. Two in the afternoon, that would be about the earliest. A lot of times we didn't even record. We'd just sit around and talk for about three or four hours or go out and get something to eat and come back. It was all very loose all the time. The Stones were always exciting. In the early days they weren't as tight as they are now. In those early days they weren't perfect but they were exciting. Nothing ever sounded the same as the first take. All those songs evolved to a nice tightness. They would change a little thing here and there but they pretty much knew the direction they were going to take a song when they came in there. My experience with all the groups I've recorded like the Jefferson Airplane and the Grateful Dead, these other American groups, when they came in they pretty seldom ever knew what they were going to do. And they weren't as dedicated as the Stones were. I think a lot of people have a misunderstanding of the Stones and look at them as a bunch of airheads." Despite the fact that the first take would sound nothing like their last, Hassinger says there would not be a huge number of takes: "They never beat it to death. Maybe ten or twelve and maybe some only three or four. We never got into the forty and fifty takes, let me tell you that." There was also a **spontaneity**: "A lot of times on a Stones record, something will happen that happened in no other take. Something would happen and just click and that would be it. It could have several

changes in it that had not occurred before that – only on that one final take. They seemed to be constantly improvising, you might say. You've been watching a controlled spontaneity."

One of Hassinger's sessions yielded '(**I Can't Get No) Satisfaction**', released as a single in the States in June and August in Britain. The contrast between this and 'The Last Time' couldn't have been greater. Whereas the former was derivative, the new Jagger/Richards-written single was massively innovative, not just for its startling roaring fuzztone guitar lick but its sheer bellicosity: it was a bellow of rage at the hassles of everyday life that captured the disaffected spirit of the Stones – and their generation – perfectly. It proved in one stroke that Jagger/Richards were now the equal of Lennon/McCartney and that the Stones were the equals of The Beatles and **Bob Dylan**, the other two artists who made up rock's holy trinity – in terms of aesthetic credibility, not necessarily sales – in the Sixties. 'Satisfaction' sailed to No.1 on both sides of the Atlantic. To this day, it remains one of the greatest rock recordings of all time.

Jagger explained at the time that the delay of the single's British release was because of their latest EP and then the release of The Beatles' '**Help!**' single – the two bands tried to schedule their releases at different times so as not to create a conflict amongst youngsters whose pocket money/wages were nothing like limitless in a country whose working class were relative paupers compared to their American counterparts. Almost as significant as the qual-

Brian and The Man, during the latter's 'Judas' tour. Photographer Bent Rej has described how Brian would submit astronomical telephone bills to Easton's office, resulting from hours-long transaltlantic conversations with Bob.

ity of the A-side were the merits of the UK flip, 'The Spider And The Fly'. Though the instrumentation was fairly ordinary 12-bar blues, the lyric was cutting edge stuff, being a tale of a groupie – of the horrifically advanced age of thirty. It inaugurated a tradition of great UK B-sides (naturally unavailable on UK albums), only helping cement their growing reputation.

However, as if to prove that the Stones were fodder for the masses as much as they were great artists, the same month saw the release of *Got Live If You Want It*, a UK-only in-concert EP that was artistically almost totally worthless. Not to be confused with the completely different November 1966 American album of the same title (which was inspired by the Slim

Harpo number 'I've Got Love If You Want It'), it featured several UK performances that were almost entirely drowned out by high-pitched audience screaming. Matters were worsened by the inferior fidelity brought about by squeezing more than two tracks onto seven-inch vinyl. All the tracks except 'I'm Alright' were cover versions so the band – who had lately become acquainted with just how lucrative publishing income could be – hived off the girls screaming "We want the Stones!" at the beginning as a separate track and put its composition down to 'Nanker, Phelge'.

Changing the Guard

August saw a change in the band's management set-up: Eric Easton was no longer part of the picture. His place alongside Oldham was taken by a brash American named **Allen Klein**, whom Oldham appointed as a business advisor. He was authorized to negotiate for a new Stones recording contract. This came about because the initial contract between Decca and Impact Sound – the company Easton had formed to record and lease out Stones tracks – was over. Easton had negotiated a new deal and to Oldham, although he didn't know quite why, it seemed suspicious. He later learned of what he felt to be its lack of probity: Easton had moved the Stones' recordings out of **Impact Sound** and into a company pointedly titled Eric Easton Ltd.

Oldham had first met Klein earlier that year. He must have seemed to Oldham in a differ-ent league from a parochial London agent like Easton, what with his reputation for making pop star clients very wealthy by the simple-sounding but rhinoceros hide-demanding and Job-like patience requiring device of discover-ing for them underpaid record company royal-ties. This partly accounted for his ability to utterly charm people and make them think he was their greatest financial ally in the world. This charm would within a few years take hold of three quarters of The Beatles. The hold-out was **Paul McCartney**, who instigated a legal action to break up The Beatles' partnership and whose barrister David Hirst told the judge in the resulting court case, "Mr. Klein cannot be trusted with the stewardship of the partner-ship, property and assets." The recriminations engendered by Klein working for the Stones wouldn't be so bad – not quite, anyway.

Though both Wyman and Jones distrusted Klein on sight, neither they or their fellow Stones could deny that Klein's appointment brought about a fresh injection of capital, something particularly important to the three non-writing members, who despite their vast record sales were all struggling to do mundane things like buy their homes. There was a sur-real-sounding meeting at Decca's office that saw the band standing in a line behind Klein and Oldham – all of them wearing **sunglasses** and saying nothing, on Klein's instructions – while Klein made demands that included a higher royalty rate. The Decca lawyers, to use Richards' word, "crumbled". The first mani-festation of the deal he secured for them was

The Life

an advance against royalties each for £2500. Though a tidy sum in those days, their gratitude for it was in retrospect pathetic.

Early September saw a short jaunt to **Ireland**, followed by another trip across the Atlantic where RCA was once again their host as they laid down several tracks, including '**Get Off Of My Cloud**'. In its bear-with-a-sore-arse mood, hollered vocal and air-punching chorus it was a sort of sequel to 'Satisfaction', and no less brilliant for that. Released in September in the States, October in the UK, it was another transatlantic chart-topper. The UK B-side was the sweet ballad 'The Singer Not The Song' while Americans were given '**I'm Free**', which the Stones would often try to use as a kind of anti-authoritarian national anthem in concert, apparently not realizing that it was not quite good enough to earn that status, which in any case they had already achieved with their previous two A-sides.

Hassinger reveals of the '... Cloud' session, "At that same session, they did a track called 'Love's The Same As Hate' but they never finished it and it was a dynamite track. Boy, that thing really galloped along and I never understood why they didn't finish that. They had a lot of tracks that were dynamite that they never finished."

The end of the month saw the release of the band's third UK album, *Out Of Our Heads*. Though most of the songs were still covers, it was a far better effort than *No.2* and showed signs of development, or at least change, in being more soul- than R&B-oriented. Late October saw the group embarking on their fourth North American tour. Once more, they stopped off at RCA. Though true greatness

The Other Man in the Stones' life, Allen Klein.

had eluded them on their last two albums, they clearly had an almost effortless capacity to record classic singles. "It's almost a novelty record, I liked it," is Dave Hassinger's comment on one of the results of this visit: '19th Nervous Breakdown', the third in the Jagger/Richards trilogy of what we might describe as **snotty singles**. Its lyric – a conversational, second person put-down of a neurotic female – was as unusual as its blaring music. Maybe this is what stalled it at No.2 in both the UK and US upon its February 1966 release. There were differing B-sides but ones of equal high-quality on either side of the pond. UK fans were treated to the band's rendition of 'As Tears Go By'. The US flip, 'Sad Day', was a brilliant throwaway lament for a broken relationship. In America, **'As Tears Go By'** had actually been released as an A-side the previous December and gone Top Ten. It's a sweet and ornate rendition – with a chamber music section – but one gets the impression its release Stateside was prompted by the success of The Beatles' similarly flavoured **'Yesterday'** earlier in '65. Just as The Beatles didn't dare put such a 'soft' song as 'Yesterday' out as a single in their home country, so the Stones declined to make it an A-side in Blighty. Additionally, just as McCartney is the only Beatle present on 'Yesterday', Wyman reckons that Mick is the only Stone to be heard on 'As Tears Go By'.

After a blissfully quiet January, February and March saw the Stones – as well as squeezing in the TV and radio appearances necessary to promote their records, naturally – touring

Australasia, then continental Europe. After a break, they coalesced once again at RCA, there to finish laying down what would be a real milestone – the first album completely written by Jagger/Richards. It wasn't only Mick and Keith who were coming into their own, though. The sessions for this album – ultimately titled *Aftermath* – saw Brian Jones complete a blossoming from a mere guitarist into a stunningly gifted multi-instrumentalist. Bored with the guitar, he had taken to flitting from instrument to instrument and was showing an almost uncanny knack for being able to master them in a very short space of time, whether they be of the wind, string, keyboard or percussive variety. At these sessions – which also yielded the single **'Paint It Black'** – Jones played, as well as his usual guitar and harmonica, sitar, dulcimer, marimbas and harpsichord. George Chkiantz – an engineer on many Sixties Stones tracks – said of Jones' genius in this department, "That was Stu's comment, really: 'This guy is unbelievable, you wait and see. Anything that makes music, that guy'll pick up and in ten minutes he'll be getting music out of it'."

Yet despite being in the ascendancy creatively, Jones was spiralling downhill on a personal level. The reasons seem complex and multitudinous. Despite his looks, talent and popularity, he was a profoundly insecure man, something that could not have been helped by the way that his once undisputed status as kingpin of the band was being eroded. When Andrew Oldham had first approached them at the Station Hotel and asked to speak to

Sitar man ...

their leader, Watts had indicated Jones; but Jones had seen that position unexpectedly and swiftly undermined by the way Jagger and Richards had become everyone's meal ticket through their composing partnership. Though Jagger and Richards also partook of drugs – Wyman and Watts abstained – Jones was the most enthusiastic devourer, particularly latterly of LSD. Colloquially known as 'Acid', this hallucinogenic is now well known to have detrimental effects on already fragile personalities (witness the artistic ruination of other brilliant but unstable musicians Syd Barrett, Peter Green and **Brian Wilson**). Hassinger recalls Jones' decline: "Brian played a lot of things but Brian just wasn't as disciplined as the rest of the guys. Yet I got along with Brian very well. He was much more quiet and less demonstrative. I really can't honestly remember which songs he played in and which he didn't. 'Cos a lot of times he didn't play on the song. He would come in a little high and anybody would wait 'til he leaves and when he would leave, Keith would do his part. A lot of the acoustic stuff was done by Brian. He was there for 'Heart Of Stone', 'Last Time' but the more sessions I did with them over a period of about three years, the less he would be on the album. He would show up fewer and fewer times. As I remember, all the lead parts were played by Keith." Hassinger recalls Jones' colleagues responding with remarkable forbearance to his antics: "Brian would come in high and lie down on the floor and stare at the ceiling for an hour or two. They wouldn't confront him.

Everybody came in and we'd talk and they would pass time until he would get up and go, rather than create a big scene. Which I thought was incredible. I thought that was great."

The Stones at this point seem to have been an extraordinary dysfunctional but highly effective family: Mick and Keith writing songs destined to become some of the most revered in rock history, Bill and Charlie gracing them with the sterling work of one of the finest rhythm sections on the planet and Jones then adding the coup de grace in the form of exotic instrumental sweetening. *Aftermath*, the miraculously cohesive result of this screwed up family unit, appeared in the UK in April 1966 and, in a slightly different configuration, Stateside in July. It made waves for its total compositional self-reliance, its preponderance of apparently misogynistic tracks (in fairness to Mick and Keith, thumbing a nose at Moon/June songwriting clichés, one way to do which was to disparage romantic partners, was an act of the rebellion in the air at the time) and for '**Goin' Home**', a 12-bar blues whose lengthy jamming section took it past the eleven-minute mark. Of the latter track, Hassinger recalls that it was down to the nous of Oldham: "That was only supposed to be around three minutes, something like that. I was going to hit the talkback after they'd gone into this riff and he said, 'No – let 'em go'. He knew when it was happening and when it wasn't happening."

'Paint It Black' was released as a UK and US single in May. The band were mystified by the way on some pressings the track was rendered

The Life

with a comma after the second word. Wyman was also mystified, not to mention irritated, that the composition of the A-side was not credited to 'Nanker, Phelge'. It was he who came up with the haunting, Eastern melody line by imitating the cinema pit style of Eric Easton, who had once been a professional organist. Though there is no doubting the quality of the Jagger/Richards composing team this would by no means be the first time that the nature in which they laid claim to 100% of the royalties for a track was eyebrow-raising. Though Jones did not have a hand in the melody, it was really he who made the record with his unorthodox but intriguing rhythmic sitar playing. The group were accused – as they frequently were – of aping The Beatles, whose sitar-accompanied 'Norwegian Wood' had appeared on the *Rubber Soul* album in December '65. "You might as well say we copy all the other groups by playing guitar," responded Jones tartly. The transatlantic flip was a smouldering soul ballad called '**Long, Long While**'.

June and July saw the group in North America once more. Sessions at RCA followed in August, the last American session until 1969. They laid down parts for their next album and what would transpire to be their next single. It's a pity that what would be their last recording dates with Dave Hassinger did not produce something better. '**Have You Seen Your Mother Baby, Standing In The Shadow?**' was a recording as ornate and convoluted as its title. The single was an attempt at something resembling a Phil Spector 'Wall Of Sound' production but lacked a memorable tune. It was also rather murky, and its brass sections indistinct where they weren't shrill. To this day, Richards insists that the record would have been great had the wrong mix not been released. Though Hassinger says, "I didn't think it was that good a record as the others, quite frankly," he finds Keith's belief plausible: "He's probably right because I didn't really like the mix. A lot of those things I didn't mix down 'cos we'd record 'em and they'd be gone. It's, as I remember, a little bottom-heavy." More interesting was the B-side, 'Who's Driving Your Plane?', another '19th Nervous Breakdown'-style putdown. Even more interesting was the promotional film which saw the band – perhaps as a subliminal result of the way their long hair so often caused them to be genuinely mistaken for women – dressed in drag, with Wyman in a wheelchair for good measure.

"I'm not going to burst into tears if this doesn't go to No.1," Mick was reported as saying at the time. Just as well. In an age where there genuinely did seem to be a correlation between pop quality and success, the single – upon its September 1966 UK and US releases – did not do as well as the previous magnificent quartet of singles (not counting the US-only releases 'As Tears Go By' and '**Mother's Little Helper**'). It stalled at No.9 Stateside and at No.5 in the band's home country.

September saw the Stones touring Britain, something that was not to happen again for half a decade due to events that would almost destroy the group.

... guitar man.

The post-concert riot in Zurich, 14 April 1967. In fact all the European outings since 1965 had been marked by demonic levels of hysteria.

Chapter 3:
Annus Horribilis

"The Rolling Stones are one of Britain's major cultural assests, who should be honoured by the kingdom instead of jailed."

Allen Ginsberg, poet,
letter to *The Times*, 12 July 1967

Annus Horribilis
1967

Between 1963 and 1966, the level of work undertaken by the Stones in gigs, recordings and promotional activity was astonishing. This had its part to play in terms of interpersonal relations. It also made use of drugs a matter of necessity as much as personal indulgence. It was the latter that would give the Establishment opportunity to make the band's 'Summer of Love' extremely sour.

Pushing the envelope

1967 was The Rolling Stones' *annus horribilis*, the year in which such was the threat they were deemed to pose to the old order – the authoritarian and rigidly hierarchal society that Britons had only ever known – that the country's Establishment in the form of the police, part of the media and the law courts, did its best to break them. At one point, two of its members were in prison while at the same time a third faced what seemed a certain jail term. They also released, perhaps not coincidentally, what was amongst their weakest and most insincere sounding music to date. There were also **terrible fissures** created within the group on a personal level. Ultimately, Brian Jones was destroyed by the events of the year. The Stones as an entity were not – emerging as a different, arguably stronger, beast and with their rebel credentials now iron-clad.

Poetically, the year started with a record which summed up everything the establishment hated about these young men, '**Let's Spend the Night Together**'. The frankness about sex – specifically casual sex – displayed by the song was genuinely shocking for the era. Britain could just about tolerate this – the song was not banned from the airwaves and reached No.3 – but it was a little too much for America. Ed Sullivan had gone back on his vow to never have the Stones on his programme again when they had proved to be too well-liked amongst his nation's youth to make this tenable for such a populist presenter, but he insisted that the lyric of their new song be amended to "Let's spend some time together". Jagger acquiesced, although for years fibbed that he had just mumbled the real title phrase instead. Many US radio stations got round the problem by flipping the record over. Americans were not losing out, for the pastoral and elegant B-side

The Life

The London Palladium 'Scandal'

The Stones were booked to perform 'Let's Spend The Night Together' on Sunday Night At The London Palladium, a rather conservative but highly popular TV light entertainment show. The show's finale saw the stars of the edition mounting a revolving rostrum and waving to the audience as the credits rolled. Like many showbusiness traditions, the Stones found this one imbecilic and refused to take part in it – the first guests to ever do so. "Who do the Stones think they are?" barked the show's producer, Albert Locked, summing up the tenor of much of the media coverage of the story. The Stones were unrepentant. "Anyone would think that this show is sacred or something,"

sniffed Jagger. "It's not us, it's not honest and why should we?" said Richards. Always more erudite in his rebelliousness, Jones reasoned, "Our generation is growing up with us and they believe in the same things we do. When our fans get older, I hope they don't require a show like the Palladium."

All perfectly reasonable – to some. To those who weren't rebellious, Stones fans, anti-authoritarian or uptight, the incident added insult to the injury of the record they were currently promoting being allowed broadcast time at all. Many felt they deserved a come-uppance. They were very soon to get their wish.

'Ruby Tuesday', though less iconic, was aesthetically superior. It topped the US chart.

The same month as 'Let's Spend the Night Together''s release saw the UK release of the album *Between the Buttons*. (In the States it appeared in February.) It was a strange Stones record, not disgraceful by any means but with the characteristic Stones raunch replaced by whimsical and gentle stylings more suited to their contemporaries The Kinks.

The **drug squad** of London's Metropolitan Police Force had clearly decided that the bad example set by pop stars – who had recently taken to speaking about their drug use and or advocating decriminalization of soft drugs, as well as inserting only thinly-disguised drug references in their songs – must be stamped on. In 1966, they accorded folkie-turned-flower-child **Donovan** the accolade of being the first British pop star to be busted when they arrested him for possession of marijuana. They would work their way up the pop hierarchy to the previously untouchable Beatles via the Rolling Stones. A key figure in all of this was an ambitious sergeant with the strangely comedic name of Pilcher. The opportunity to obtain the Stones' **scalps** arose on 5 February when the *News Of The World* – a paper we would now call a tabloid but which then still had broadsheet-size pages – published what it claimed was an interview with Jagger in which the Stones frontman admitted to LSD use, and was seen by the reporter to possess both the amphetamine Benzedrine and hash. The story was mostly genuine but the identity of the interviewee was wrong. The hilariously unhip undercover man had come across a drug-frazzled **Brian Jones** – a state the increasingly tormented guitarist was to be found in lately – in the nightclub Blaises and had mistaken him for his completely dissimilar-looking colleague. Though hardly a drugs abstainer, Jagger was understandably irritated at the spotlight that was shone on him by the coverage, and announced he was suing for libel.

In light of the situation, it was perhaps unwise of Keith Richards to open his Sussex house Redlands the following Sunday to a man whose nickname was 'The Acid King'. David Schneiderman, also known as Dave Britton, is a mysterious figure whom the Stones had met in New York in '66. It was subsequently suggested by some that he was a **paid informer** of the *News Of The World* and that this is how the police were able to obtain a search warrant for the premises for that day. (The paper denied this). Amongst Richards' guests were Jagger, Marianne Faithfull, George Harrison and his wife Patti and friends antiques dealer Christopher Gibbs and art dealer Robert Fraser. A measure of the way that The Beatles were then almost royalty in Britain is provided by the fact that the police waited for Harrison and his wife to leave before raiding the premises. There were plenty of drugs about the place, mostly – those present have recalled – in Schneiderman's **briefcase**. The police didn't look in there when Schneiderman asked them not to on the ground that it contained unexposed film. On Schneiderman's person they found cannabis. Fraser was discovered to be in possession of heroin. Four amphetamine capsules were found in a jacket pocket. They in fact belonged to Faithfull, but Jagger **chivalrously** said they were his. It is also said that there was cocaine aplenty on the premises, though the police didn't know what it was and so ignored it. Though Richards was not found to have drugs about his person, he was informed he could face charges of allowing his property to be used for illegal drug consumption after chemical analysis of the seized materials.

This was an era when the law made no distinction between soft and hard drugs, and little distinction between users and dealers. **Harsh sentences** were commonplace. The Stones were naturally worried about the events. It has been claimed that they were told that a £7000 bribe would solve the problem, and that this was paid but to no avail. Marianne Faithfull has said the story is not true. Richards has said it is, acidly remarking, "In America, you pay off the cops as a matter of course. It's business. But in Britain you pay them off and they still do you." (No corruption charges were ever brought against any officer over the allegation.)

Trials and tribulations

A week later the story hit the papers. Perhaps to avoid the publicity or escape the worry, or both, Richards, Jagger and Fraser, as well as Faithfull, Brian Jones and Jones' girlfriend, model/actress

Anita Pallenberg departed to Morocco for a holiday. They travelled as separate groups, with Richards, Jones and Pallenberg journeying through France together. Jones fell ill and told his companions he would catch them up. By the time Richards and Pallenberg had reached Valencia, they had embarked on an affair. Jones was furious when he found out and, not for the first time, beat Pallenberg up. This prompted Richards to take Pallenberg away to Spain, **abandoning** Jones without notice or luggage. Pallenberg never went back to Jones and friends and family say that Jones never recovered from this. That it was real love between Pallenberg and Richards – they ultimately remained together for a decade and had three children (one of whom died in infancy) – can't have been of much consolation to Brian, who had now lost not just the leadership of the Stones but the love of his life.

There was a European tour in March and April but it was difficult for Jagger and Richards to escape their dilemma: customs officials, cognizant of recent developments, were now giving them a very hard time. Stone aide Tom Keylock has said that continental policemen were literally **spitting** at Jagger while he was on stage. On 10 May 1967, Jagger, Richards and Fraser appeared in court at Chichester in West Sussex and were remanded on bail. Brian Jones had been due to come down to Redlands on the day of the bust with Pallenberg but was phoned and warned to stay away after the police came. If the guitarist thought he had made a narrow escape from the turmoil his lax mouth had caused, he

Keith and Anita shortly after the rupture with Brian.

was in for a surprise. On the very same day of his colleagues' hearings, his London flat was raided by the police and he was subsequently charged with possession of cannabis resin, cocaine and methedrine and for allowing his home to be used for cannabis consumption.

Suspicians of an orchestrated campaign against the leading figures of the counter-culture deepened when, three weeks later, **John 'Hoppy' Hopkins**, co-founder of hippie bible *International Times* (*IT*) and underground music-gathering organizer, was given a nine-month prison sentence for possession of a small quantity of pot. The trial judge made reference to his remark to the court that the drug was harmless and should not be illegal when he sent him down, and said 'You are a pest to society,' a rather heavy hint that he was being punished for having a certain opinion as much as his victimless offence. This was the kind of savagery the Stones generation had grown up under, and why their contempt for their elders and alleged betters seemed so attractive to their followers. This was in some ways the real backdrop to the **'Summer of Love'** that history portrays the whole year of 1967 as being: some elements of young society might have been revelling in the feeling that for the first time they were free to speak without censure, have sex with whom they pleased, and face a life not hamstrung by church and conventions like marriage – but their generation was not yet in power.

The harshness of the older generation was revealed at the trials of Jagger, Richards and Fraser in late June. Things got off to an extremely bad start when the judge directed the jury to find Jagger guilty on the first day on the grounds that verbal advice Jagger claimed he received from his doctor about the amphetamine capsules did not constitute a prescription. Richards' case was heard the next day. There was actually **no real evidence** that Richards had allowed his house to be used for the consumption of illegal drugs. The police therefore emphasized the merry mood that a woman named as Miss X – in reality Faithfull – seemed to be in, and also made sure to mention that she was nude beneath a rug (Faithfull had just taken a bath). On this basis, Richards was sentenced to a year's imprisonment. Jagger got three months and Fraser six months. Schneiderman meanwhile had not even been charged and had been allowed to leave the country. He has never been identified since. Jagger was despatched to Brixton Prison, Richards to Wormwood Scrubs.

Though **riotous demonstrations** of Stones fans took place outside the *News Of The World*'s offices on the evening and night the sentences were passed, it would be a mistake to assume that Jagger and Richards had anything approaching universal public sympathy. The hundreds of thousands – or more – of Stones fans in the country were outnumbered by people who disapproved of what they felt the Stones represented. An opinion poll of the time found that 46 per cent of people thought Jagger had got what he deserved.

However, a supportive editorial in *The Times* (see panel) started something of a snowball.

Seeing that *The Times* had gone unpunished, other newspapers – except the *News Of The World* – followed suit in condemning the sentences. In the first week of July *The New Law Journal* criticized Jagger's jailing for a first offence and the way the talk of the **'nude girl in the rug'** had seemed to be used to prejudice the jury. Late July saw a full page advertisement in *The Times* – stating that the cannabis laws

were "immoral in principle and unworkable in practice" and was signed by doctors, MPs, writers and pop stars.

Nervously awaiting their appeal date, Jagger and Richards joined the rest of the Stones at Olympic to record their next single. Olympic engineer George Chkiantz recalls a strange situation in the studio, where the rhythm section was usually punctual and the songwriting axis

Would you trust these men? Mick and Keith suitably attired for court upon receiving bail pending their appeals.

The Life

Who Breaks a Butterfly on a Wheel?

Outrage at what had happened – both at people being punished for victimless crimes and for the unusual severity of the sentences – was deep and widespread. Hugo Young wrote in Establishment paper *The Times* that the legal process had been "a show trial." The Who quickly announced that their next single would be a coupling of two Jagger/Richards songs, 'The Last Time' and 'Under My Thumb', and that they would be releasing only Jagger/Richards songs until the pair were free to record themselves. A nice gesture but one that it is safe to assume left the legal establishment unmoved. Said establishment would have been somewhat more interested in, and perturbed by, an editorial in *The Times* on 1 July. Though Jagger and Richards were both released

after a day each in prison pending an appeal, the editorial was still sub judice, the laws governing comment on cases extending in those days even to appeal cases. Written by The Times editor, William Rees-Mogg, and headlined Who Breaks A Butterfly On A Wheel?, it condemned Jagger's sentence. (The more severe and more unfair one imposed on Richards was strangely ignored, as was Fraser's.)

"Who breaks a butterfly upon a wheel?" was a phrase – slightly modified by *The Times* – from Alexander Pope's *'Epistle to Dr. Arbuthnot'*, in which Pope described the torture of criminals. The saying came to be widely used to describe massively disproportionate punishments.

would always arrive late: "That was the one session on which Keith and Jagger arrived on time and everybody was waiting for Charlie. We were told by the office that we had to be half an hour earlier 'cos this one was going to start on time. So we duly did and all waited in trepidation for Charlie to turn up. There was a lot of tension in the room. Everyone was longing to talk about this and nobody dared ask. So there was this unbelievable conversation going on in the control room with everybody not talking about the one subject that they were interested in." Chkiantz recalls that the laconic Watts, upon his arrival, looked around the room and asked, "So how are the two jailbirds?" Asked if at this juncture the Stones felt that they needed to deliver a manifesto, Chkiantz says, "Oh yes, I think so." Said manifesto was '**We Love You**', a message of solidarity to their fans couched in the love-infused argot of the season.

On the last day of July, the appeal courts quashed Richards' conviction on the grounds that the judge did not warn the jury that the evidence that the guitarist knew drugs were being consumed on his premises was scant. Jagger's conviction was upheld but his sentence reduced to twelve month's probation. However, the long-held consensus by many that it was Rees-Mogg's editorial that saved the Stones is probably an incorrect assumption. As soon as Jagger and Richards asked for bail, for instance, they seemed to be pushing at an **open door**. Their counsel was told by the prosecution counsel that he had been instructed not to oppose it. Additionally, their

appeal dates were brought forward to 31 July, the last day of the present law term (in an age where there was such a thing) following the direct intervention (admittedly possibly after the Rees-Mogg editorial) of the **Lord Chief Justice**. It would seem that someone in authority – either legal or political – was embarrassed by the injustice or even, possibly, moved by genuine compassion.

That day, Jagger took part in a televized debate with, amongst others, a former home secretary, a bishop and William Rees-Mogg, all of whom listened attentively as he expounded on his worldview. For many of those watching who disapproved of The Rolling Stones, it was the first time they had heard Jagger talk in anything other than the banalities required by pop interviewers – many had no doubt never heard him speak at all – and it must have been something of a surprise to them how intelligent and articulate he was. "That's a textbook definition of the English constitution," he chided his opponents at one point.

By the time 'We Love You' was ready for release, Mick and Keith had learned that they would not be going back to jail. Banging cell doors and the sounds of footsteps walking to freedom were dubbed onto it. A stunning, rippling, exotic confection, 'We Love You' was one of the greatest things the Stones had recorded up to this point. Everyone was expecting it to soar to No.1, not least because a promotional film made by the band, which cast them as modern day Oscar Wilde-type martyrs, was banned by BBC TV (or at least by *Top Of The Pops* producer Johnny Stewart, essentially the same thing in those days), something that one would assume would create an even greater feeling of solidarity amongst their supporters. In fact, in only climbing to No.8 it was, excepting 'Have You Seen Your Mother, Baby, Standing In The Shadow?', their worst chart performance since 'I Wanna Be Your Man'. 'Dandelion' was the side played in the States, and that made only a miserable No.14.

Satanic Majesties

Late August saw Jagger and Faithfull join luminaries like **The Beatles** at a Transcendental Meditation weekend in Bangor, Wales hosted by the Indian Maharishi Mahesh Yogi, one of the many alternative figures suddenly (and briefly) given a plausibility and fashionability by the psychedelic age. It was the Maharishi's type of love vibe – as well as Eastern-sounding soundscapes – that the Stones tried to inject into their music when they returned to London to continue work on their latest album, which would ultimately be titled *Their Satanic Majesties Request*. However, there wasn't much love in the air when Oldham was in the room. Some have alleged that the Stones were aggrieved that a shaken Oldham had **absented** himself from the country while the world had been falling on the heads of Jagger and Richards, others that they just felt they had outgrown him. Whatever the reason, Oldham and the Stones parted company during the album's sessions.

The Stones decided to collectively produce the album themselves. "The whole of *Satanic Majesties* was a complete shamble," recalls Chkiantz. "[It] took forever to record." As well as the mental exhaustion felt by Mick and Keith, there remained the worry over the forthcoming trial of Jones and the possibility that Jagger's conviction would stop the Stones playing in the States. The record is perhaps summed up by the fact that the disarray in the camp led to Wyman's one and only songwriting credit on a Stones album (excluding the legal obligation odds and sods album *Metamorphosis*).

Brian's case came up at the end of October. Though found **not guilty** of possessing cocaine and methedrine, he was convicted of cannabis possession and of allowing his home to be used for its consumption. Court Chairman Seaton took the same line that Lord Chief Justice Parker took at Jagger's and Richards' appeal by telling Jones that he needed to set a good example to his followers. He imposed a £750 fine and a nine-month prison sentence. Like his colleagues had done, Jones had to spend a night in prison before being released pending an appeal.

Their Satanic Majesties Request, was released in the UK and US in the second week of December. It was the first Stones album to have **identical content** on both sides of the Atlantic. It came in a multi-coloured, exotic sleeve (originally in 3-D) that, went the general consensus, was as much a pale imitation of the lush jacket of *Sgt. Pepper's Lonely Heart's Club Band* as the contents were a poor man's version of the music of that Beatles masterpiece, which had been put out in June.

At the end of what had been an awful year for the Stones, and a particularly awful one for Jones, there was at least something from which to take relief when, on 12 December, Jones' prison sentence was set aside and he was instead given three years' probation and fined £1000 plus £250 costs. A condition of his probation was that he continue to receive psychiatric treatment. One of the **psychiatrist witnesses** at the appeal hearing had said Jones was "frightened ... anxious, consider-ably depressed, perhaps even suicidal." This was probably not exaggeration. How must it have felt for Jones to have to turn up in the studio each day and face Richards, the man who now had the woman who had been the love of his life? It's little wonder that Jones' involvement in Stones recording sessions from hereon was sporadic, where it wasn't simply non-existent. His conviction also railroaded the Stones: as he had pleaded guilty, he would not be able to obtain a visa to America, which meant touring there was out of the question for the immediate future.

Too many hands...
Satanic Majesties style.

The publicity shoot for *Beggar's Banquet* presented a new phenomenon, the album release as an 'event'.

Chapter 4:
The Stones Mach II

"The only performance that makes it, that makes it all the way, is one that achieves madness"

Turner (Jagger) in *Performance*, Douglas Cammell, 1968.

The Stones Mach II
1968–69

In March 1968, Mick Jagger – in possibly the only conspicuous display of ideological solidarity in his life – joined a protest against the Vietnam war outside the American embassy in London. Such were the heady times. 1968 was a very different year to '67, for both the world and the Stones generally. Whereas western youth had basked in ideals of love the previous year, it was anger that was the flavour of '68.

Heady Times

It was a year when people were demanding, not asking – and cities and campuses erupted into riots when demands were not being seen to be met. It's even alleged that the Queen at a dinner party that year said she thought revolution of some sort – and hence the end of royalty – was imminent. To illustrate their defiance of prevailing mores, young men – encouraged by the examples of the increasingly hirsute Stones, as well as other stars – were growing their hair longer and longer. Scorning the 'short – back and sides' was already a symbol of rebellion but as rebelliousness grew more intense, hair was now reaching shoulders. Meanwhile the use of recreational substances became as much a political act as (for many) a social norm.

That said, the Stones were more concerned with trying to put back on track their wayward career than changing the world. To this effect they recruited a new producer, **Jimmy Miller,** having found the strain of overseeing *Satanic Majesties* themselves too much. Miller would remain the Stones' producer for the next five years, and would be highly influential on their metamorphosis from a singles band into an album-driven rock band – indeed into the ultimate rock band archetype.

The group rehearsed and recorded sporadically with Miller in early March. But it was effectively a four-man Stones that was doing the recording. Deeply immersed in his pain, **Jones** was absent as often as not, and seemed increasingly incapable of contributing when he was around. Richards had to overdub second guitar parts, although Jagger – beginning to become proficient on the instrument – **Traffic's Dave Mason** and, rumour has it, even **Eric Clapton** were able to lend a hand. Nevertheless, Jones was still able to provide some nice slide work on the track **'No Expectations'**.

As an entity, the band did little but record and rehearse in '68. Their one gig was at the **NME Pollwinner's Concert** on 12 May. That same month (June in the US) saw the release of what was acclaimed as their comeback single, '**Jumpin' Jack Flash**'. "Everything went wrong on the sessions," says Chkiantz of its genesis. This difficult birth also extended to the record's promotional film. Chkiantz says of the song: "Stu told me: 'This is going to be huge'. I said, 'Why?' He said, 'Because of all the curses on it'." Ian Stewart was right. Although nobody could know it at the time, 'Jumpin' Jack Flash' was effectively the first record of the new Rolling Stones, or the "**Rolling Stones Mach II**" as Richards would later term it. Big, brutal, riff-driven, anthemic – the adjectives one could use to describe it were ones that could be used to describe most great Rolling Stones music from hereon as they set about inventing their own generic style and, while they were about it, what would come to be considered the template for any self-respecting rock and roll band. Perhaps understandably, this first foray was not as good as much of what was to come, but it still shot to the top of the UK charts and went US top three, their best chart performance for a single in Britain for two years and for sixteen months Stateside.

The success of 'Jumpin' Jack Flash' was helped in no small measure by a promo film that was as disquieting and devilish as the lyrics to the record itself, featuring the Stones carousing in the dark with their faces daubed with tribal-looking paint. Directed by **Michael Lindsay-Hogg**, it not only proved a more than worthy successor to the imaginative film clip shot for 'We Love You' but was the first step in the Satanic image the band in general, and Jagger in particular, would acquire over the following few years.

Dealing With The Devil

Three days before the UK release of '**Jumpin' Jack Flash**', Brian Jones' world fell in once more when he was arrested on suspicion of possession of cannabis. His flat had been raided after the police had strangely managed to obtain a search warrant without having any evidence of wrongdoing. Jones, already being on probation, knew that if convicted he faced almost certain imprisonment. This would have been painful enough had he been guilty, but all the evidence that subsequently emerged suggested that the cannabis had been planted. Jones – a man previously described by **psychiatrists**, lest we forget, as "considerably depressed, perhaps even suicidal" – was understandably distraught as he was released on bail. The Establishment was clearly still out to get the Stones. Richards and Jagger (the latter also still on probation) could easily be next.

The band tried to concentrate on their music, which was going well. Cult film-maker **Jean-Luc Godard** was allowed in to capture the development from beginning to end of a track originally titled 'The Devil Is My Name'. "The thing went on for a week," recalls Chkiantz. "I

One Plus One/Sympathy for the Devil

French *avant-garde* radical film-maker Jean-Luc Godard set out to make a back-to-back and back-to-basics anti-narrative film combining two sections, one about creativity (the Stones recording a song – 'Sympathy for the Devil') and one about destruction (the suicide of of a white politico when her black lover defects to an extreme Black power movement). With him eventually editing and integrating the two sections together, apparently arbitrarily, the film became a modernist mess, but very much a piece of its time, and the linking of the Stones with the political activism (however juvenile or banal) of the moment had the effect of helping sustain the illusion of the Stones as genuine

radicals. A later version, in which the producer Iain Quarrier added the completed version of the Stones' song remains a fascinating account of the evolution of one of the band's most peculiar and emblematic songs, but appalled M. Godard.

Jean-Luc Godard (second from left) at the 'Devil Is My Name' sessions.

did some nights, Andy [Johns] did some nights. It went through some extraordinary changes. Quite extraordinary." The engineer is not just referring to the song title's metamorphosis into '**Sympathy For The Devil**' but the way a modest-sounding ditty, penned by Jagger after reading Russian dissident novelist Mikhail Bulgakov's *The Master and Margarita*, ballooned into a grandiose and magnificent epic. How fortunate for Godard that he should happen to be

present with his cameras not at the recording of a B-side, or even outtake, but a 24-carat classic of the new Stones era. Its scale did not reflect the rest of the contents of album, which would be called *Beggar's Banquet*. This was an album unlike anything bearing the Stones' name before or since, a blues-folk hybrid with acoustic guitar to the fore.

Completed by July, the general public would not get to hear *Beggar's Banquet* until

The Life

Performance

This highly unusual, hallucinogenic and controversial film depicted an androgynous, hedonistic retired rock star named Turner and the effect his unconventional morals, magic mushrooms, and louche lifestyle have on an East End gangster who is hiding out from his murderous former associates in Turner's house. Jagger played Turner and prominent British actor James Fox the gangster. Anita Pallenberg was cast as one of Turner's two live-in lovers. Although set in (the then) seedy Powis Square off the Portobello Road in Notting Hill Gate, it was in fact filmed on location in a house in Mayfair. Drugs and real-life criminals infested the set.

The filming of *Performance* almost did what the authorities the previous year failed to: destroy the Rolling Stones. It was during the shoot that Jagger and Pallenberg took their explicit lovemaking scenes together to a sort of logical conclusion by embarking on an affair. Though it could be pointed out that Richards was merely having done to him what he had done to Jones, Richards was nonetheless devastated. His bodyguard/driver/drug procurer Tony Sanchez recalled him as too scared to come into the film location when the two drove to pick Pallenberg up, terrified of what a confrontation might lead to. Certainly the stakes were high: Richards could theoretically lose his woman,

Identity crises: Pallenberg, Fox and Jagger.

his best friend – Jagger – and his band. Even the heady sexual nature of the times – an entire generation briefly sex-mad as they collectively threw off the prudishness and circumspection about sex imposed upon them by their elders – doesn't seem to offer much of an excuse for the profound betrayals of both Jagger and Pallenberg. (The latter, incidentally, was best friend of Jagger's partner, Faithfull, though it seems that Jagger's and Faithfull's relationship was not monogamous by agreement.) Amazingly, there doesn't seem to have been any confrontation nor long term fall-out caused by the affair – although suspiciously anguished, even apocalyptical, lyrics would characterise some of Keith's contributions to the next album.

This absence of collateral damage proved not so true for some of the others involved: while co-director Roeg went on to a glittering career, Cammell decayed in Hollywood, creating a sporadic handful of weirdly fascinating movies before literally filming his suicide; Jagger's other co-habitee, Michele Breton, developed a heroin habit and drifted around Europe, while James Fox gave up acting completely for over a decade, to become a vacuum salesman. Meanwhile, outtakes of Jagger's sex scenes with Pallenberg – in which the sex was palpably not simulated – turned up at a Dutch erotic film festival in the early '70s, and won first prize.

December, though America did at least get to hear the track '**Street Fighting Man**' in August. Some of them anyway: many US radio stations banned it, fearful of dire consequences in a year which saw the assassination of figures like **Bobby Kennedy** and **Martin Luther King Jr.** and would see riots that very month at the Chicago Democratic Convention. In fact, the song was Jagger's wry observation that in his sleepy home country, manning the barricades wasn't really the done thing. His wimpy lyric was counterpointed by a roaring musical backdrop that was quite extraordinary considering its acoustic nature. Chkiantz again: "They had this bright idea. They bought this **Philips 3302**. You remember the cassette recorders which had a sort of joystick on the front? Keith had bought the Philips extension speaker and figured out that this thing had an amazing crunch when the batteries were partially flat. It just sounded great so he wanted to use this. So they recorded the basic tracks in a kind of acoustic version sitting on a carpet. Charlie had a fibre suitcase, which was a street drummer's kit, which is like small clip-on drums. So it had sort of tom-toms and things which clipped on round the edges. So he's playing that. Bill was sometimes playing. **Ronnie Lane** had an acoustic bass guitar. They borrowed it. The roles changed: Keith on acoustic, Jagger doing percussion and what have you. Sitting there pushing this one joystick. Then came the moment so we put this machine on, then we carefully wound the batteries down to the magic level, stuck a mike in front of the speaker and recorded the result.

That provided the core, the kernel, to which they then overdubbed an electric version of the track. As an idea it was great. It certainly gave rise to some amusing spectacles as well."

Early September saw Jagger begin acting work on a movie that would eventually be released as *Performance*, in 1970. Directed by Nicolas Roeg and Douglas Cammell, it was avant garde in style, and dealt with organized crime, decadence, unbridled sexuality and drug-taking. A perfect vehicle for Jagger (his only good acting role), like *Beggar's Banquet* (see below), it engendered a long, draining battle with the financial powers behind the project. The distributors were shocked at the nudity, immorality, violence and profanity of the movie and held up its release for two years after its completion, demanding extensive cuts.

Down By Law

In the last few days of September '68, **Brian Jones** was found guilty of possessing cannabis. This verdict was to the astonishment of many who attended court, including apparently the court chairman Seaton who – in contrast to his severity at Jones' court case the previous year – did not hand down the prison term of at least a year expected by a terrified Jones but merely imposed a £50 fine plus costs. Though relieved, the already brittle Brian was mentally wiped out by his ordeal. **Jagger** would later say of the harassment the authorities had directed at the Stones, "They destroyed Brian in the process."

The Life

Some might contend that, as the Stones were drug users and, as drug use was against the law – leaving aside the allegations of evidence-planting and the arguments about victimless crimes – they were not really standing on solid ground in objecting to their treatment. However, few could contend that Jagger's treatment by one establishment member upon the public announcement in October that Faithfull was pregnant was utterly despicable. The **Archbishop of Canterbury** greeted the happy news by asking people to say prayers on Faithfull's behalf on the grounds that the pair weren't married. This was the type of morality that still held sway in Swinging England as the Sixties drew to a close. Perhaps it would be unkind to suggest that the archbishop might well have been pleased that Faithfull miscar-

ried at the end of November – although not implausible.

The release of **Beggar's Banquet** had been delayed since the summer because Decca Records would not allow its release with the cover the group wanted: a disgusting Los Angeles lavatory wall graffitied with the track-listing and musicians' credits as well as various in-jokes and smutty comments.

A Mexican stand-off ensued for six months, but it was finally released in the first week of December when the Stones, having realized that they could not win against a mighty corporation like Decca, capitulated over the cover design, swapping their preferred artwork for a white, party invitation sleeve in elegant copperplate. It was one of the albums of the year, chiming with the back-porch rusticness of several albums of the time such as The Band's *Music From Big Pink* and Dylan's *John Wesley Harding* and with the social concern in the air (even if the latter element was often illusory in the Stones' lyrics).

A few days later, the Stones and a host of assorted famous friends began filming a TV special called **The Rolling Stones Rock And Roll Circus**, a way of presenting the Stones to the public in the absence of their ability to tour. The main reason for that inability – Brian Jones – looked haggard at the two-day event, although he alone can't be blamed for the fact that the Stones were upstaged by their guests, especially **The Who**. The Stones' previous two gigs had been in May 1968 and April 1967, and they were understandably very rusty. The

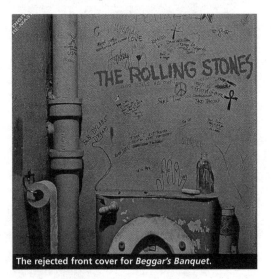

The rejected front cover for *Beggar's Banquet*.

The Life

The Rolling Stones Rock And Roll Circus

Mick Jagger's concept for a Stones-funded TV special could be, once again, compared to a Beatles' idea – their *Magical Mystery Tour* TV film of 1967. Nevertheless, this was a quintessentially raggedy-assed Stones show. Additionally, unlike the Fab Four's effort, it set the Stones in their musical context, by inviting along the great and the good among their friends and peers, not least John Lennon (with new squeeze Yoko in tow). The Who, Jethro Tull, Eric Clapton, Jimi Hendrix Experience drummer Mitch Mitchell, Marianne Faithfull and, for good measure American roots music polymath Taj Mahal, all mixed in alongside dwarves, circus performers, a tiger, classical musicians and musical directors Jimmy Miller, Glyn Johns and Tony Visconti.

'Dirty Mac': Lennon joins the Circus between Clapton and Keith.

Purportedly costing the Stones £20,000 (but with worldwide licensing revenues projected at £250,000), the fact that they didn't shine put the boys in a sulk, and the finished product was tanked. The album and video were eventually released in 1996, with a DVD released in 2004: it remains an iconic, if shambolic, mirror of a moment.

band subsequently buried the project, much to the amazement of **Pete Townshend**, who was impressed that the Stones had the power to ensure that something that cost so much money could be written down to experience.

Notwithstanding this minor setback, the band were already thinking of their next album, which would emerge as *Let It Bleed* a year later. Mid-November had seen them recording at Olympic studios with well-known multi-instrumentalist sessioner **Al Kooper**. The latter had been invited by Jones, who attended the recording himself but simply lay on the floor reading a magazine throughout. This was symptomatic of Jones' role in the band now: he was like a ghost wandering purposelessly around the locales of the life he had once led. The track recorded at this session was '**You Can't Always Get What You Want**'. Though still in its early stages, it was a hell of a start to the new album: a grand statement and musical extravaganza that would help finally prove to anyone who still doubted it that the Stones were neck and neck with The Beatles artistically.

It was the last Stones recording session of the year, though the songwriting axis remained creative. The end of '68 saw Jagger, Richards, Faithfull and Pallenberg take a holiday to South America. Whilst holed up on a ranch in Brazil, Mick and Keith began writing a song that would ultimately become '**Honky Tonk Women**' and be acclaimed as an iconic Stones classic. However, as if to emphasize what his supposed best friend had recently

done to him, when recording re-commenced upon their return, Richards laid down a track called '**You Got The Silver**', a song of devotion to Anita with a pretty acoustic vibe which belied its torment. It was around this time that Jones' appeal against his last conviction was thrown out, making it out of the question that he could be a part of an American tour that the Stones were already publicly speaking about. Jones' days as a member of the Stones – the band he had co-founded and once led - were now numbered.

1969: *Vale* Brian

Jones was rarely present as the group continued working on the clearly powerful music for the new album in 1969. The band tried to fill the gap by roping in sessioner and future solo recording artist, **Ry Cooder**. Cooder had laid down most of the (Turner/Jagger) guitarwork on the soundtrack of *Performance*, but would only be heard on '**Love In Vain**' on the album (although his contribution to '**Sister Morphine**' would surface on 1971's *Sticky Fingers*). He would later denounce the Stones to *Rolling Stone* magazine as "a reptilian bunch of people", claiming that while he was playing, Richards would leave the room and surreptitiously record his licks for the group's own later use. Cooder walked out of the sessions in disgust. Richards later said he was "amazed" by his claims. During another holiday that combined recreation with writing – this one in Positano, Italy – Jagger and Richards came up with the menacing '**Midnight**

Rolling Stone Magazine

A slight confusion has often attended the link between the rock journal *Rolling Stone* and The Rolling Stones.

Rolling Stone was set up in 1967 by Jann Wenner, a music fan in his early twenties, and the considerably older Bay Area music critic Ralph J. Gleason. It was the first professional, mainstream magazine (as opposed to underground paper) to treat rock seriously, featuring writers as diverse as Tom Wolfe, Hunter S. Thompson and Cameron Crowe and photographers such as Annie Leibovitz, Herb Ritts and Richard Avedon. Well written and irreverent, it grew quickly. In 1973, the group Dr Hook released a song that summed up how crucial a main feature in its pages had become to an artist's record sales, 'The Cover Of Rolling Stone'.

The public often assume that the magazine was named after The Rolling Stones and/or that the Stones owned it. The public are partly right in both cases. The magazine's title was a tip of the hat to the band – amongst other things. To quote from the letter from the editor in the first issue: "You're probably wondering what we are trying to do. It's hard to say: sort of a magazine and sort of a newspaper. The name of it is ROLLING STONE, which comes from an old saying: 'A rolling stone gathers no moss.' Muddy Waters used the name for a song he wrote; The Rolling Stones took their name from Muddy's song,

and 'Like a Rolling Stone' was the title of Bob Dylan's first rock and roll record." In its heyday, the magazine's logo featured a performer's graphic profile, easily identifiable as Mr. Jagger.

As to the ownership question, Jagger took a stake in the British edition of the magazine but, in November 1969, it was announced that the British edition was to cease publication owing to Jagger withdrawing his money because he didn't have sufficient time to exercise control over its contents. Nevertheless, the Stones easily hold the trophy for the most *Rolling Stone* covers of any band in the magazine's first 30 years of publication – 23 in comparison to local heroes Grateful Dead weighing in with 12, pursued by Dylan (11) and John Lennon (who had featured on issue No.1), with 10.

Down the years, both *Rolling Stone* and The Rolling Stones have changed considerably. Just as the band have been accused of selling out their once radical beliefs – becoming tax exiles, making increasingly conservative, audience-pandering music, Jagger accepting a knighthood – so the magazine has been accused of abandoning its leftist principles, both by gearing the content more and more away from music and by such corporatist acts as employee drug testing. For what it's worth, both The Rolling Stones and *Rolling Stone* are today massively profitable operations.

The Sacking of Brian Jones

Even had he been allowed into the States, Brian Jones' fragile constitution would probably not be up to a tour. He was also increasingly a passenger, scornful of much of the group's current music, still the only one of the band with the mentality of someone who looked down slightly on "rock 'n' roll" as opposed to R&B, even though the Stones were one of the artists who in the previous years had helped massively expand the boundaries – and definition – of rock. It was no easy decision: Jagger, Jones and Richards went way back, had lived together and had collectively gone through an incredible amount down the years. Accordingly, on 8 June, Jagger, Richards and Watts were very quiet when they embarked on the long car journey to Jones' Sussex home, (Wyman wasn't present because he hadn't been in the studio when the trio decided on the spur of the moment to make the trip.) Richards recalled that when the three arrived, Jones seemed to know what was coming and appeared relieved when it did. Jones'

The beginning of the end. Brian leaving the Court of Appeals in December 1967 after his first sentence for drug possession was reduced. Nevertheless, such a conviction jeopardized his ability to ever tour or work in the US again.

girlfriend at the time, Anna Wohlin, has confirmed that Jones had already made up his mind to leave: partly because it would never be the same with Keith now that Pallenberg was with him, partly because he resented not being allowed in on the songwriting, and partly because he didn't think much of their current direction. His interests, when he could concentrate, had drifted towards increasingly ethnic musical forms and idioms, the beginnings of 'world' music. However, he must have felt ambivalent about the severing of this now painful but long-standing relationship, to say the least. Watts later described the whole matter as "the worst thing so far that I've ever had to do." A couple of bland statements followed, in which Jones and the Stones insisted that the guitarist's departure was amicable and was due to him no longer seeing eye to eye with the band over the discs they were cutting. Thus was born that now standard cliché surrounding a musician leaving a rock group: 'Artistic Differences'.

Rambler' and the studiedly obnoxious '**Monkey Man**'. Like several tracks on the album, these songs exulted in and played up to the band's image as social outlaws.

Speaking of which, another Stones drug bust took place on 28 May, when Jagger and Faithfull had their Chelsea home raided. (Not long before, the police had unsuccessfully tried to engage in a search of Jagger's car). As with the last Brian Jones case, it had the hallmarks of a fit-up. Also like the Jones case, it potentially put in jeopardy a US Stones tour. In fact, the band were able to mount a tour before the court case took place. Though now in one of the same boats as Jones, Jagger – and the rest of the Stones – decided that the time had come to erase him from the picture.

The Stones had picked Brian's replacement even before Jones's dismissal. On 31 May, a young guitarist named **Mick Taylor** attended Olympic at the Stones' invitation to work on a couple of tracks, 'Live With Me' and 'Honky Tonk Women'. The 22-year-old veteran of **John Mayall's Bluesbreakers** wasn't nervous, assuming he was merely wanted for a bit of session work. He proceeded to add the *coup de grace* to '**Honky Tonk Women**', his and Richards' guitar lines twining beautifully on the lead-up to the chorus. Taylor was promptly asked to join the band and the Rolling Stones Mach II had reached completion.

'Honky Tonk Women' was scheduled as the Stones' new single on 4 July, more than a year after their previous UK 45, 'Jumpin' Jack Flash'. The following day, the Taylor line-up was to play its inaugural public performance at a free gig at London's **Hyde Park**. In the early hours of the morning of 3 July, the Stones were doing some overdub work at Olympic. **Alan O'Duffy**, the engineer working with them that night, noticed something of a commotion, with the band members leaving the room to take phone calls and gathering in anxious huddles. Gradually, it emerged what the problem was: news had come through from Sussex that Brian Jones was dead. Journalist and band friend **Keith Altham** happened to be present that evening and readily acknowledges that one of the first things that must have flashed through Jones' former colleagues heads was that the guitarist might have committed suicide over his sacking. He recalls Jagger's reaction to the news almost as a strange one. Though clearly upset – as was everyone present – he seemed almost angry as he said through clenched teeth, "**It goes on, it goes on**". The mild mannered Alan O' Duffy, meanwhile, found it "extraordinary" that the group then carried on with their recording work.

Jones hadn't committed suicide. He had drowned in his swimming pool at his home. Despite the fact that there were already many suspicious facts about the events leading up to and following the discovery of his body, the coroner's verdict was death by misadventure due to drugs and alcohol. (The latter itself was suspicious to **Wohlin**, who said Brian did not take drugs that evening.) But then, people in positions of authority were ready to believe the worst about a dandified, hedonistic pop star. At Brian's memorial, the Reverend Hugh Hopkins used his platform to preach against the values of the young generation: "Brian was the rebel," he lamented. "He had little patience with authority, convention, tradition. Typical of so many of his generation who have come to see in the Rolling Stones an expression of a whole attitude towards life". And this hijacking of someone's memorial presumably displayed the superiority of the values of Hopkins' generation?

Down the years, more and more details have emerged about the murky facts of the night of Jones' death, the most significant of which is the alleged death-bed confession of builder **Frank Thorogood** – then living on the grounds of Jones' house and bearing a grudge because Jones had recently sacked him – to Jones' murder.

There was talk of abandoning the Hyde Park gig. Watts suggested that instead they do it as a tribute to Brian. Accordingly on a sunny afternoon on 5 July, 1969, the Stones walked out onto the stage at Hyde Park to a crowd estimated to be between 250,000 and 500,000, either way their largest audience up to that point. Jagger read a poem to Brian's memory – an eulogy from Shelley's **Adonaïs** – and the band's first number was Johnny Winter's 'I'm Yours And I'm Hers', which had been Jones' favourite song at the time. As with the **Rock And Roll Circus**, the wisdom of performing publicly after such a long lay-off was open to question, especially with a new member to

On stage in Hyde Park just as 3500 white butterflies were released during their opening number.

The Life

incorporate. However, the event's vibe was a happy one and the crowd didn't seem to mind the Stones' raggedyness.

Jones' funeral took place on 10 July. Jagger and Faithfull were unable to attend, being in Australia where both had contracted roles in a Tony Richardson movie, **Ned Kelly**. No sooner had they arrived, though, than Faithfull attempted suicide by taking a massive sleeping pill overdose. The reasons seem to be a not-quite-rational mixture of anguish over her decaying relationship with Jagger, her miscarriage and her sadness over Brian's death. Jagger saved her life by calling for help. Faithfull was in a coma for six days as headlines flashed around the world of yet more turmoil in The Rolling Stones' world.

Vale the Sixties

In June, the Stones had announced that they were planning to release two new albums in '69, one (to be titled **Sticky Fingers**) in September, the other in December. Though this didn't happen, it could technically have been achieved: the group had more than enough songs and an 8-track acetate of *Sticky Fingers* was prepared. In the event though, only **Let It Bleed** was released, in late November Stateside, and early December in the UK. It's possible that the only reason the group did not put out two albums in 1969 (and released no studio album at all in 1970) is that they didn't want **Allen Klein**'s publishing company to own their compositions.

Klein – the sole manager of their affairs since Oldham's departure – was a man the Stones were highly anxious to get rid of. The band blamed Klein for the fact that they didn't have easy access to their cash. Though Klein had secured them massive advances against future royalties and a huge advance for a feature film of the novel *Only Lovers Left Alive*, it has been alleged that the group had severe difficulty getting hold of any of this money. Jagger and Richards, with their increasingly substantial songwriting royalties, gathered for them not by their record company or Klein but by performing rights organizations, were in large part insulated from the financial hardship Watts and Wyman were going through, but they were still affected. In '69, Richards sent Stone employee **Tom Keylock** to Klein's New York offices to collect the deposit he needed on his new Chelsea house. The loyal Keylock vaulted the receptionist's desk and told Klein he would not leave his office until the money was in his hands. For once, the Stones got what they asked for from Klein.

Jagger and Richards were also not unaware of the irritation, even fury, engendered in the Stones camp by the fact that there was no money to pay even small bills. For instance, the group was threatened with court action from production company Colourtel – who had shot *Rock and Roll Circus* – when an invoice was not settled. **Jo Bergman**, manager of the Stones' office, wrote a memo to Jagger in which she complained, "The Klein problem is more than a drag. We're puppets. How can we work or run the office if we have to spend so much

The new line-up, with Mick Taylor second from the right.

time pleading for bread?" Matters wouldn't have been so bad if Klein had been instantly contactable but he was based in New York and – in a day and age before email and fax and when the cost of Transatlantic telephoning was astronomical – the band had to resort to the cumbersome method of telex to get information out of him. **Klein** responded only sporadically, whether it be about a field recording Brian Jones had made of Moroccan musicians and which record companies were interested in (the project did not see release before Jones' death) or personal finances. Communication and accounting rigour alone were not the issue. Klein also seemed to be non-responsive to the band's wishes. When artwork for the Stones compilation album *Through The Past Darkly* (released in September) went missing in May, Jagger had cabled Klein with the message, "Your inefficiency is a drag. What the fuck did you do with all the photographs, not the press cuttings, the photographs? They were supposed to be delivered to Andy Warhol. We await your reply."

However, reluctant though they may have been to give Klein any of their songs, the band had to release something new, both to give any kind of meaning to being a functioning group and to have something to sell other than the new compilation on their upcoming American tour, now set for November. The band actually finished the new album in the States, re-recording the track '**Country Honk**' and overdubbing some parts and remixing at Sunset and Elektra studios in LA.

The tour was a triumph, a rejuvenation and reinvention of the band, with Jagger now coming into his own as a performer, giving a camp twist to Presley's original rock 'n' roll sexual rituals and injecting it with a Satanic menace through his crowd baiting in numbers like '**Midnight Rambler**'. *Let It Bleed* was stunning. Topped and tailed by two epics that remain amongst the Stones greatest achievements – '**Gimme Shelter**' and '**You Can't Always Get What You Want**' – and addressing adult issues and concerns, it fulfilled all the yearnings of the generation who insisted that rock was an art form, not noisy pap for adolescents as it had always been portrayed by their elders.

The Stones were criticized throughout the tour for their unusually high ticket prices, most notably by *Rolling Stone* magazine co-founder **Ralph J. Gleason**. Clearly stung by this, the band planned another Hyde Park-style free event on 6 December, this time in San Francisco's Golden Gate Park. San Francisco's city fathers objected, and a last minute switch was made to a remote wasteland 50 miles outside the city – **Altamont Raceway**. As with the Hyde Park event, Hell Angel's provided the security but there the similarity ended. Instead of the sunny, happy atmosphere of the London gig, there was menace in the air, mainly from the Angels, although there was a bad vibe generally, with the Stones appearing some four hours late. Jagger was punched in the face by a crowd member when he got out of the helicopter that flew the band in. Four people died at the event, including Meredith Hunter,

Disaster At Altamont

Back in 1967, Brian Jones had enthusiastically attended the first, and for many the best, major rock festival, at Monterey. It was an offshoot of the Happenings and Love-Ins that had blossomed in San Francisco from 1965 onwards. Although the Stones, like Dylan, had eschewed Woodstock in August 1969, two weeks later Dylan showed for a star-studded bill at the Isle of Wight, which Keith Richards visited; all this, with the success of the Stones' free Hyde Park concert (following on a similar concert the week

Angels invading the stage during the Stones' set.

before headlined by Blind Faith) had given everyone a taste for Big Events.

The Stones contacted open-air West Coast concert veterans the Grateful Dead to arrange a similar bash in Golden Gate Park, off Haight Ashbury, SF, to round off the US tour in December. Civic permissions were refused at the last minute, and the event shifted east to the remote Altamont Raceway track. The Dead recommended using the local Oakland chapter of Hell's Angels for security (a very different tribe from the British bikers hired to police Hyde Park). The set-up was a shambles, with a 4-foot high stage and far too few facilities for the 300,000 people who turned up. The Angels ran roughshod from the beginning. Santana kicked off – late, followed by

Jefferson Airplane (during whose set guitarist Marty Balin was attacked by an Angel). The good natured country-rock of Gram Parsons' Flying Burrito Brothers and sweet harmony vocals of Crosby, Stills, Nash & Young were soothing but the effect was transient. Tensions between the performers, the pool-cue wielding Angels and the crowd reached a horrifying climax while the Stones were on stage. The concert staggered to a close with the Stones aware of the hugely bad vibes but not of the fact that the Angels had stabbed an audience member to death. The Grateful Dead – who refused to play when they saw what was going down – flew home to write a bitter anthem about the grisly affair, 'New Speedway Boogie' which appeared on *Workingman's Dead* the next year.

a black man knifed by one of the Hell's Angels as he apparently brandished a gun. Something else also began to die: the idea of the 'Love Generation'. The belief amongst the young in the Sixties that the blissful mass gatherings at the San Francisco 'Love-Ins' and the Monterey and Woodstock festivals proved that they were a new, different breed was proven this day to be erroneous.

The early 1970s saw a new, leotarded and uniquely androgynous Jagger emerge from the chrysalis of the late 60s.

Chapter 5:
The Swaggering Seventies

"They are the biggest draw in the history of mankind"

Bill Graham, promoter.

The Swaggering Seventies
1970–74

As the Stones entered the 1970s, they also strode into their role as 'The Greatest Rock and Roll Band in the World.' With a triumvirate of seminal albums behind them, their main rivals for the trophy now history, the job in hand was setting the template for what would become known as STP – the Stones Touring Party.

Biding Time

1970 was a year of relative inactivity for The Rolling Stones. Not because they were not churning with ideas. As well as unused tracks from the *Let It Bleed* sessions that they had in the can, they also already had other new songs, including a fabulous new creation called '**Brown Sugar**' that Jagger had come up with during the *longeurs* of filming *Ned Kelly*. However, they were extremely reluctant to issue those recordings or any other new songs because of who the beneficiaries would be: Decca, with whom they had had endless hassles and clashes of mentality, and Allen Klein, with whom their hassles had been of a different nature but just as infuriat-

ing and draining. The Decca contract expired on 31 July 1970. They were also planning to jettison Klein. The Stones needed to sit the Decca contract out out and to not let word get to Klein of any recordings they had made in the meantime in case Klein decided he had a legal claim to them. The band remained active – and solvent – by planning a European tour. They also began making plans for **The Rolling Stones Mobile Recording Unit**, an ingenious idea which would enable them to record wherever they wanted, and which would be hired by many of the top rock acts over the years.

Jagger's and Faithfull's cannabis possession trial took place in January. Despite Jagger flatly stating that he had been framed – Brian

Back in the dock: Faithfull and Jagger had been charged once again with drug possession in May 1969. Seven months later they got off with a slap on the wrists.

Jones' QC had only gone so far as insinuating such in his case – and, despite alleging that he was offered a way out if a bribe was paid, Jagger was found guilty. This may have been partly because he attended court looking like a resplendently outfitted caveman, his hair flowing now to a length that western civilization had not known on men in living memory. Faithfull was acquitted and Jagger fined £200.

Because of the **censorship issues** over *Performance*, it was actually Jagger's second film that premiered first, *Ned Kelly* opening in Melbourne in July 1970. Jagger wasn't expecting a rapturous reception: he had burst into tears at a preview, so dismayed was he by its quality. It was panned and naturally – because this was Jagger's acting debut as far as the public was concerned – those pans were accompanied by 'don't-give-up-the-day-job' jibes. Later, Jagger would denounce the movie as a "load of shit".

On 29 July 1970, The Rolling Stones put out a terse statement about Allen Klein, and his company ABKCO Industries Inc., which stated that neither had "the authority to negotiate recording contracts on their behalf in the future." As they left the Sixties behind them, the Stones also had to cut significant losses. Klein now owned all of their Sixties masters and publishing rights. They would continue to receive performance royalties from them – Jagger and Richard's publishing money was beyond even Klein's reach — but they were waving goodbye to what they had imagined to be ownership of classic recordings. It wasn't all bad news though. With the Decca contract coming to an end, the Stones could virtually dictate their terms with any new label. By 1970, it was known in the industry that The Beatles were on the ropes and would be putting out no more group recordings, something made official by **McCartney**'s December 1970 application to dissolve the band's legal partnership. Bob Dylan, meanwhile, had retreated from cutting-edge brilliance into soporific examinations of his marriage. Only **The Who** could now approach The Rolling Stones for the position of World's Most Important Artistes. Record companies were queuing up to sign the Stones, including Decca. Naturally, the band had no intention of

agreeing a new deal with their corporate nemesis. Still owing them product to finally see out their contract, they supplied them with a live album from tapes of their US tour. A new song was also required. Contemptuously, Jagger and Richards delivered '**Cocksucker Blues**'. Actually a pretty good 12-bar blues exploring London's seamy underworld, it was deliberately designed to be too obscene for Decca to even countenance releasing. The live album, *Get Yer Ya-Yas Out!* appeared in September. It is not known whether the suits at Decca, with whom the Stones had locked antlers so many times, appreciated that in releasing it they were putting out an album that would come to be considered by many the greatest live album of all time. The week before its release, the Stones kicked off their twenty-date European tour in Sweden.

Performance opened in the States in mid-September and the powerful work by Jagger in it surprised anyone who saw it whom had also seen *Ned Kelly*. There was no Stones music on the soundtrack, but the movie's sleazy set-piece song '**Memo From Turner**' featuring Mick accompanied by a stellar line-up of talent including Traffic's Steve Winwood and Jim Capaldi was issued as a Jagger solo single. According to director Douglas Cammell, Richards had been too upset by Jagger's dalliance with co-star Pallenberg to allow it to become a proper Stones recording. Nonetheless, it contains over the rather lumpen instrumentation some of the best songwords Jagger has ever written.

Gimme Shelter, a movie by the Maysles brothers which had been intended as nothing more than a document of the last Stones tour, but whose Altamont footage ensured it became an exhibit in a murder case, was premiered on 5 December. Little over a week later, the trial of Alan David Passaro for the killing of **Meredith Hunter** began. He would be acquitted in February the following year, on the grounds of self-defence.

Expatriate Blues

The month after Passaro's acquittal, an announcement came from the Stones' camp that shocked many to the core. The band announced they were leaving the country *en masse* to live in France. The real reasons were not actually given at the time. In retrospect, the press statement by the Stones' PR man Les Perrin was remarkably mealy-mouthed. It spoke of the move as something prompted by their love of France and its nice climate, plus the fact that they had an affinity with the country because it was the first continental territory in which they achieved success. The real reason for their emigration would have been scarcely more believable to the public, not least because of a *Daily Telegraph* article earlier that year, which estimated their income from recordings alone at around £83,000,000. The Stones were broke. Wyman alone owed £118,000. With income tax astronomically high (it would reach 83 pence in the pound), and with the previous management allegedly maladroit in

ensuring their taxes were paid, they were deeply in debt to the Inland Revenue. Their recently-appointed and improbably aristocratic financial adviser **Prince Rupert Loewenstein** had advised them to take a 'year out' (actually 21 months in their case) – valuable time away from the rapacious grasp of the UK tax man. Even to those to whom it wasn't obvious what the motivation was, it was clear that the Stones' new life on the French Riviera was a jet-setting existence which was making their 'Men of the People' image increasingly tenuous, as did the twenty-shilling ticket prices they were currently charging on their nine-city UK 'farewell' tour, which started in March.

However, it wasn't just this that fuelled the rumblings in the press at this time. With new stars like **Marc Bolan**, **Elton John** and **Slade** in chart ascendancy, the Stones couldn't help but seem a little old hat. This was a time before the idea of people making a long-term career out of being pop or rock stars had taken hold. Rock was so intertwined with the idea of youthful rebellion that the public – and in truth many pop and rock artists – had yet to get their heads around the idea of recording artists carrying on towards their thirties (the Stones were mostly now in their late twenties). It probably isn't exaggeration to say that some of the people who bought tickets for their UK tour were seizing what they felt might be the last chance they would ever have to see them on a stage.

That the Stones were still cooking was confirmed emphatically in mid-April 1971 with the release of 'Brown Sugar'. Released almost two years after their last official 45, it was a stunning re-entry, a rock anthem as iconic as anything they had ever recorded. It reached No.2 in their home country and topped the American chart. Proving that they had learned a lot from the way their wealth had previously been lost to others, it was the inaugural release of Rolling Stones Records, the label on which all their new product would now be issued. The Rolling Stones label was initially distributed by Atlantic. The distribution would change hands many times over the following decades as the band leased it to the highest bidder. The single's label saw another new arrival: the 'lapping tongue' band logo that would come to be the most famous symbol in rock.

Sticky Fingers, the new album, appeared in April (June in the States). It featured 'Brown Sugar', representing the fact that the rock industry was entering a new era where artists – or at least established artists like the Stones – now only released singles as a form of promotion for the parent album. There would never be another official stand-alone Stones single. Daringly – for the time – the album was housed in a sleeve depicting a pair of jeans with a real zip. Pulling down the zip revealed a card inset with occupied men's underwear. Just as daringly, the entire album dripped with drug references, the band now fully into a decadent image that would, for the next several years, help maintain an outlaw status when their increasing distance from their fans might otherwise have rendered them 'sell-outs' according to the values of the day. The first Stones studio album for which **Mick Taylor** was present throughout, it was musically superb and at a stroke rendered ludicrous the growing feeling that – like The Beatles and Dylan – they would not manage to remain relevant and important artists in the Seventies.

In Exile

In May, something happened which many never thought would. Mick Jagger got married. His wife was a Nicaraguan woman named Bianca Perez Morena De Macias. Many have pinpointed this moment as the one when the Stones' anti-establishment credentials were

Decca's Sulk

On the very same day as the release of *Sticky Fingers*, Decca Records embarked on probably the longest recorded sulk in history by putting out *Stone Age*, a Stones compilation which included four tracks previously unavailable in Britain in an attempt to lure those who already had most of the selections into spending their money. As though deliberately taunting the group, it was housed in a sleeve that was a toned down allusion to the rejected *Beggar's Banquet* graffiti artwork. The Stones took out full-page adverts in the music press condemning the album. There would be many more such releases by Decca in the coming years, the only ones of which to possess any real value being the B-sides-and-obscurities mop-up *No Stone Unturned* and the double, chronologically-arranged, compilation *Rolled Gold*.

The Tongue Symbol

On April 29 1970, Jo Bergman of The Rolling Stones' office wrote to a design student named John Pasche. She said, "Further to our recent discussion, I would like to confirm that we have asked you to design a poster for the forthcoming European tour by The Rolling Stones. We have also asked you to create a logo or symbol which may be used on note paper, as a programme cover and as a cover for the press book. I will speak to you on Friday to let you know when it will be possible to speak to Mr. Jagger."

Bergman spelt Pasche's surname incorrectly in the letter, but if he took umbrage Pasche must have quickly forgiven her, for the logo or symbol she mentioned quickly became not something that would be used on anything so modest as notepaper or as temporary as a programme cover. Instead, it became the symbol of The Rolling Stones *per se*, appearing on their every record release, and the most instantly recognisable graphic icon in rock.

The idea for a logo had come from Marshall Chess, president of Rolling Stones Records, after he had seen the yellow-and-red symbol of Shell Petroleum and thought that it would be good to have a logo for the Stones that was instantly recognisable as such despite featuring no words.

"At this time, I was in my final year of a graduate design course at the Royal College of Art in London," says Pasche. "Jagger's office rang the Royal College of Art and I was suggested as the most suitable student to take on the job. I was very honoured when Mick Jagger turned up at the College to see my final degree show. A short time later, I met with Mick again to discuss a logo or symbol for The Rolling Stone's record label. The letter from Jo Bergman was sent after the first meeting I had with Mick… Mick showed me an image of the Goddess of Kali which was the starting point to our discussion regarding the design of the logo. The mouth in the Kali image was the starting point." Pasche came up with a brilliant, glossy and superbly appropriate lascivious mouth and lapping tongue in bold red and white. Pasche explains, "The design concept for the Tongue was to represent the band's anti-authoritarian attitude, Mick's mouth and the obvious sexual connotations. I designed it in such a way that it was easily reproduced and in a style which I thought could stand the test of time."

Mick displays the brand.

The Life

"I was paid £50 for the design which took me about a week to complete. In 1972 I was paid an additional £200 in recognition of the logo's success." Down the years, the Tongue – now usually referred to as the Lapping Tongue, although this title didn't come from Pasche - has often been erroneously credited to Andy Warhol. Pasche explains, "The first use of the logo was the inner sleeve for the *Sticky Fingers* album. The outer sleeve was designed by Warhol, hence the mix-up with the credits." He adds, "The logo was not fully registered in all countries and a German jeans company registered the logo in Germany for their own products. This situation, and the fact that the tongue was getting used by unauthorised manufacturers of badges and t-shirts, prompted proper registration and a merchandising agreement with myself to capitalise on the success of the logo. Due to its immediate popularity, the Stones kept with it over the years and I believe that it represents one of the strongest and most recognizable logos worldwide. And of course I'm proud of that. The simplicity of the design lent itself to many variations which were done by other designers and not myself. Obviously, I would have preferred to have done the variations myself. The Stones ultimately bought the copyright, but I still own the hand-drawn artwork. My busiest time creating artwork for the Stones was from 1970-1974, including four tour posters."

Pasche went on to do design work for The Who, Paul McCartney and many other artistes. He subsequently spent eleven years as Creative Director of the South Bank Centre Arts Complex in London. He now works as a freelance designer from his home studio and is "still enjoying rock music".

For more information see: www.johnpasche.com.

rendered meaningless, both by the very fact that he had embraced the supposedly outdated concept of betrothal and by the jet-set nature and location of the ceremony: celebrity guests were flown in for the glittering occasion in **San Tropez**. Richards was in fact now the only original Stone who had never tied the knot. Richards' and Pallenberg's marriage remained a common-law one, despite the birth of their son Marlon the previous August.

Because of the rubber-neckers and would-be gatecrashers, one report described the wedding as "hippie chaos". Much the same could be said about the sessions for the next Rolling Stones album, ultimately titled *Exile On Main St.* For many years it was erroneously assumed that the entirety of this double (vinyl) album originated at Nellcote, Richards' rented mansion in the south of France. Though recording did commence there in July '71, Jagger later admitted that some of it was "bits and pieces left over from the previous album recorded at Olympic studios and which, after we got out of the contract with Allen Klein, we didn't want to give him." Nonetheless, half of the basic tracks were done at **Nellcote,** and Watts has said that the offcuts Jagger mentions had overdub work done to them there too. The band were using the Mobile Recording Unit for the first time, cables leading from the wheeled studio down into Richards' sweaty basement. Witnesses have described a house brimming with both good and bad company. Though there were gifted friends like saxophonist Bobby Keys and ex-Burrito and now solo star Gram Parsons

– from whom Richards picked up many tips about country music – there were also numerous freeloaders and drug dealers. Richards' drug of choice over the last couple of years had become hard, he and Anita having drifted into a full-blown heroin habit. Mick Taylor was also dabbling with the hard stuff, as was Jimmy Miller. This was having negative creative consequences. Despite the fact that they were being held in his own home, Richards would sometimes fail to turn up for the album's sessions. In retaliation, an annoyed Jagger would sometimes then not turn up the next day. Jagger himself began to annoy the rest of the band within a few weeks by taking leaves of absence to visit Bianca, who was **pregnant** and refused to come to Nellcote. It was so humid in the basement that guitars would spontaneously go out of tune. Conditions elsewhere in the house weren't much better: engineer Andy Johns recalled a guitar part being overdubbed in the kitchen while around him people were chatting and knives and forks clattered. Jagger mixed the results in LA, isolated (Miller was no longer considered reliable) and up against a deadline.

Amazingly, out of this chaos emerged what many consider to be the band's masterpiece. Or, rather, it is now. Upon its release in late May 1972, *Exile on Main St.* got mixed reviews. 'Tumbling Dice' was released on single as a taster. As with a lot of the album, on first hearing, it baffled many listeners. 'Tumbling Dice' sounds initially like the musical equivalent of an out-of-focus photograph, the margins of this funk-soul ballad alternately blurred and fading as the song lurches, as though inebriated, from tempo to tempo, and an alternately slurred and strangulated Jagger complains incomprehensibly on the vocal track. It's only after a few hearings that everything slips into place, although some were understandably not inclined to grant such sloppy delivery and production techniques a second chance. If one perseveres, one will discover a worthwhile song. Still, a bizarre choice for an A-side and one can only assume that the Stones' stature is what led to it reaching the Top Ten on both sides of the Atlantic. The album nevertheless topped the album charts in both the UK and the US.

The Stones Touring Party

The Stones' 1972 American tour was probably their first tour as modern audiences understand the term, involving both playing to the gigantic venues necessary in order to accommodate their massive and by now two-generation fan base, and employing a veritable army of staff to transport the lavish stage sets the punters expected for their steep ticket prices, all of this planned with military precision. Jagger admitted he was nervous about the band's first visit to the country since the horrors of **Altamont**, for which many still blamed them, but the American audiences seemed very willing to forgive. The tour was probably The Rolling Stones Mach II at their zenith. They

Getting publicly hitched in San Tropez: "The worst day of my life" said Bianca.

cut a swathe of decadence through the country, partaking of drugs, groupies, hotel-trashing and Hugh Hefner's Playboy mansion along the way. Oh, and they also played some magnificent music and presented some stunning stage spectacles. Mick Jagger was now utterly unselfconscious as a frontman, taking rock performance into new areas with his then-unique **male tart stage persona**. Friends who had known Jagger since the early days might have been embarrassed to see him pouting his lips and wiggling his hips like a woman, but

the audiences lapped it up.

Documenting all of this were author **Robert Greenfield** and filmmaker **Robert Frank**, working on separate projects. Greenfield's emerged as the book *STP: A Journey Across America With The Rolling Stones*. Frank came up with the documentary *Cocksucker Blues*. The contents of the latter were about as palatable to mainstream society as the title would be – although not unrepresentative of the goings-on on the tour – and the Stones understandably banned a full release. Also hovering was **Truman Capote**.

The Rolling Stones Record Label

Tapes were made of some of the 1972 American concerts for a live album, for which overdubs were recorded and artwork prepared. However, as if to prove that, despite now having their own label, the Stones were not all-powerful, the project never materialized because Decca and Allen Klein exercised their veto over new live recordings of the songs to which they owned rights.

Nonetheless, in its early years Rolling Stones Records did engage in a relatively energetic release schedule. 1971-1972 saw the appearance on the label of Brian Jones' Moroccan field recording (*Brian Jones Presents the Pipes of Pan at Joujouka*), *Jamming With Edward* (a Stones jam minus Richards but with Ry Cooder and Nicky Hopkins present, recorded at the *Let It Bleed* sessions) and *The London Howlin' Wolf Sessions* (the titular bluesman backed by Watts, Wyman, Eric Clapton and others). Unfortunately, after paying their respects to Brian and Howlin' Wolf – and Hopkins, for whose benefit *Jamming With Edward* seems mainly to have been issued – The Rolling Stones' record label then stalled almost completely, ex-Wailer Peter Tosh being the only outside artist that the Stones mustered the energy to issue the product of, although they did sign a band called Kracker and are said to have toyed with the idea of signing Rory Gallagher.

Apart from Tosh, Bill Wyman was the only artist to record more than one album for Rolling Stones Records, venting his creative frustration with a brace of mid-Seventies solo albums.

Though his planned article on the band for *Rolling Stone* never materialized, the fact that a serious, non-rock writer like Capote (still basking in the praise for his ground-breaking New Journalism book *In Cold Blood*) wanted to be in the band's orbit demonstrated their status as a social phenomenon.

In The Soup

After a drugs-related *contretemps* with the authorities in France, the Stones relocated to Jamaica for the recording of their next album, *Goat's Head Soup*, the venue chosen partly because Richards was a big reggae fan. Additional work was done in American and

British studios, with live dates interspersing the recording. In their tenth year as a band, the acclaim from their '72 tour ringing in their ears, the Stones were finally beginning to achieve financial security and bestrode rock as unassailable titans. The result was – for the first time in their existence – complacency. Jagger later said, "I think we got a bit carried away with our own popularity and so on." Engineer Andy Johns admitted, "There are a couple of examples on there where just the basic tracks we kept weren't really up to standard." Richards eventually dismissed the album as "marking time". Richards also claimed that **Jimmy Miller** was now more of a hindrance than help, his heroin addiction making him so unproductive that he spent his time carving swastikas into a wooden console when sessions relocated to Island Studios. More than one of Richards' Stones colleagues might have a thing or two to say about that example of the smack-addled pot calling the strung-out kettle black. Nonetheless, the band went along with the idea to dispense with Miller's services before the record was completed.

The group played a benefit concert for victims of a recent earthquake in **Nicaragua** in January '74, helping to raise $500,000. A Pacific tour – Hawaii, New Zealand and Australia – took place from late January to late February. On 26 June, with the new album nearing completion, Richards was busted at his house in London's Cheyne Walk, charged with a veritable grand slam of offences: possession of cannabis, heroin, mandrax and firearms. This came as a

surprise to his colleagues, who were under the impression that his drug problems were over. Exactly one month later, Jagger turned 30. It was quite a big deal at the time. In the Sixties, one of the slogans of part of the Stones' audience – the hippies and the radicals – had been, "Never trust anybody over thirty." For many, the milestone brought home the absurdity of men of the Stones' age continuing to play rock music. This was a separate matter from the disillusion felt by many fans – including those who had themselves turned thirty – over the way that the Stones seemed to be turning into a mere vehicle for entertainment rather than the zeitgeist-encapsulating social phenomenon they had once constituted. This kind of disillusion would colour Stones reviews for several years, until such time as reviewers got used to the idea that the Stones now saw their role as simply a working rock band, not the figureheads for societal change that they had never claimed to be (though had sometimes flirted with being).

To the majority of the public, though, this sort of stuff clearly didn't matter a jot. When *Goat's Head Soup* appeared in late August in the UK and early September in the US, it not only topped both album charts, but became the band's fourth-highest selling album. It was preceded by the single 'Angie' which, because it was a ballad, was perceived by some ex-loyalists as another example of the Stones going soft. The wider public recognized it as an achingly beautiful love song and made it a phenomenal success. Though only reaching No.5 in their home country, it topped the charts in countries all over the globe, including America, and became probably their first 'crossover' record, i.e. bought by people who wouldn't normally purchase Stones product. Only a band of the Stones' calibre could – when putting out an album recorded in an atmosphere of complacency – still manage to produce such a classic song. Additionally, the band were able to keep their collective bad-boy image going a little bit longer by the controversy surrounding the album's closing track '**Star Star**', whose refrain "You're a starfucker" referred to a groupie, and which Atlantic refused to distribute until actor Steve McQueen gave an undertaking that he did not object to appearing in the song as a recipient of fellatio by said lady.

September and October saw the Stones touring Europe, including Britain. However, Richards found time during the last week of September to attend, with **Marshall Chess**, President of Rolling Stones Records, a clinic in Switzerland. Both men were attempting to wean themselves off heroin.

On 24 October, Richards was fined and given a conditional discharge on the charges arising from the 26 June bust. What might have seemed like an amusing incident to some – heroin chic etc. – was cast in a different light that very evening when a fire started in the hotel room of Richards and Pallenberg. A shaken Andy Johns recalled, "One side of the double bed was on fire. It was incredible. We'd already been to court,

Keith nearly got done, and here we are and the kids nearly get it. I thought, 'I'm getting out of here, man!'"

But It's Only Rock 'n' Roll

Having not worked with the group since *Sticky Fingers*, George Chkiantz was pleased to be asked in 1974 to work on the Stones' latest album project. Sessions took place at Jagger's country house **Stargroves**, Island Studios and (on one occasion) the home of Faces member Ronnie Wood. The band were now being produced by Jagger and Richards, using the pseudonym '**The Glimmer Twins**', a nickname they'd acquired on their 1969 South American trip ("Give us a glimmer" asked their fellow boat passengers, unsure of who they were but perceiving their glamour). Chkiantz found himself in the midst of a disillusioned Taylor, a drug-addled Richards and a feuding pair of Glimmer Twins: "The band was in a pretty poor state because the whole thing was breaking up over Mick Taylor leaving," he says. "Some of those sessions at Stargroves were just lunatic." Chkiantz remembers "trying to persuade Keith not to overdub Charlie's drums, trying to persuade Mick not to overdub Bill's bass. It was all kind of, 'Oh, I don't think he's got it quite right..' I thought the band was in a terrible state. I was heartily glad to get out of Stargroves – nice though it was, great time though we had in some ways – but a lot of the

Taylor/Jagger. Where's Angie?

time was spent just in internecine band fights that basically left me personally with absolutely horrific decisions to make or to try and subvert. If somebody's going to do something which you think is likely to do permanent damage to the tapes, what the hell do you do to stop them? There was nobody in authority to say 'no'. Who was in authority? Keith Richards?"

In reaching No.16 in the US and No.10 in the UK respectively, '**It's Only Rock 'N' Roll (But I Like It)**' became the lowest-charting new Stones single since the Sixties, discounting unofficial releases and second singles from albums. Ironically, it was a song that would become one of the few iconic post-*Exile* Stones anthems. The track bore the Jagger/Richards publishing credit despite the fact that it was in reality a collaboration between Jagger and Ronnie Wood. This seems to have been due to a deal that Wood made with Jagger over the credit on another of their co-writes. Mick Taylor, however, had made no such deal and was dismayed that credits for his own contributions to the single's parent album were non-existent.

For some time, it had been obvious to those who could be bothered to care – which apparently did not include Jagger and Richards – that Mick Taylor was an unhappy Rolling Stone. Wyman has recalled how, several years before, he had found screwed up notes written by Taylor saying he no longer wanted to be in the band. Taylor's partner Rose told Wyman as far back as December 1972 that he was

thinking of defecting to the band **Free**. The reasons for Taylor's disenchantment with being in the world's most famous rock act seem to be numerous. Though Taylor has subsequently revealed that the story put about that he was a teetotal vegetarian on joining the Stones was false, it's certainly true that he wasn't a heroin user before his arrival. It has also subsequently emerged that Taylor's wife had a reason for wanting him to leave: she was convinced he was having a gay love affair with Jagger.

'74 had been a **soporific year** for the Stones, with them doing no live work at all (the first time this had happened since their formation) and this had been another cause of frustration for Taylor. There also seemed to be a certain contempt felt toward him by the band's songwriting axis: Andy Johns has recalled Richards barking at Taylor at one recording session "Fuck you! You play too loud. You're really good live, but you're no good in the studio. So you can play later…" There was also the fact that he had mysteriously only received one co-songwriting credit so far. Indeed, the final straw for Taylor seems to have been the fact that when *It's Only Rock 'N' Roll* – the album – was released in mid-October '74, once again all the original songs were credited to Mick and Keith. Judging by comments journalist Nick Kent later recalled Taylor making to him just before the album's release, he had been expecting this album to correct a **recurring grievance**. When told by Kent that the finished sleeve artwork he had seen bore no admission that numbers to which Taylor

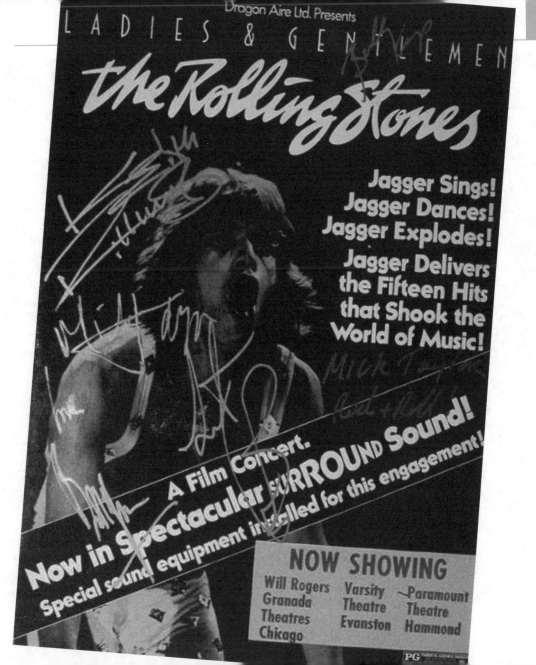

Charlie and Mick, waiting for time?

had contributed heavily, like the ornate 'Time Waits For No One', 'Till the Next Goodbye' and 'If You Really Want To Be My Friend', had anything to do with any composers but Jagger and Richards, Taylor had said "We'll see about that!"

Taylor did attend a band meeting in **Switzerland** in the last week of October, but stormed out when he felt that once again his contributions to the band were not being given enough credit. About a month later – according to Wyman's estimation – Taylor rang the Stones' office to say he was leaving the group. "I was a bit peeved about not getting credit for a couple of songs, but that wasn't the whole reason," Taylor later said. "I guess I just felt like I had enough... I never really felt, and I don't know why, I was gonna stay with the Stones forever, even right from the beginning."

The **middle period** of The Rolling Stones – in which many feel they made their greatest music – was over.

In the air and in the round, the new gang of five at
Madison Square Garden, NY with Billy Preston on keyboards.

Chapter 6:
The Stones
Mach III

"When I consider it coolly, I think it's more than possible that they've peaked. I wonder what I'll think of them in 1978."

Philadelphia Inquirer, 1975.

The Stones Mach III
1974–78

By the mid-Seventies the strain of the rock 'n' roll lifestyle which was effectively epitomized by the Stones was beginning to show. They had achieved a seemingly unassailable position as the world's most popular, prolific and successful band. But changes were afoot – changes in line-up, in lifestyle and, more importantly, in popular music tastes.

Exit Taylor

Taylor left at an ostensibly strange moment. *It's Only Rock 'N' Roll* was better received than *Goat's Head Soup* had been. Though no classic, it was a solid and occasionally adventurous effort, was housed in an intriguing **Guy Peelaert** sleeve, and contained some of the controversy that a Stones album still felt incomplete without, albeit amounting only to the allusions to assassination of the vocalist contained in the title track. At the very least, it showed the band as old masters whose product was still better than that of most of the competition in 1974.

Wyman has claimed that at first they thought Taylor might be **bluffing**. If so, this makes the annoyance that Jagger subsequently expressed in interviews about the short notice Taylor had given the band understandable, for they had tried calling his alleged bluff. They were

then plunged into something of a crisis, for recording dates had already been booked in Munich. Instead of cancelling the sessions, the group decided to go ahead with them. The sessions almost collapsed at the beginning when the now ever-unreliable Richards didn't bother turning up for the first couple of days. The band decided to cancel the sessions if he didn't show on the third day, but Richards finally emerged. **Glyn Johns** was overseeing the sessions and recalled a marvellously productive opening couple of weeks, with the group getting down the basic tracks of nearly a dozen songs before the proceedings broke for Christmas. When the sessions recommenced in **Rotterdam** in January, the band had decided to use them for a dual purpose, not only laying down an album, but auditioning people to replace Taylor in the process. Johns found these sessions less enjoyable and walked out on them.

Just about every axe-slinger of note who didn't already have a regular job was considered for the vacant guitarist role. **Jeff Beck, Rory Gallagher** and **Wayne Perkins** auditioned in Rotterdam. The sessions returned to Munich at the end of March, and Wayne Perkins (again) and **Harvey Mandel** played with them there, although these were by no means the only people considered. The group had just about decided on Perkins when Jagger's and Richards' mate **Ron Wood** had his turn on 1 April, contributing dagger-sharp lines to the sparky 'Hey Negrita'. A chemistry was obvious immediately, Wood's style meshing with Richards' in a manner reminiscent of the interweaving, interchangeable guitar work of Richards and Brian Jones back in the olden days. That Wood also had the same kind of mindset, background and humour as the Stones was also a plus factor. As Richards later said, "This is an English band". Richards recalled that even Woods' fellow auditionees Mandel and Perkins saw the natural rapport and urged them to give Wood the job. Trouble was, Wood already had a job, being the guitarist of **The Faces,** the five-man rock combo fronted by Rod Stewart, that so many had compared to the Stones since their 1969 formation. The Faces had had their troubles of late – original bassist Ronnie Lane had left in 1973, partly because of the increasingly prima-donnish behaviour of Stewart – but Wood was loathe to break up the band by defecting to the Stones. A compromise was reached when Wood agreed to tour with the Stones as a temporary fill-in when The Faces weren't working, but such was his love for the Stones – he was, like so many millions of others, a fan – that he spent the rest of the year agonising about the situation.

Enter Wood

That the Stones elected to go on the tour on which Wood first accompanied them at all – starting 1 June 1975 – was a strange decision. Though the Stones had helped pioneer the idea of a tour as a **multi-million dollar pay day,** this was a day and age when the main reason for touring was still considered to be a mechanism for promoting product; and the new studio album was nowhere near complete. Putting out a new compilation album as they did was hardly a solution: for *Made In The Shade* they only had access to their post-Decca records. Allen Klein 'helpfully' put out his own Stones album during the tour in the shape of *Metamorphosis,* a collection of rejects and outtakes they were obliged to give him as part of the settlement in extricating themselves from his clutches. The Stones announced the tour by performing on the back of a flatbed truck on **New York's Fifth Avenue.** The announcement was greeted with the 'May this be the last time?' headlines the Stones had by now been used to for a few years. Things on the tour were as grandiose as the fans had come to expect them to be, with the group performing to massive audiences whom they treated with an extravagant set, including a giant inflatable

Ronnie Wood slipped into his new role in a way that his predecessor could never have achieved.

penis which popped up during the performance of 'Star Star'. The latter ensured that the band's frayed and creaking bad-boy image staggered on just a little longer when they were threatened with police action in various states if they brought it out. Richards later claimed that on this visit to the States, he was supplied with top-grade heroin by people who identified themselves as **FBI agents**, a scenario supposedly arranged because certain people with money invested in the Stones were anxious to protect it by ensuring Richards wasn't arrested while trying to score himself. If true – and Richards doesn't particularly seem a liar about such things – then it surely marked the definitive transformation of the Stones from outlaws to commodity and institution.

A week after the tour ended in August, Wood was off on the road again with The Faces. Wyman and Jagger meanwhile were recording work for respective solo albums. Wyman had already put out a solo record the previous year but Jagger's solo material – recorded in Toronto – would not see the light of day, and it would be another decade before the world heard a Mick Jagger album. Jagger spent late October adding the vocals to the tracks recorded at the previous Stones album sessions.

In December, Wood was given the perfect get-out from his dilemma when **Rod Stewart** announced he was leaving The Faces. Though Stewart gave as one of his reasons the fact that their band's guitarist "seems to be permanently 'on loan' to The Rolling Stones", Wood could have a clear conscience because most observers

agreed that so drunk was Stewart on fame at the time – he had a far more successful parallel solo career - that he would have found an excuse to jettison his colleagues in any event. The '**Rolling Stones Mach III**', as Richards might have termed it, had arrived.

Young Pretenders

The album resulting from the audition process appeared in mid-April 1976, titled *Black And Blue*. Wood appeared on two tracks. The record surprised many in the way it constituted a volte face on the generic Stones sound of much of the previous album, embracing funk, reggae and jazz. It wasn't altogether successful aesthetically, but the Stones couldn't be accused, as they had been on the previous two albums, of treading water. However, the reviews were mixed, no doubt subliminally affected by a feeling best expressed in critic Lester Bangs' appraisal of it for *Creem*: "The heat's off because it's all over, they really don't matter anymore or stand for anything, which is certainly lucky for both them and us. I mean, it was a heavy weight to carry for all concerned. This is the first meaningless Stones album, and thank God."

It wasn't just for Bangs' generation that The Rolling Stones had lost something that was more than the sum of their music. It was at this precise juncture – April 1976 saw their first major press coverage via a Jonh Ingham *Sounds* article – that a group of young musicians in Britain called the **Sex Pistols** began to attract notoriety. Part of the reason for their notoriety would be the fact that they did the previously unthinkable by publicly dismissing the Stones, the epitome of the rebel, as Establishment. Moreover, *Black And Blue* was accompanied by an advertisement campaign depicting a **heavily-bruised female** adherent of bondage tied up atop the album artwork. Whereas the dismissal of women precisely ten years before on *Aftermath* had been a spurning of songwriting convention and hence a rebellious act that even women could relate to, this campaign simply seemed gratuitously offensive and indicated people marooned in the past. However, it wasn't just the tarnished image that dismayed the once-loyal. The fact that '**Fool To Cry**', the single from the album, was a slow, almost sentimental ballad – parts of which Jagger sung in a falsetto – only confirmed many people's feeling that musically the Stones had lost their edge.

Nonetheless, releasing 'Fool To Cry' as a single was the correct decision. Now that the consumer knew that any single by a band of the Stones' stature was going to shortly end up on the parent album, there was little incentive for them to buy their singles. The Stones had to choose songs that would '**crossover**', and classy ballads were perfect for this. It was a UK No.6 and US No.10 and, as 'Angie' had been, was a big hit in many overseas territories.

It should in no way be assumed that punk had any detrimental effect on the Stones' career. Yes, punks made headlines and obtained TV coverage through their disrespect to their musical elders, but it was only prog rock acts like **Emerson, Lake and Palmer** who seemed to experience a sudden loss in ticket and album sales as a consequence. Unlike ELP, the Stones' music does not suffer from a invisible demographic syndrome – the phenomenon of not being able to find outside the climate of the time people who obtain genuine pleasure from listening to their music. When the Stones embarked on a European tour in late April, demand for tickets was huge. For their six shows at London's Earl's Court, postal ticket applications topped **one million**. They closed the tour with a triumphant marathon performance in front of 200,000 people at the **Knebworth** festival on 21 August.

"Keith... where are you?"

Richards though was probably somewhat unmoved by the reception at Knebworth or anywhere else after June 4. That was the date on which Tara, his and Pallenberg's third child, died of respiratory problems. The instant suspicion was that Pallenberg's ingestion of drugs during pregnancy was partly to blame, not least because Richards had wandered through the tour like a zombie and had been arrested and charged with cocaine possession in mid-May. Pallenberg admitted as much to Victor Bockris in his biography of Richards where she said, "I am sure that the drugs had something to do with it. And I always felt very, very bad

The Life

The Arrival of Punk

By the mid-Seventies, rock audiences were becoming dissatisfied. The Sixties pop stars had become the rock aristocracy. They were remote, insulated by their vast wealth from their fans' concerns and lifestyles, and from the need to record or tour with any great regularity. It seemed that they were also insulated from the desire to prove anything any more, their blunted artistic ambitions revealed by the mediocre quality of their work when they did deign to release albums, the ever greater gaps between which were emphasised by their refusal to release those stand-alone, state-of-the-union singles anymore. By 1976, the prospect of a new album by Bob Dylan, Rod Stewart, The Rolling Stones, Eric Clapton, The Who or any ex-Beatle was still an intriguing prospect but only because of their past work. The release of their albums was almost always followed by disappointment. Even when the music was good, it was music to which only an older age group could relate – witness Bob Dylan's fine album about divorce, *Blood On The Tracks* (1975). Meanwhile, the 'progressive' likes of Genesis, Emerson, Lake & Palmer, Pink Floyd, Yes, even Led Zeppelin – with their endless extemporization and po-faced lyrics - had so fallen in love with the idea of being Serious Artists that they seemed to have lost any interest in pleasing an audience.

The younger artists who came in to fill their shoes – such as the groups in the UK glam rock scene of the early Seventies – did not replace them as such, their talent – with the exception of David Bowie, who had also by now become remote - being too meagre to translate the status of chart sensations into major artists. Despite game attempts by the likes of the New York Dolls (too much a Stones pastiche) and Bruce Springsteen (too American and too wrapped up in

myth for Britons to take seriously), the music scene was boring and stagnant.

Then came punk. In New York, it revolved around the venue CBGB's, where Television, the Patti Smith Group, the Heartbreakers, Talking Heads, the Ramones and Blondie, as well as several others who never got signed, were bringing a youthful enthusiasm and primal energy back to popular music. The spirit of that scene made its way over to London, partly through Malcolm McLaren, a frequent visitor to New York both as the proprietor of a clothing shop and the manager of the New York Dolls in their latter stages. British punk centred around McLaren and another manager, Bernie Rhodes, and the main groups of the movement were initially the Sex Pistols and the Damned, with The Clash making a late rally in assuming importance. British punk was a lot less varied than New York punk, aggressive and sometimes brutal, making a virtue of musical and philosophical simplicity, as well as speedy tempos. However, very few of the UK punk bands – or at least the ones that got signed – were actually musically tal-

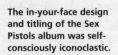

The in-your-face design and titling of the Sex Pistols album was self-consciously iconoclastic.

entless and the movement produced several classic albums and many fine singles in its first wave.

UK punk rockers also made a virtue of disparaging their predecessors, a marked contrast to the way the Stones themselves had paid homage to Howlin' Wolf and Chuck Berry *et al*, whenever they could. Some of

Latterday punks would rival the Stones in outlandishness.

this disdain was genuine – for the reasons outlined above – and some of it was done for the sheer gleeful youthful pleasure in making an outrageous statement. Rod Stewart aroused much of the punks' ire for the way he had turned from an "everyman" of rock into a preening, strutting ball of self-regard but the Stones were also

natural targets for the way they had become unproductive and lazy and – in Jagger's case – a social climber who seemed anxious to go the parties thrown by Ladies and Princesses.

Punks also displayed a social conscience, The Clash and The Jam especially specializing in denunciations of poverty and injustice that stood in stark contrast to the decadent image the Stones had increasingly acquired in recent years, and which made their previous flirtations with politics in their art like the 'Salt Of The Earth' begin to seem a very long time ago. Additionally, the way that punk frontmen like the Sex Pistol's Johnny Rotten, The Clash's Joe Strummer and Mick Jones and The Jam's Paul Weller pointedly sang in their own English accents suddenly made Jagger's (and everybody else's) vocal Americanisms seem not a badge of cool but phoney – yet another sign that the rock rules were being suddenly, and unexpectedly, rewritten.

The Stones affected nonchalance to all this at the time. Many years later though Jagger said that the hostility of punks toward them was "very shocking at the time". It would also be patently obvious when the Stones' next album – *Some Girls* – emerged that punk had given the band a kick up the backside.

On stage and on song at Kebworth in 1976.

The Life

about the whole thing." (He would receive a fine for the cocaine charge the following January.) Both she and Richards seem to have been unimaginably devastated. Journalist Nick Kent saw the couple after a show in Paris, to which Anita had flown after the tragedy: "Anita was crying and seemed to be having difficulty moving. Keith was shepherding her along but he was crying too and looked all of a sudden to be impossibly fragile. I honestly never thought I'd see them alive again." Richards and Pallenberg lived – they had two other children to care for – but anyone assuming that this would constitute a wake-up call for the pair were mistaken. Possibly they were drowning their grief in drugs, but their mutual heroin addiction continued.

So did the Stones' career. They signed a deal with **EMI** in the UK that would see Rolling Stones Records moving all its product over to that company for distribution. (They signed a new deal with **Atlantic** in the States.) Tours of America, Australia, Japan and England were discussed, starting in the Spring. The group still owed an album from the previous deal and decided to meet the debt with a live double recorded on the last tour. In addition, some club dates were arranged in Toronto in order to facilitate one vinyl side set in an intimate atmosphere. Ironically – considering subsequent circumstances – Canada was chosen because it was feared that with his current court case, Richards might have trouble getting into the States. Richards, as was now becoming the norm, failed to show for the first few

days of rehearsals in Canada. The band sent him an exasperated telegram: "WE WANT TO PLAY. YOU WANT TO PLAY. WHERE ARE YOU?"

The Mounties Get Their Man …

Richards and Pallenberg finally arrived in Toronto on 24 February. Pallenberg was busted before she was even out of the airport, arrested for, amongst other things, possession of cannabis. Richards spent three days rehearsing with his colleagues for the club dates, at which – in an unusual display of sentimentality by the Stones – the band were planning to play some old numbers owned by the Chess publishing company, inclusion of which on the live album would be a lucrative golden goodbye to **Marshall Chess**, who was leaving Rolling Stones Records after seven years as its president. On 27 February the **Royal Canadian Mounted Police** raided Richards' hotel room and found a comatose Richards plus heroin, cocaine and various drug paraphernalia. Richards was so out of it that, he said, it took the police half-an-hour to wake him up in order to tell him he was being arrested. Richards was a drug-bust veteran, but this was no ordinary drug-related arrest. At his court hearing that day before his granting of bail, it emerged that the quantity of heroin Richards had in his room made it possible for the police to charge him with possession of the drug with the intent to traffic, a crime that carried a maximum life sentence.

Richards was able to carry on as normal that evening, attending another band rehearsal. By the next day though, he was frantic with withdrawal symptoms. Wyman and Wood found him in his hotel room literally writhing in pain and were so moved they each went out and scored some heroin for him to alleviate the symptoms. Over the following week or so, the case made headlines around the world. People discussed what could genuinely be the end of the group – the new record contracts were jeopardized, and they had to gradually acknowledge that more than a couple of years in prison for Richards would necessitate a replacement or a split. The Stones did the only thing that anybody in the situation really could: try to maintain a **semblance of normal life**. Rehearsals continued through late February and early March. On March 4, Pallenberg was given a fine after pleading guilty to possession of heroin and cannabis.

On 4 and 5 March, the Stones played to two of their smallest audiences since the days of the Richmond Station Hotel at Toronto's El Mocambo Club. Considering the circumstances, they were pretty good gigs musically and a highly enjoyable nostalgia trip for a band who had long ago become too big for venues where the front row of the audience was brushing their legs. In the audience on one of the days was **Margaret Trudeau**, 28-year-old wife of Canada's prime minister Pierre Trudeau. Before long, rumours were sweeping the country that she was having a affair with Jagger. This alleged scandal was not good news for Richards, who needed to get in good odour with the Canadian authorities if he had any hope of having his drug-trafficking charge dropped. The charge, of course, was ludicrous – nobody genuinely believed that he needed to supplement his superstar income in such a way – but people can be charged with offences for a variety of reasons, including a desire to nab a famous scalp. When Richards returned to court on 7 March, far from his troubles being eased, he had another charge added, namely possession of cocaine. He was in court again the next day where his passport was confiscated and he was informed he now had to pay $25,000 bail. Jagger and Wood left town for New York to begin work on the live album. Richards, Wyman and Watts went into a Toronto recording studio to lay down some overdubs on the El Mocambo recordings. By 11 March though, Watts and Wyman had gone home and Richards was the only Stone left in town. Only **Ian Stewart** stayed with him.

Cold Turkey

Richards was saved from the prospect of having to spend the time awaiting trial stranded in a strange country when his passport was ordered to be returned to him on 14 March, although he still faced the task of obtaining a visa from whichever country he decided to go to. Surprisingly, it was America that granted Richards a visa. He and Pallenberg left Canada at the beginning of April to take a **treatment** in Pennsylvania for their joint heroin addiction. Known as the 'black box treatment', this was a method which supposedly sent electrical signals to the brain and tricked it into thinking the drug needs were being met, therefore ensuring **no withdrawal symptoms**. Under his bail terms, Richards was only allowed to travel within a six-mile radius of his place of treatment, so he and Jagger booked into the local Sigma Sound Studios in April to mix tapes for the live album. Richards and Pallenberg went to the more familiar environs of New York in May to receive further treatment and while there the Stones did some overdubs on the live tapes.

Richards' trial did not take place until October 1978, during which time he twice failed to show for court appearances, though his bail was surprisingly not forfeited. Mid-September 1977 saw the release of the in-concert album, *Love You Live*. A double-set, it was accompanied by a series of photographs which featured the band biting each other in a way that somehow seemed obscene and showed that in the year of punk – which employed shock tactics in name, image and song subject as a matter of course – the Stones were still the elder statesmen of outrage.

However, there was still a lot to prove to the punks and to those who considered the Stones to be **irrelevant old farts**. Accordingly, when the Stones convened in Pathé Marconi Studios in Paris, France, in the second week of October, both Jagger and Richards had a new sense of purpose.

As Richards' trial date seemed to grow further and further away, the band had to just plough on with their careers. Mid-May 1978 saw the release of the first product of the Pathé Marconi sessions in the shape of the single 'Miss You'. (Considering its subject matter it was perhaps appropriate that it was released within a week of Bianca filing for divorce against Mick.) It was a magnificent record, its slinky groove carrying a lyric of unusual vulnerability for the Stones. Quite deservedly, it was a smash, hitting No.2 in the UK and topping the American singles chart. The parent album *Some Girls* followed in June. It too showed a vitality that many had given up ever hearing in Rolling Stones music again, the band purveying disco, country, punk and classic Stones rock anthems like they'd fallen in love with the idea of making records all over again. The lyrics meanwhile were often streetwise and self-aware. It ultimately sold eight million copies, their biggest success up to that date, even despite the hiccup of the album having to be recalled when various celebrities objected to their depiction on an elaborate cover that came in the form of a parody of a shopping catalogue. The band kicked off their US tour on 10 June, and although many of the tickets were no doubt bought because once again – and for the soundest reasons yet – some people thought this would be the last chance they would ever get to see the band in the flesh, only the most churlish punk (or ex-hippy come to that) could doubt that this was a band that people

The Some Girls Sessions – Something to Prove

During the making of the Stones album that would eventually be titled *Some Girls*, Mick Jagger was determined to fit in with the speed that punk had once again made modish in rock. "The whole thing was to play it all fast, fast, fast," he later said. "I had a lot of problems with Keith about it, but that was the deal at the time." Richards could be forgiven for giving his colleague "problems".

Not only did he think a lot of Jagger's new fast songs sounded samey, his sense of artistic mission came out of far more desperate circumstances than a bruised ego caused by the younger generation not paying him the respect he was used to. As he later noted, "I'd been through the bust in Canada, which was a real watershed.. for me. I'd gone to jail [sic], been cleaned up, done my cure, and I'd wanted to come back and prove there was some difference... some reason for this kind of suffering. So *Some Girls* was the first record I'd been able to get back into and view from a totally different state than I'd been in for most of the Seventies."

One thing that Jagger and Richards were unanimous on was that they had been coasting since 1973, and it was now time to prove that they really did deserve the title 'Greatest Rock 'N' Roll Band In The World'. Not that punk was the only bandwagon on which Jagger wanted to jump. He also brought with him a song called 'Miss You'. His tribute to model Jerry Hall, who had replaced estranged Bianca in his affections, it had a four-on-the-floor tempo that was in step with the rhythms of the current disco craze. Ronnie Wood

Out clubbing with 'er indoors.

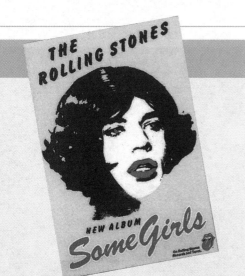

meanwhile would have been anxious to prove his worth on the first Stones studio album on which he was present from the beginning of the sessions – maybe partly because he had publicly said in September that he expected a fifth share of the Stones' income, not a salary. This latter ambition took another thirteen years to be realised, possibly because he was too subservient. One of the numbers cooked up at these sessions was the blues number 'Black Limousine'. It would eventually turn up on the 1981 album *Tattoo You* credited to Jagger/Richards/Wood. Apparently the hold-up was caused by Wood wanting to be credited. Wood observed, "One of the lessons I had to learn was that if you want to get a credit, it has to happen there and then in the studio, as you're recording it. I didn't go about it professionally enough to get a credit, so I let it go." Clearly, the same problems that partly led to Mick Taylor quitting were still present. Accompanying the group at these sessions was engineer Chris Kimsey, who would bring a new brightness and freshness to the Stones' sound.

mainly wanted to see because they were on a **creative roll.**

On 23 October 1978, Keith Richards pleaded guilty in Toronto to possession of 22 grammes of heroin. All the other charges, including drug trafficking, were dropped, much to the amazement of many. Richards was given a year's probation on the proviso that he continue his drug therapy. He was also ordered to play a benefit concert for the blind. The last proviso was made, it is said, because a blind female Stones fan who followed the band on the road had knocked on the door of the judge's home and told him how Richards had always displayed a paternal concern for her, making sure she got safely from venue to venue. Some sources have suggested the girl was in fact the judge's niece. With their joint-most-important-member saved from imprisonment, their new line-up clearly gelling, their latest album their most successful ever, and their nemesis the Sex Pistols now history – **Johnny Rotten** had left the group and bassist **Sid Vicious** was facing a murder charge – it seemed that now nothing stood in the way of The Rolling Stones continuing to make great and important music for the rest of their collective existence.

Never one to keep his mouth shut, Jagger's capacity for increasingly energetic and expressive behaviour on stage remained undiminished.

Chapter 7:
World War III

"The truth of the matter is that Mick is having a sex-change operation and the rest of the group don't want to play with a girl."

Keith Altham, Stones' PR man, 1979.

World War III
1979-1992

The Life

Tensions, in terms of personal direction and ambition, bubbled to the surface in the late Seventies, with Jagger seemingly mesmerized by the bright lights of celebrity, and Richards pondering the musical future of the band. Their differences would come to dominate the next decade and threaten the very existence of the Stones.

Expensive Habits

The high hopes that long-term Stones fans had harboured for an ongoing creative resurgence were rather dashed and quite quickly. All the good signs upon the release of *Some Girls* proved to be a false dawn. Putting it bluntly, *Some Girls* is the last major Rolling Stones album, and it is now unlikely there will ever be another.

The reasons for this relative decline seem to be many and varied. Firstly, there were Ron Wood's drug problems. No sooner had the band been celebrating the fact that they now had a **fully-functioning** Keith Richards for the first time in many years than Wood got himself addicted to freebase cocaine; an addiction he swore he would overcome but kept returning

to. This repeatedly threatened his position in the band. By 1984, his cocaine habit was costing him $5000 per day. Though the Stones made some classic music when Richards was on smack, Richards has the constitution of an ox. It's hard to believe that Wood's **addiction** was not partly responsible for the deterioration in the band's music. Then there was a problem that had been afflicting the group since 1973, when they first began living in different countries. With them no longer all a short car journey away from each other, the opportunities for the band to play together became scarce and indeed had to be carefully planned. Though the Stones, more than most bands. had always been able to gel quickly when facing each across their instruments in a room after a hiatus, they now had an increasingly high mountain to climb whenever they reassembled.

The deteriorating relationship between Jagger and Richards didn't help either. The ongoing battle of wills caused by Jagger's populism and Richards blues-oriented purism was now compounded by other things. Jagger wasn't amused when a newly *compos mentis* Richards began to take an interest in the Stones' business affairs, previously the preserve of Jagger and **Loewenstein**. Jagger also increasingly gave the impression of seeing music as merely one aspect of his professional life, becoming interested in cricket and films, whereas – apart from his family – Richards lived only for music. Jagger also seemed to realize that a Rolling Stones comprised of 40, or 50, or even 60-year-olds, might look ridiculous and so began to conceive of a musical career outside of the Stones. In the mid-Eighties, the relationship between the former best mates literally became a **feud** because of this.

One further reason for the deterioration of the Stones' art may also have been that old ennui, indicated by Jagger's comment about their 1980 album ***Emotional Rescue***: "You know, *Emotional Rescue* is a lot of leftovers from *Some Girls*." How disappointing that the Stones should be resting on their laurels again so soon after the genuine determination that attended the *Some Girls* sessions to drag themselves out of the doldrums. Amazingly, *Emotional Rescue* – released in June 1980 after a long and bitty recording process – was their biggest seller to date. Clearly, being living

legends and having a back catalogue stuffed with classics engendered significant goodwill amongst the public.

The album ended with an awful song called 'All About You' which was widely interpreted as Richards' bitter-sweet kiss-off to **Anita Pallenberg**, with whom his relationship, after twelve years, three children and many drug busts, had ended spectacularly in summer 1979 when a 17-year-old boy shot himself in the head in Richards' South Salem house when Pallenberg was present and Richards absent.

Things between the Glimmer Twins were deteriorating to such an extent that when, in January 1981, **Wyman** discussed a US tour with Loewenstein, he felt that if it happened it might be the group's swansong. Watts actually reached the conclusion that the Stones were finished that year: Richards had failed to turn up for a band meeting in New York, despite insisting that everyone fly in for it. After about a week of waiting for him, a disgusted Wyman flew home. Things were patched up by the summer, but at that point Ronnie Wood's colleagues got so worried about his drug intake that they told him he had to clean up, not least because the band's US tour started in September.

There would be an album, ***Tattoo You***, to accompany the tour, but that album would not contain much new material. With Jagger and Richards unable to stand being in an enclosed space together for a prolonged period of time, it was largely a vault-raiding exercise. Inspired by a *Some Girls* outtake called 'Start Me Up',

The Life

Jagger and Jerry ligging with NY artist Andy Warhol, at the time publisher of *Interview* magazine, the ultimate jet-set wannabe rag.

Chris Kimsey had got the idea of finding gems on the endless reels of tape he had recorded of the band working in the studio over the last few years. He reasoned that if there was such good stuff discarded, he could put together a whole album. It wasn't quite as simple as that, though. Much of the material Kimsey was having to wade through was uncatalogued. In addition, the material that he was pulling out after listening to endless reels – from sessions going as far back as *Goat's Head Soup* – was

not comprised of finished songs but 'basic tracks', the term for recordings which feature rhythm section work, riffs, chord changes and sometimes lead guitar but no vocal. Vocal melody lines would still need to be devised. There was a further problem to sort out, namely the fact that recordings of such varying vintages and featuring different engineering personnel was going to result in an album with several different sonic textures. Jagger decided to employ producer/engineer **Bob Clearmountain**

By the early Eighties, as the quality of the music began to decline, the elaborate stage sets and outfits grew exponentially – as did the stadium-filling audiences.

The Life

– who had previously done the disco mix of the 'Miss You' single – to remix the record to create a uniform sound. **Richards** was not consulted about this appointment, nor the fact that at the last moment the title of the album – released in August 1981 – was changed from *Tattoo* to *Tattoo You*. The title was a reference to the cover art which, like *Goat's Head Soup*, featured Mick on the front and Keith on the back, only this time with tattoo-like patterns painted on their faces. In contrast to the elaborate jacket, the design of the inner sleeve was ultra-minimalist, with no written credits or 'thank-yous'. This was quite simply because a form of deception was going on. Though the Stones later became relaxed about acknowledging it, at the time they were not openly admitting that *Tattoo You* was a ragbag of tarted-up discards. Few journalists had the courage to confront the band members in interviews about the mellifluous guitar solos on the album which were clearly neither Richards or Wood.

On the Road Again

Not that the public would have cared if the truth had been widely known. 1981 was the Stones' year. As they began their American tour come September, they were amazed to find that they simply couldn't keep up with demand for tickets, second and third shows often being added to cities where they had originally planned to play only once. '**Start Me Up**' meanwhile – released as a lead-off single – was hailed as a return to the band's classic riff-driven rockin' style and went Top Ten both sides of the pond. In fairness, *Tattoo You* was actually quite a good listen, even if Clearmountain's mix – heavy on the drums – was often boring. Not even the uniquely Eighties garish costumes sported by Jagger – latex and puffy jackets in primary colours – could turn the public off, nor the fact that he was for the first time clearly fighting a losing battle for his looks as wrinkles began to appear on that hitherto ultra-fresh face. As they made their way round the States, the Stones increasingly began to **win over journalists**. The press started to shrug their shoulders at the group's lost political import and embrace them as simply a good-time, high-quality rock 'n' roll band. By its end, the tour had become the highest grossing in history – helped by the fact that it was underwritten by Jovan Musk men's perfume, the first such example of sponsorship in rock – and *Tattoo You* had become the Stones' top seller.

Summer 1982 saw a momentous event in Richards' life when he was reconciled with his father, Bert, following two decades in which the pair had had no contact. Richards had originally moved out of the family home because he couldn't stand being under the same roof as his dad anymore. His mother and father had actually split up shortly afterwards. Richards was encouraged to patch things up by his girlfriend (and later wife), **Patti Hansen**. Father and son subsequently became inseparable.

The Stones began their European tour in the last week of May. It included a couple of dates at London's gigantic Wembley Stadium but they also managed to arrange an unpublicised gig at that city's tiny **100 Club**. *Still Life*, an album document of the American leg of the tour, appeared at around the same time. Naysayers to the trend of showering the band with hosannas pointed out how badly this perfunctory collection of live performances compared to the sizzle and danger of much of *Get Yer Ya-Yas Out*. Nonetheless, it became a transatlantic top five.

Night Work

The Stones reconvened at Pathe Marconi in November that year to work on a new album – a real new album this time. Despite the unconditional love with which the Stones had latterly come to be showered – how else to describe the massive sales for the hardly classic *Emotional Rescue* and *Tattoo You*? – it's interesting that these sessions indicated that the band, Jagger in particular, still had some artistic ambition. June 1983 marked the twentieth anniversary of the release of the Stones' first record, while on 26 July Jagger turned 40. Only Jagger knows whether the impetus for the unusual care he took with the recording of their new album was these two milestones – significant respectively because the Stones were the first rock band to reach the two-decade mark as an active (as opposed to nostalgia-peddling) unit, and because Jagger had once been the *de facto* leader of the world's youth. The fact is, however, that it was Jagger who insisted that the Stones make a break with the now long-prevailing Stones recording *modus operandum* – he or Richards bringing in a song fragment and the band bashing away at it, often interminably, until it took shape – and instead suggested that he and Keith get together separately beforehand to work up the new numbers. Jagger would also seem rather anxious to point out in interviews to promote the album upon its release that it wasn't another Tattoo You. "Actually all these songs are all new," he insisted. "They were all written this year, last year." (Wyman reckoned this was out of necessity: everything else in the vaults had been **bootlegged**.)

'Undercover (Of The Night)' was chosen as the album's lead off single in November 1983. It was an urgent, percussive number with a genuinely relevant lyric – the death squads that were turning Latin America into a bloodbath – and was accompanied by an atmospheric video supervised by trendy director **Julien Temple**. It indicated to some that the band had embraced the new video technology – but only those unaware that they had in fact pioneered it with the promo films for 'We Love You' and 'Jumpin Jack Flash'.

The single's quality augured well for the album, called *Undercover*, and issued at the end of the same week. However, whereas 'Undercover (Of the Night)' had been the most exciting Stones single since 'Miss You' there was little as impressive on its near-namesake parent album. Nonetheless, it was leagues ahead of the last pair of studio albums in terms of application. The brittle, rattling production may have sacrificed Stones crunch for modernity, but it showed a band – or perhaps Jagger – willing to keep pace with the times. There was even a theme of sorts: violence. The blood-soaked songs were attended by some good tunes and memorable riffs and lots of horns and percussion in an exercise that can overall be considered an interesting failure.

Undercover would be the last Stones album for EMI in the UK and Atlantic in the US. Three months before its release, they signed a deal with **CBS**. The guarantee was $28m. Though CBS were getting the massively lucrative back catalogue (1971-onwards) as part of the deal, it was still a staggering amount of money for four new albums. **Walter Yetnikoff**, the larger-than-life head honcho of CBS, was also for some reason excited by the idea of a Mick Jagger solo career. Jagger was game. The result was the closest the band had ever come to breaking up in its two-decade existence.

Dirty Work was released in March 1986. Not surprisingly, considering its tortured genesis (see page 134) the album contained little worthwhile material. The sweeping '**One Hit (To The Body)**' was good stuff and 'Back To Zero' demonstrated, as 'Undercover (Of The Night)' had, that they could still write protest songs set to danceable contemporary rhythms. Much of the rest however was negligible, although that didn't seem to warrant making 'Harlem Shuffle' the first non-original official Stones single (apart from live tracks)

The Life

The Rolling Stones or the Biff Hitler Trio?

The recording of *Dirty Work*, the Stones' first album under the CBS deal, seems to have been chaos.

That Jagger was making an album on his own was perhaps something his colleagues could live with – after all, they didn't own each other – but what galled the others, Richards especially, was the detrimental impact they felt it had on the Stones. *She's The Boss*, recorded by Jagger in Nassau (self-produced but with Dave Jerden engineering), was perilously close to the next scheduled Stones sessions at Pathé Marconi, which started in January 1985. So close in fact that they ended up overlapping – Jagger arrived late for the Stones album and didn't seem to be concentrating on the work at hand. Or, as Wyman put it, "We messed around for weeks because Mick was still buggering around with his solo album instead of working with us. He would fly back to London in the middle of it which … is a thing that nobody else has ever done, because when it's Stones work, everybody drops solo projects." Charlie Watts, meanwhile, was amazing those who had always known him as the sensible Stone with a mid-life crisis that saw him addicted to heroin for a while. He also cut his hand during the sessions and flew home for a period (his drumming on the album was understandably sub-standard) although some have said he departed in disgust at the feuding. Wyman is not present on several tracks. Jagger's, Watts' and Wyman's various absences made parts of the product barely Stones music at all but, instead, the work of what Richards contemptuously labelled 'the Biff Hitler Trio': Richards, Wood and session drummer Steve Jordan.

Additionally, Bobby Womack – band friend and composer of their '64 hit 'It's All Over Now' – seems to have been a big influence on the record. Certainly, when Jagger made his belated appearance, he was empty-handed, having used all his material on his solo venture, which meant that the ideas Richards and Wood – who lived around the corner from each other in New York – had been knocking together on acoustic guitar came in handy. Wood got his highest ever number of credits on a Stones album. Some of the songs – 'Had It With You' for instance – showed the seething resentment Richards felt over what he considered the disloyalty of Jagger.

After the group had been recording for about three months, the band decided to bring in an outside producer for the first time since dispensing with Jimmy Miller's services in 1973. The man chosen was the highly successful Steve Lillywhite, who had worked with Peter Gabriel, U2 and Simple Minds. Lillywhite was dismayed by the fractious atmosphere he encountered and was reluctant to talk about the record to the press after it was finished – which process took a year, final mixing being done in New York in December. However, Lillywhite did say (and was at pains to emphasise), "It was a Keith Richards-inspired record." Though they have not used his services again, the band have been complimentary about Lillywhite, Richards impressed by his refusal to gush over what he was hearing and his helpful impartial viewpoint. The only real problem between Lillywhite and the Stones came during the mixing process when Lillywhite varispeeded a track without consulting anyone. Richards briefly went ballistic.

since 'Little Red Rooster'. The album ended with a ghostly snatch of boogie woogie piano played by **Ian Stewart** that was included as a tribute to him: he died of a heart attack in December 1985.

Rock Bottom

The tensions between Jagger and Richards over the former's perceived conflict of interest were so obvious that the video of the second single from the album, 'One Hit (To The Body)', utilised it for dramatic purpose, showing them almost talking swings at each other as they mimed the song. Such aggression had a resonance with the viewing public for by this time – due to caustic remarks by Richards to the press – it had long been public knowledge that he was not best pleased with his fellow Glimmer Twin. However, Richards' simmering resentment turned to **real anger** when Jagger proved reluctant to take part in a tour to promote the album (which, like its predecessor, didn't sell that well for a Stones album). Even Wyman later acknowledged that Jagger was right to not tour *Dirty Work*, despite it being their first album for their new distributor. What with Watts' condition, Woods' recurrent drug problems and the rock-bottom state of affairs between Jagger and Richards, Jagger's contention that the tour could have meant the end of the band seems plausible. Richards, though, wasn't impressed by these arguments, feeling that there was little point in being in a band if it wasn't touring, and that there was a rather sad

reason for what seemed to him Jagger's attempt to explore the possibility of carefully extricating himself from the Stones. When promoting his own solo album *Talk Is Cheap* (1988) – a project in which he only engaged because he was not able to make a Stones album due to Jagger's absence – Richards told journalist Lisa Robinson that Jagger was, "afraid The Rolling Stones could turn into some kind of nostalgia dead end." If Richards' analysis is correct, it may have been a fear of Jagger's that went quite a long way back. He was already telling journalist **Stanley Booth** in 1969 of his doubts about how long the Stones could continue in the medium as they grew older. Certainly Jagger has made comments to journalists in recent years about his fear of the Stones becoming a "**comedy act**", and many people who loved what the Stones stood for in the Sixties would actually be sympathetic to that worry. (In Jagger's mind it can't have been helped by some of the hostages to fortune he has left: for instance, he told a journalist in 1972 that if he was still singing 'Satisfaction' when he was forty, he would kill himself.)

The Stones maintained a public show of unity for a couple of events in late February '86. The first was a memorial show for Ian Stewart at the 100 Club, London. Such a good time was had by all that Jagger and Richards left with their arms around each other and an unnamed band spokesman said that a tour within the next eighteen months might be possible, adding "A week or so ago I would have said there was no chance at all." Two days later, for the first time ever – bizarrely for an act of their stature – the Stones won a Grammy, being given a lifetime achievement award. However, by the following April, with it now official that Jagger would not tour for the foreseeable future, and with the singer planning another solo album, Richards was reduced to telling an interviewer, "If Mick tours without us, I'll slit his throat." At a band meeting in **Amsterdam** a few months later, even the angelic Watts was driven to distraction by Jagger, although has admitted this was more to do with the crisis in his life at the time than the anger caused in him by a drunk Jagger ringing his hotel room at five o' clock one morning and asking "Is that my drummer?" Watts went down and decked Jagger – although curiously took the trouble to dress immaculately before doing so.

The End of the Stone Age?

By early 1987, it genuinely seemed that The Rolling Stones were finished. Down the years, Stones fans – and the Stones themselves – had become inured to press stories and speculation about the demise of the group and utterly bored by the 'The Last Time?' headlines, but the stories that began appearing at this juncture were more than the usual slow-news day extrapolations upon an aborted session or on a whimsical aside from Wyman that he had only expected all this to last a couple of years. Open warfare between Jagger and Richards

was being waged in the press. Richards would later dub the situation "**World War III**".

Jagger's second solo album, *Primitive Cool* hit the shops in September 1987. It was preceded by a grisly single called 'Let's Work', which seemed to extol the virtues of **Thatcherism** ("The world don't owe you" lectured its lyric.) From this distance, it is difficult perhaps to remember how offensive such sentiments were to many in a country with massive unemployment and still smarting from the divisions caused by the 1984/1985 miner's strike. It was also hardly likely to endear Jagger or the Stones to rock critics who now sneered at them as the epitome of

World War Three

In early March, the UK tabloid *Daily Mirror* carried an interview with Jagger in which the singer complained that Richards wanted to run the band "single-handedly" and said, with quite breathtaking baldness, "I don't feel we can really work together anymore." The *Mirror*'s main competitor *The Sun* carried an interview with Richards the very next day. Its contents were even more sensational in their apparent boats-burning intensity than Jagger's: "He should stop trying to be like Peter Pan and grow up... We were that close. I didn't change but he did. He became obsessed with age... I don't see the point of pretending that you are 25 when you are not... Until this time last year, there was still a chance... He has told me to my face that he cannot work with me, but he cannot say why. I don't think he knows himself." A couple conservatism in music. Ironically, in an interview in mid-September to coincide with the release of the single's parent album, Jagger rationalised his solo career as a reaction to Richards' musical conservatism: "Keith sees The Rolling Stones very much as a conservative rock 'n' roll band with very strong traditions and as he gets older his ideas have become more conservative… I used to tell people that I would never need to make a solo album because I could do whatever I wanted to do within the band, but it started to get narrower so I no longer felt that." Richards, however, felt that Jagger's concern was motivated by a desire to be seen to be trendy, stating elsewhere, "Mick is more involved with what's happening at the moment.. He has to go backwards and compare himself to who's hitting the Top Ten at the moment."

Despite Richards' contempt for Jagger's alleged anxiety to keep pace with the young things, he couldn't really make the same complaint about *Primitive Cool* that he had about *She's The Boss*, namely, that for there to be any point to it, it should be completely distinct in style from a Rolling Stones record. *Primitive Cool* had a reflective, confessional flavour that the Stones may have flirted with before but which it was nigh on inconceivable would ever be found on a new Stones album in such measure. A genuinely

of weeks later, Wyman was asked by MTV's *Music Box* whether the Stones were finished. "It looks that way," he said. "It's a pity we didn't go out with a big bang. Instead we went out with a whimper." Though Wyman has backed Jagger's insistence that touring *Dirty Work* with the band in its present state would have been a bad idea, he still pinned the blame for the feuding within the group on Jagger: "He has decided to do his own thing and be famous in his own right."

It wasn't long before the principals began to pull back from the brink. Wyman asked MTV not to repeat the broadcast of his interview, arguing that his comments were "misquotes, off the cuff remarks that were taken out of context and blown out of proportion." A spokesman for Jagger insisted, "There is no official end to the group. You know the Stones – they go through these tribulations. Hopefully things will settle down to where people can talk again. You can never write off The Rolling Stones." Only Richards – ever intolerant of artifice – refused to toe the party line, saying in another interview, "Mick lost touch with how important the Stones were for him. He thought that he could just hire another Rolling Stones and that way he could control the situation more, rather than battling with me." Richards may have been referring here to the fact that Jagger had indeed hired a band to tour his debut solo album. Their jaunt of Japan in 1988 featured Stones songs as well as his solo material. Whatever the truth of the matter, Richards was having to face the fact that making music with the Stones was not going to happen in the foreseeable future and accordingly signed a solo deal with Virgin.

The Life

Can Rock Music Be Mature Music?

It's interesting that, following his scabrous comments about Jagger's fear of being part of an ageing joke to Robinson, Richards then launched into a soundbite which became a favourite of his around this time and which he has continued to come out with – or variants of it – to this day: "I see the Rolling Stones on the cutting edge of growing this music up, and the only band in the position to do it." The guitarist was referring to the fact that The Rolling Stones were the first – or at least most important – rock group to make a career out of something that had once been considered musical juvenilia. Previously it had been assumed that rock could not sustain an income for more than a couple of years, at which point an artist would fall out of favour because his fan base had grown out of the music and the younger consumers were interested only in purchasing the product of newer artists. (Keith is overlooking a solo artist like Dylan,

The two key albums of Dylan's post-1970 career proved that rock could age both gracefully and with dignity.

who cannot 'split up' like a group, but you get his point.) This process of decline happened to 'Fifties artists – mainly because rock n' roll was a stagnant medium at the time – but not to artists of the Stones' generation, precisely because, as the fans got older, they found that the music of their heroes was maturing with them: the arc traced from Jagger/Richards compositions 'Tell Me' to 'Gimme Shelter' is one of

progress from callow immaturity to world-weariness.

Yet Richards was overlooking the fact that, since 1969 or perhaps 1971, the Stones had themselves been if not regressing then certainly not moving forward. Songs of the magnitude or profundity of 'Gimme Shelter' or 'You Can't Always Get What You Want' were few and far between in the modern Stones canon. In fact, it was Bob Dylan – whatever his inconsistencies – who had helped rock music grow. *Blood On The Tracks*, a 1975 album about the agony of divorce, would have been inconceivable in rock ten years previously. Similarly, his 1997 album *Time Out Of Mind* pushed the envelope by addressing mortality as he entered late middle age. The Rolling Stones' contributions in the areas tackled by Dylan were 'Respectable' ("Go take my wife, don't come back") and 'Time Waits For No-One' (which achieved a certain poignancy but only with received imagery). There's even an argument that the type of maturity exhibited by Dylan is something that is not possible within the context of a rock group, for a variety of reasons including the inability to give an album a theme due to two or three different writers contributing songs and the ridicule that the fellow gang members might pour on overly-morose subject matter (there was nobody to mock Dylan as he sank into self-pity with *Blood On The Tracks*, thank goodness, and we are left with a heartbreaking classic).

good album, its insensitive preview single is probably what led to it being panned in the press.

Said press were talking sides in the Jagger-Richards 'feud', and excitement was in the air in music journalist quarters at the prospect of Richards' forthcoming solo album. "I'm a musician and I need to work," Richards explained. "If the Rolling Stones were together, then I would be doing it with them." He was a bit taken aback to be informed, by Jagger, during the recording of said album, that Mick wanted to make a new Rolling Stones record. Considering his public complaints about Mick's disinclination to make music with the Stones recently, it was hardly an **olive branch** he could refuse. Nonetheless, Richards emphasised to journalists that the approach came from Jagger, not him, and noted, "Maybe what we've found out is that Mick really needs The Rolling Stones more than The Rolling Stones needs Mick." Richards' debut solo album – which couldn't help but be perceived as riposte to Jagger's solo career – appeared in October '88. Titled *Talk Is Cheap* it was without doubt a decent effort, but if journalists were honest with themselves the ratio of good to mediocre in the songs (at least one of which, 'You Don't Move Me', was a broadside at his estranged Glimmer Twin) was no greater than on *Primitive Cool*. In fact, had the best six songs from both *Talk Is Cheap* and *Primitive Cool* been used on a Stones album, it would have constituted the best Rolling Stones platter since *Some Girls*. Richards toured his album with his band the **X-Pensive Winos** in November and December.

Making Up

Mid-January 1989 saw Jagger and Richards hook up in Barbados. Face to face, their recriminations seemed less bitter. "When you actually get back together again and start working, and it's just the two of you in a room, you're lying on the floor laughing," recalled Richards. "'Remember when you said that I was a this, and I called you a that?' And then we start cracking up." The idyllic surroundings helped of course, but so did the fact that they decided to adopt a strict schedule for this album and tour. Jagger wanted 1989 dedicated to both recording and touring but wanted it all finished by the end of the year, an unprecedentedly rapid work rate by modern Stones standards. "We had got into a terrible habit of meandering and being disorganised," said Jagger. To that object, it was decided that they would rehearse any new album before going into a studio to formally record the songs. "I never thought it would work – but it did," Jagger said. They got cracking immediately, working up half a dozen songs within a couple of days, some of which were embryonic numbers Richards hadn't had time to develop for his solo album. On 18 January, Jagger and Richards went to New York to be inducted into the then new **Rock 'N' Roll Hall Of Fame** awards. Wood attended as well. Mick Taylor also got an invite from the hosts. Graciously, Jagger paid tribute in his acceptance speech to Ian Stewart and Brian Jones.

The Life

Proper recording of the album began on the Virgin island of Montserrat in March. One of the most interesting new songs was 'Continental Drift'. Based on a Jagger keyboard riff which Richards found redolent of Moroccan sounds, it was a song on which Jagger was toying with the idea of overdubbing the master musicians of **Joujouka**, with whom Brian Jones had recorded in 1969, when a letter from them to him arrived out of the blue. It was written by the chief, who had been seven years old when Jones had met him in Morocco. Jagger couldn't ignore that sort of kismet and the Joujouka musicians added some of the most exotic instrumentation heard on a Stones track in recent years at a studio in Tangiers in June. It was tracks like 'Continental Drift' that seem to have been the reason that the album, *Steel Wheels*, got good reviews upon its September 1989 release, although frankly a certain pleasure at having the old warhorses back after their recent travails seems to have been the subliminal motivation behind a lot of the raves.

The massively successful **Steel Wheels/Urban Jungle** tour on which the band embarked in Philadelphia at the end of August rather illustrated that the quality of new Stones product was almost irrelevant. Budweiser beer were the exclusive sponsors for the tour, which cost them £3.7m. Wyman revealed that one of the conditions attached to this was that the Stones agree to meet-and-greet sessions with VIPs backstage. Snide comparisons here between the Stones' refusal to hop on board the *Sunday Night*

At The London Palladium carousel and their willingness to press the flesh with dignitaries might be predictable but would not be unfair, especially as their by now vast wealth made it all unnecessary. Speaking of vast wealth, just before the band embarked on the Japanese leg of the tour in February, **Ronnie Wood** was finally taken off his salaried status and given equal money after Watts and Wyman said that they would not participate otherwise.

January had seen the Stones return to the recording studio. It was not to lay down a new album – the days of new Stones studio albums within two years of each other were long gone – but to record a couple of tracks they could append to *Flashpoint*, the in-concert document with which they wrung a few more pennies from the tour. One of the songs – released as a single in March, the same month as the release of the live album – did at least have a certain integrity to it. 'Highwire' pointed out that in the recently-ended (first) Gulf War, Saddam Hussein's men had had access to arms that had been sold them by the West.

Bill Bows Out

One final bit of revenue was milked from the **Steel Wheels/Urban Jungle** tour in late '91 with the release of the video *Rolling Stones At The Max*. A month later, the band were finalizing a three-album deal with Virgin worth £25m. Naturally, Bill Wyman's name was on the contract along with his four colleagues. Yet to the disbelief of many, including his bandmates, Wyman said that he would not be signing it. Nearly three decades of working with his colleagues – and waiting upon the convenience of **Richards** – seems to have played its part in his retirement if his later comments are anything to go by. As does a feeling of the same-old same-old: "I didn't see anything new happening in the future," he said. "I realised if we played for another ten years, I'd still be playing 'Jumpin' Jack Flash', 'Honky Tonk Women', 'Street Fighting Man' until we packed up." He is also said to have developed a belated fear of flying, a real impediment for a member of a rock band. Moreover, he wanted to start a new family. Yet Jagger and Richards continued to exude hope in public that they could persuade him to stay. However, the nature of their entreaties were hardly likely to prove persuasive to a man who had endured endless humiliations in trying to get his songs on Stones records and in even getting his contributions to Jagger/Richards

compositions acknowledged and seeing inferior bass players like Richards and Wood often hijack a track's bass part. Jagger said that if necessary he would play bass, adding "How hard can it be?" for spiteful good measure. Richards' contribution to the 'charm offensive' was "No-one leaves this band except in a coffin." This kind of comment seemed to mask – or perhaps betray – a real concern. **Wyman** recalled later that the Glimmer Twins adopted a nice cop/nasty cop routine in their increasingly desperate attempts to make him change his mind. How ironic that the man whose efforts had always been slighted where they weren't frustrated should now suddenly hold this power. In the end, the Glimmer Twins bowed to the inevitable and accepted that one half of one of rock's greatest ever rhythm sections was departing. Wyman's retirement from the band was officially announced at the end of 1992.

And Age Shall Not Wither Them...

Chapter 8:
Life After Bill

"*I give the Stones about another two years.*"

Mick Jagger,

Ipswich Gaumont Concert Programme,

2 November 1963.

Life After Bill
From 1992

For many, Bill Wyman's departure from the band signalled the end of the road for 'The Greatest Rock 'n' Roll Band In The World'. However, the road, and increasingly elaborate tours upon it, was to prove much longer and more lucrative than anyone could anticipate. As the remaining band members approached their pensionable ages they were still topping up their retirement funds by cavorting on stages world-wide.

A Major Upheaval

In the year preceding Wyman's departure, the individual Stones were quite busy. Richards' band the X-Pensive Winos released a live album recorded at the Hollywood Palladium. Jagger and Richards spent part of the year working on their third and second solo albums respectively. Richards' *Main Offender* appeared in October and he went off on a world tour to promote the album in November. Jagger's new solo album *Wandering Spirit* appeared in February 1993. In early June the two Glimmer Twins were inducted into the songwriters **Hall Of Fame** in New York. By that time, Jagger and Richards had got together with Wood and Watts to begin the new Rolling Stones album.

The process began in Barbados, with occa-sional days and weeks off. However, there was still what Richards described as a "cloud on the horizon". They needed a new bass player to begin their post-Bill Wyman professional career. "Thirty years, the same rhythm section – this is a **major upheaval**," Richards had to concede.

Not that the new bass player was going to be a proper member of The Rolling Stones. Even before the official announcement of Wyman's departure, Jagger had responded to the rumours of it by saying that he didn't envisage the group wanting a permanent replacement. Perhaps this was because a brand new fixture in that job would seem strange after so many years. Equally plausible is the money factor, the group (not just Jagger, as has often been portrayed) being notoriously careful with the

The Rolling Stones

for ever

Possibly…

pennies. Wyman's departure brought about another significant change in the Stones' camp. Though he had already been granted equal money, it was at this point that the "employee" (Richards' word) status of Ronnie Wood finally came to an end when he was also given equal voting rights.

June saw the Stones auditioning in New York for what we might call the new Bass-Playing Employee role. Understandably, they took the process very seriously. Twenty bassists were given the task of playing along with them to archetypal Stones riff rocker 'Brown Sugar' and to 'Miss You', another Stone classic, but uncharacteristic in its rhythm stylings. Then a jam would take place. **Doug Wimbish** of Living Colour briefly seemed to be a favourite, but he wasn't in the party when the rehearsals relocated to Wood's home studio in Ireland in the summer.

A 31-year-old black Chicago bassist called **Darryl Jones**, hearing that the job was still open, rang the Stones camp asking for an audition. He had previously worked with Eric Clapton, Peter Gabriel, Madonna, Sting and Miles Davis. The band were impressed when he came over to Ireland to audition in September, but left the final decision up to the man who would be his partner in the Stones' rhythm section. **Charlie Watts** didn't like being put in the hot seat but it was gently pointed out to him that this was not something that was asked often of him. Jones got the job and he was in the bassist's seat as recording proper on the album started, with **Don Was** – producer of,

amongst others, Bonnie Raitt and Bob Dylan – supervising the album. The resultant record, *Voodoo Lounge*, released in July 1994 began with 'Love Is Strong', which took many Stones fans back twenty years or more with its blasts of mouth harp. This was the influence of Was, who wanted a retro sound. Jagger later said that although he went along with the idea, it was a mistake as Was would steer them away from anything too un-Stonesey.

Globe Trotting

It had been **five years** since *Steel Wheels*, the longest gap between Stones studio albums to date, and in that time the compact disc had taken over the world. With an upper time limit of 74 minutes, albums were well on their way to being hour-long affairs by default. The Stones' new album, *Voodoo Lounge*, would feature fifteen, not ten, songs. It wasn't an effort – Richards has spoken of the group being in danger of being buried by the avalanche of material they were working up early in the sessions – but frankly, the album would not have suffered aesthetically if five songs had been left off. But this wasn't going to stop the album topping the charts in the UK and reaching No.2 in America, nor picking up sales from satisfied customers on their new **globe-straddling** tour, which began in August '94. Actually, the tour was a little shaky in the beginning, with empty seats at some venues and a noticeable, if understandable, hesitancy to the newly-constituted band. Nonetheless, the tour grossed half a billion dollars and played to eight million people. A live album called *Stripped* appeared in November 1995. "I believe it's definitely the best-sounding live Stones record there is," Richards said. Well... It certainly didn't sound appreciably better than their performance on the 1968 *Rolling Stones Rock And Roll Circus* TV special (page 75), an album of which containing some of their performance there appeared in October 1996 on Allen Klein's ABKCO label. (A video of the same material as the CD, but with visuals, appeared the following month; a DVD of the event appeared in 2004 with additional material.)

At the end of 1996, the Stones were preparing another album. It's a measure of how the work rate of this band – who had released eight studio albums in their first five years, as well as enough singles and B-sides to fill a couple more – had slowed that Jagger argued with Richards that it was too soon to go back in the studio. With the newly-powerful Wood also insisting that they not allow another half decade to go by as they had last time, Jagger's had to acquiesce – although he did so on the condition that the writers could use their own producers on their tracks. "I thought if we at least had some different producers we would stand a chance of not sounding exactly the same on every track," reasoned Jagger. Naturally the kind of producers he was speaking of were the producers of the moment, the likes of the Dust Brothers and **Babyface**. Richards had only contempt for them, imagining them to be nothing more than non-musical knob twid-

dlers. He also can't have been unaware that many people's instant reaction upon hearing the news would be that it smacked of desperation: why did men of the Stones' talents need help from people so patently less gifted than they, just because they were young? There was some merit to those points of view but at the same time Jagger was at least exhibiting a still surviving artistic ambition in his anxiousness to keep the Stones contemporary and relevant. He said as much to journalist **David Sinclair** before the album: "I want to do something that's a bit more groundbreaking. Producers and engineers always want you to do another *Exile On Main St.* but I want to move on to something that's different and new and a bit more exciting."

The album was named *Bridges To Babylon*, and it appeared in September 1997. It was the second album in succession that seemed to exhibit a nervousness about putting the band's extremely weathered faces on the cover, but there was little sign of decrepitude in the contents. Amazingly, considering a heated and convoluted genesis that saw Jagger and Richards overdubbing and remixing without the consent of the other (reflected in tortuous producer credits) it was a fair album. Contrary to Jagger's hopes, there was nothing particularly 'groundbreaking' – unless we count some **overdubbed rapping** on one track and Mick's voice being put through a sonic blender on another – although this may have been a casualty of the warfare over competing mixes. Like its studio predecessor, it clocked in

The Death of Rock?

Jagger's concern about remaining up-to-date can't have been uninformed by the fact that, by the mid-1990s, something was happening to rock music that nobody had ever envisaged before: it was in danger of dying. Since the early Eighties, the synthesizers and electronic gizmos that could create a orchestra (albeit a weedy, watery one) in anyone's bedroom had rendered it in bad health. The business of gathering a group of people in a room in order to create music had come to seem to some cumbersome and unnecessary. Before, nobody had even thought about it because there was no alternative. Bands were suddenly old-fashioned. As were the rhythms and tempos of rock. Some modern dance producers actually laugh at rock drummers for their inability or unwillingness to maintain metronomic patterns the way a machine can. Considering that this very inconsistency is the kind of humanity that made rock attractive to its fans, this was clearly a massive culture gap. By the end of the Sixties, the very word rock had come to be an umbrella title for all popular music. The phrase 'rock 'n' roll' itself had been more than merely a description of a musical style: it had also summed up an attitude to life, one that was anti-authoritarian and alternative. (This fact lives on in the way that 'rock 'n' roll' is still used colloquially as an expression meaning – loosely – admirably wild and crazy.) Rock will never disappear completely – though now a niche market, it's a very large, multi-million dollar niche – but its fall from grace was swift and unexpected. Anybody suggesting in, say, 1969 that within twenty years rock would be outsold by discs made by people who neither sang nor played instruments and who instead of composing original songs merely electronically cannibalised pieces of old rock songs – i.e. hip-hop artists – would have been laughed at. Nonetheless, that is what has happened. Today, that once-so-important accolade – Greatest Rock 'n' Roll Band In The World – is something that many recording artists would in no way be interested in acquiring.

at an unwarranted hour, but there was more life in the material than anyone had a right to expect from men in their mid-fifties, especially after the unimpressive *Voodoo Lounge*. It even had, in the shape of the lovely ballad 'Already Over Me', a song that almost constituted that Stones Holy Grail: a modern day Jagger & Richards classic.

Just before the tour started in August 1997, people in the Stones' camp noticed how **unwell** Richards seemed. Very sadly, it seems that he had succumbed to heroin again. Perhaps only Richards will ever truly know why somebody who nearly got a life sentence over smack and who theoretically could have lost a child because of it would drift back into its awful embrace – if briefly – but there had been talk of his marriage to **Hansen** no longer being as blissful as it once was, with his wife taking interest in her staunch Christian roots and insisting that their daughters be brought up in the faith. Still, that he was not the one-dimensional embodiment-of-rock-and-roll character that he had often been portrayed as was illustrated by the fact that the opening of the European tour had to be postponed when

Richards sustained an injury in a fall. The location of his accident? His home library. The guitarist had been reaching for a Da Vinci tome and had found himself buried under an avalanche of Encyclopaedia Britannica volumes and other books of similar weight. During the tour, Jagger's relationship with **Jerry Hall** came to an end, at least physically. Jagger had been proven to be the father of a Brazilian model's baby, and the fall-out from this was something Hall seems to have felt constituted a public humiliation of a different quality to Jagger's many well-known dalliances during their time together. She was to file for divorce in January 1999. It wasn't only Jagger who was pilloried by the media during the tour. UK dates had had to be rearranged in the middle of 1998. New tax laws brought in by Britain's **Labour government** would have penalised the group and their touring staff had they gone ahead with their scheduled British concerts in that tax year, so they were rescheduled for 1999. That the main objection to the tax change was that it was retroactive – an unfair imposition considering that there was no way for the group to plan for it when they put the tour together – and that it would have hit the relatively low-paid touring staff got buried in the denunciations of the band's 'greed'.

Billion Dollar Babies

The statistics for Stones tours are almost boringly more record-breaking each time around but, for the record, the **Bridges To Babylon** tour – which lasted for a year and nine months off and on – saw them play to twenty million people and gross a billion dollars. There was yet another tour-generated live album, *No Security*, in November 1998.

There was very little collective Stones activity in the following few years. Jagger kept himself busy by producing the movie of the **Robert Harris** novel *Enigma*, the rights for which he had fought in a bidding war. In interviews, he spoke of being involved with the movie – which starred Kate Winslet – with a joy he had not publicly expressed about making music with the Stones for a long time. Late 2001 saw the release of Jagger's new album *Goddess In The Doorway*. The weakest thing he'd yet done, it allegedly had shockingly low sales.

In the June 2002 honours list, it was announced that Mick Jagger had been awarded a **knighthood**. Some considered it nothing less than what he deserved as both someone who had helped to do massive amounts for British industry by shifting millions of record units and for being the figurehead of a generation that had wanted to shrug off the stale and cruel assumptions of a previous era. Some smiled in amusement at the sight of the old rebel being clutched to the bosom of the Establishment in this way. Others tutted with contempt at his willingness to be so embraced. The reaction of Keith Richards was closest to the latter: "**Blind stupidity**" was the way the guitarist described Jagger's acceptance, saying that he threatened to pull put of their next tour over it. Whether his opinion was right or wrong, it couldn't be

...Nor The Years Condemn

denied Richards was entitled to it. He and his one-time best friend had been though much together in the previous four decades, including imprisonment. It was the latter experience that motivated what Richards admitted was "**cold, cold rage**" at Jagger's knee-dip. "I thought it was ludicrous to take one of those gongs from the Establishment when they did their very best to throw us in jail," Richards said. He also commented, "It sent out the wrong message. It's not what the Stones is about, is it?" Countered Jagger, "It's a great recognition of what the band's achievements have been over the years we've been together."

There was another tour starting in September 2002 and lasting a year. The band decided to play at a variety of venues – small, medium and large. Alarmingly, this jaunt was not accompanied by a new studio album, despite the fact that it marked a half decade since the release of *Bridges To Babylon*. Instead, a compilation album was released. This one was something special. For the first time, the band had negotiated a deal with **Allen Klein** whereby they could put material whose ownership rested with him on a release that also featured their post-1969 material. *Forty Licks*, issued in October 2002, was therefore the first Stones compilation that was truly comprehensive. It also featured a pointer to the future, in the shape of four new tracks recorded in the early summer of 2002. It was in October as well that Allen Klein's **ABKCO** company put out the new remasters of the Stones Decca-era catalogue. Hitherto, the Rolling Stones had experienced the crummiest transfer from vinyl to CD of any major artist. Only the inferior and nonorganic American configurations of albums had been made available and the sonic quality of the transfers was widely considered to be poor. Now, Allen Klein allowed both UK and US albums to be released simultaneously (except the first two UK albums), all with new remastering, and all dual-layered so that they could be heard in SACD by people who had the relevant kit. Richards himself conceded that the new versions were superior to even the vinyl editions.

An album from the tour – *Live Licks* – appeared with monotonous predictability in November 2004. In the months prior to its release it had been revealed that **Watts** was being treated for throat cancer. He made a full recovery.

An Even Bigger Bang

By the end of 2004, work on the new Stones studio album had been completed. Don Was – now clearly a man with whom they felt as comfortable in the studio as they had once Jimmy Miller – was in the producer's seat. The album was recorded in Paris and seemed to mark a return at last to The Rolling Stones working as a cohesive band. "Mick and Keith are writing songs together in a collaborative fashion that probably hasn't been seen since the late Sixties," Was reported. Naturally, a new tour – this one to start in August 2005 – was announced. Released in September 2005, the album was titled *A Bigger Bang*. The official explanation was that it reflected the band's fascination with the **origins of the universe** but few doubted that it was juvenile sexual innuendo in the classic Stones tradition.

Illustrating the advantages afforded by the compact disc, it was actually just two minutes shorter than *Exile On Main St.* had been, despite the latter having required four sides of vinyl. Of course, nobody was expecting the new album to be as grand a statement or artistic classic as that aforesaid 1972 release. Nonetheless, it got good reviews. "Best since *Some Girls*" was the general consensus. Frankly, that assessment will quickly become as embarrassing as all the other claims for greatness made about post-*Tattoo You* Stones albums by journalists intoxicated by great-to-have-them-back sentimentality and/or being granted an audience with one of the Glimmer Twins. The more measured Simon Hattenstone of *The Guardian* got it about right when he said, "*A Bigger Bang* is a pretty good record, and a couple of the songs could become mini-classics." There was a core of at last half a dozen high quality tracks on the album that proved the group were not dead yet. As did, naturally, the rush to buy tickets for their new tour, attendances at which proved they were still as popular a live attraction as ever. In February 2006 they played to one of the largest entertainment crowds ever assembled when a million people saw them on Brazil's **Copacabana Beach**.

At the time of writing, The Rolling Stones have passed milestones that many people, including themselves, would once have considered it absurd that they might reach. In the film *Performance*, the gangster character Chas played by James Fox says to Turner, Jagger's outlandishly dressed androgynous rock star character, "You'll look funny when you're fifty." That Jagger was happy for that line to be in the script – or at least happy enough not to demand its removal – indicates that he never thought it would come back to haunt him. Perhaps he was thinking that by that half century, courtesy of a gradient of which *Performance* was the ground level, he would be not a rock musician but an established movie actor. Maybe he just had that contempt for worrying about the future that often afflicts (or blesses) the young. For many former fans,

he had become a funny figure long before reaching fifty, not merely for the lines that are now etched deeply into his face in a way that is considered inappropriate for a medium so associated with being young (even as rock itself celebrates its half century of existence) but also for the way he has supposedly made a mockery out of former ideals.

Certainly the sight of Jagger, Richards and Woods with **suspiciously dark hair** dressed in finery and or alternative clothing far more appropriate to men in their twenties than men who seem to be inordinately lined even for their ages is a sad spectacle. Ironically, Charlie Watts – who refuses to hide his bald spot and has let his hair go completely grey – looks better than his colleagues, his disinclination to fight the ageing process giving him a quiet dignity. None of this necessarily means that the Rolling Stones make art that is worthless. There are no rules about how old a rock star should be. As Jagger himself once noted, all of his blues heroes when he was young were already middle-aged.

It would also be absurd to suggest that the Stones in their early sixties would ever hold as much importance for young people as they had possessed when they were in their twenties. New generations desire icons adjacent in age to them, firstly because they are easier on the eye and secondly because they think broadly like them. Adults with children do not have the same mind-sets as teens or twenty-somethings.

Nonetheless, being neither young nor relevant to the youth market does not prohibit

The Life

making important music. Witness the likes of **Bob Dylan, Bruce Springsteen** and **Neil Young,** who despite having aesthetic ups and downs in their careers have continued to sporadically release major artistic statements which have been accepted as being worthy of at least being spoken of in the same breath as their classic vintage recordings. That has not happened to the Stones. They have remained **living legends**, a huge box office attraction, and have continued releasing studio albums (albeit at an ever slower rate) which contain interesting music and even the occasional heavyweight song. However, though they always sprinkle their set with numbers from the latest album, more than anything else they resemble not functioning, vital recording artists but a gargantuan version of acts like **The Searchers** and **The Hollies,** who play their old hits to the nostalgia circuit.

Irrelevance?

Lester Bangs was probably right when he said as far back as 1976 that the group's latest effort was the first meaningless Rolling Stones album. Interestingly enough, he also said in his review "They are still perfectly in tune with the times (ahead sometimes, trendies)." He couldn't deny the aesthetic qualities of what he was hearing even as he lamented the lack of anything in it that would hearten people manning metaphorical or even real barricades. Without wishing to put words into the late Bangs' mouth, by his estima-

tion, the only way to critique The Rolling Stones over the past three decades is not as a social phenomenon or – to use Andrew Loog Oldham's phrase – "a way of life" but as a rock band, nothing more, nothing less. On one level, they've done badly. As far back as 1981, Jagger admitted that once the current tour was over, he wouldn't even think about the band for another six months. By the 21st century, it would seem that band members could go years without the group crossing their mind for any great length. The **eight-year gap** between *Bridges To Babylon* and *A Bigger Bang* is, when one considers it, jaw-dropping. No-one seriously expects grown men to live in each other's pockets or to live for the music the way Mick, Keith and Brian did back in the Edith Grove days, but it is a shame that by their late thirties, The Rolling Stones seems to have become an occasional job to which the individual members return when they get a hankering to make some more music or to make some more money (the two things now seem completely intertwined, although one should point out that even in the late Sixties – his most radical period – Jagger stated that he was not a socialist). There's also the fact that even when recording, it would seem appropriate to put the term 'Rolling Stones Album' in inverted commas. If, as happened on *Bridges To Babylon*, Jagger doesn't appear on some tracks and Richards doesn't appear on others, is there not a case for saying that the respective Glimmer Twins are coming perilously close to using The Rolling Stones brand name to put out **solo material** that would not sell anything like as much if it were to appear under their individual identities? There is also the fact that Wyman's departure left the very concept of the group rather fractured. Jones being replaced by Taylor being replaced by Wood were transitions that were easy to accept, the same role being filled each time. But seeing four instead of five faces staring out from Rolling Stones record covers and posters just strikes one as being wrong. It's a missing tooth, a reminder that the band is not self-contained any longer and has to hire an outside musician when they want to record.

Does it really matter if they're producing the goods? Maybe not, but there now seem to be barriers to them doing that. The first is a problem in the band unselfconsciously attending to their art. In the 1990s, Jagger said to journalist Alan Lysaght, "The Stones is such a big project, especially if you're thinking about touring behind it. The album becomes a bit of an adjunct to a tour, so you're thinking, 'Can I do this on stage? Will this work?' and all that and it becomes part of something else… With a solo album, you can do a folk song with just a fiddle if you want, because no-one's going to say anything." The formulaic methodology Jagger describes is a stark contrast to the band who once paid such **little attention** to public reaction that their every Sixties studio album, except their second, sounds completely different to its predecessor.

Another barrier is the consequences of ring-rustiness. Despite their undeniable technical proficiency and effortless knack for turning out material that is at least professional – *Dirty Work* is their only truly disgraceful album and there were mitigating circumstances – the Stones seem to have lost that ability for the incontrovertibly special song, the number destined to become iconic. There is no set pattern to such numbers – 'Miss You' and 'Angie' sounded utterly un-Stones-like but have become every bit as iconic as 'Satisfaction', 'Honky Tonk Women' or 'Brown Sugar' – other than the fact that the listener's heart leaps every time the opening bars sound and he has it running through his head afterwards. There is no getting around the fact that this lost talent, logically, seems related to the infrequency of their get-togethers. Not even the self-styled Greatest Rock 'n' Roll Band In The World is immune to ring-rustiness.

Nevertheless, they will always be the **Greatest Rock 'n' Roll Band In The World** to many of their fans – and this is not just due to the shrunken status of rock music itself and the consequently fewer candidates for that role. The **back catalogue** of The Rolling Stones is amongst the richest in the history of post-Elvis popular music. It is this that means that it is now inconceivable that their star will wane in what remains of their working lives, and unimaginable that when their working lives are over they will be forgotten. It is this, in other words, that makes them immortal.

Part Two: The Music

"God – if I commit suicide, I'm gonna miss the next Stones album."

Patti Smith
New Musical Express.

The Albums

This section presents a catalogue of all albums released by The Rolling Stones, in chronological order. All albums are available on CD unless indicated.

THE ROLLING STONES

UK, Decca, April 1964; US, London (with surtitle *England's Newest Hitmakers*), May 1964.

(GET YOUR KICKS ON) ROUTE 66/ I JUST WANT TO MAKE LOVE TO YOU / HONEST I DO / I NEED YOU BABY (MONA) / NOW I'VE GOT A WITNESS / LITTLE BY LITTLE//I'M A KING BEE/ CAROL / TELL ME / CAN I GET A WITNESS / YOU CAN MAKE IT IF YOU TRY / WALKING THE DOG

The US version substituted 'Not Fade Away' with Bo Diddley's 'I Need You Baby'. Recorded Regent Sound Studios, London, January- February 1964. Producers: Andrew Loog Oldham & Eric Easton for Impact Sound. Engineer: Bill Farley. Cover design and photography: Nicholas Wright.

As with many debuts, *The Rolling Stones* was the nucleus of the artist's current stage set, honed to perfection at countless dues-paying gigs, hence its superb quality.

We can't attribute to it the artistic significance that we can The Beatles' debut, for that platter was already fifty per cent self-composed whereas the Stones were still tentatively dipping their toe into the waters of songwriting on their premiere album. However, the Stones not only displayed technical prowess on their eponymous album but an imagination regarding arrangement, production (such as they could) and song selection that drew on the same kind of original vision that would ultimately provide the well-spring for their own writing. To illustrate this, debut albums by R&B/pop bands crammed with American songs were ten a penny in 1964. Few of them are as listenable today as this one.

Regent Sound studio doesn't sound like an inspiring recording venue, with its egg-box lined walls, cramped space and mono recording facilities. However, the Stones were probably as much worried about that as Mick, Keith and Brian had been by the squalor of Edith Grove: everything was background to the mission of playing the blues to the best of their abilities. Highlights are the anthemic 'Route 66', the then-slightly daring 'I Just Want To Make Love To You', the dream-like 'I Need You Baby (Mona)', the sensual 'I'm A King Bee' and the novelty closer 'Walking The Dog' (to which Jones contributes comedic gruff backing harmonies). Even the derivative original songs – the chugging 'Little By Little' and the naïve but sweet 'Tell Me' – are highly listenable.

The Albums

Note: Although the original UK configuration of this album is not available on CD, its contents can be found spread across *England's Newest Hitmakers* and *The Rolling Stones Now!* (The version of 'Tell Me' on *England's Newest Hitmakers* is faded earlier than on the eponymous UK debut.)

THE ROLLING STONES NO. 2

(UK only), Decca, January 1965

EVERYBODY NEEDS SOMEBODY TO LOVE / DOWN HOME GIRL / YOU CAN'T CATCH ME / TIME IS ON MY SIDE (UK VERSION) / WHAT A SHAME / GROWN UP WRONG // DOWN THE ROAD APIECE / UNDER THE BOARDWALK / I CAN'T BE SATISFIED / PAIN IN MY HEART / OFF THE HOOK / SUSIE Q
Recorded RCA Studios, Hollywood, Chess Studios, Chicago, Regent Sound Studios, London, June-November 1964. Producers: Andrew Loog Oldham & Eric Easton for Impact Sound. Engineers: Dave Hassinger. Ron Malo, Bill Farley. Cover photography by David Bailey.

Considering their talent and their proven recording abilities, there really was no excuse for the Stones not making another great album with their follow-up effort. After all, the 'Difficult Second Album' syndrome (first album the result of a set honed to perfection; second the consequence of the success of the first album not allowing them time to develop new material properly) hardly applies when a band have their pick of a bottomless well of R&B classics to choose from (the single greatest advantage of being covers merchants). Nonetheless, the Stones managed the achievement of coming up with a second album that stank almost as much as the excreta to which the title was a schoolboyish allusion. Probably unrelated, but conceptually interesting, is the fact that it is the only Sixties Stones album that was not a stylistic departure from its predecessor, underlining the lack of any sense of adventure in its creation.

The opener 'Everybody Needs Somebody To Love' dismally fails to be the lovers' anthem it strives to be – its tempo leaden, its structure clunky and Jagger's vocal mannerisms suddenly as irritating as they had been sweetly naïve on the debut. The group's attempts at self-composition – 'What A Shame', 'Grown Up Wrong' and 'Off The Hook' – are really just the sort of generic blues exercises they had to work their way through in order to learn how to write real songs and should have been left on the cutting room floor. 'Time Is On My Side' is beautiful but apart from that, the only thing approaching a classic is a version of The Drifters number 'Under The Boardwalk', which – though its pure pop nature may have appalled the purists, including some in the Stones – is well crafted and infused with sweet post-coital mellowness.

Note: Though currently unavailable on CD, the album's contents can be found spread across the CDs *The Rolling Stones Now!*, *12 x 5* and on CD compilations *Big Hits (High Tide And*

Green Grass)/Hot Rocks/More Hot Rocks. The version of "Everybody Needs Somebody to Love" on *The Rolling Stones Now!* is different to the one that appeared on the original *The Rolling Stones No.2.*

OUT OF OUR HEADS

UK Decca, September 1965.

SHE SAID YEAH/MERCY, MERCY/HITCH HIKE/THAT'S HOW STRONG MY LOVE IS/GOOD TIMES/GOTTA GET AWAY//TALKIN' 'BOUT YOU/CRY TO ME/OH BABY/HEART OF STONE/THE UNDER ASSISTANT WEST COAST PROMOTION MAN/I'M FREE

US London, July 1965.

MERCY, MERCY/HITCH HIKE/THE LAST TIME/THAT'S HOW STRONG MY LOVE IS/GOOD TIMES/I'M ALRIGHT (LIVE)// (I CAN'T GET NO) SATISFACTION/CRY TO ME/ THE UNDER ASSISTANT WEST COAST PROMOTION MAN/PLAY WITH FIRE/ THE SPIDER AND THE FLY/ONE MORE TRY

Recorded RCA Studios, Hollywood, Chess Studios, Chicago. November 1964-September 1965. Producer: Andrew Loog Oldham. Engineers: Dave Hassinger, Ron Malo, Glyn Johns. Cover photography (both releases): David Bailey

Though the opening cover of Larry Williams' 'She Said Yeah' has an impressive metallic, buzzsaw bite to it, the rest of this album will have come as a shock to those who were expecting a dozen shots of gritty rhythm and blues. The Stones had gone soul. By 1965, Motown and Stax were the sounds of young black America and they were sounds that had evolved from R&B. The Stones on *Out Of Our Heads* were moving with the times. It was also the first UK Stones album to be released in stereo.

Not that they completely embraced all the attributes of soul. There were no horns for a start. However, they otherwise smoothly made the transition with a complete authenticity. 'Mercy, Mercy' has an impressive swing to it. 'That's How Strong My Love Is' is a true tearjerker. Ditto for Bert Russell's 'Cry To Me'. Sam Cooke's 'Good Times' is simply an uncanny act of impersonation – never have either Jagger or the Stones sounded so silky. Even Chuck Berry's 'Talkin' Bout You' is given a slinky soul treatment. While the Nanker, Phelge-credited 'The Under Assistant West Coast Promotion Man' takes the easy option of plastering witty lyrics over a hackneyed 12-bar blues progression, the other originals are getting incrementally better. 'Gotta Get Away' is a song whose spiteful lyric is the type that Jagger would perfect in the following year or so. 'Heart of Stone' is a fine song of defiance. 'I'm Free' is an early attempt to provide an anthem for the generation who looked up to their anti-conventional spirit and though it's really too gentle to work on that level is diverting enough and features some

nice wobbling instrumentation.

David Bailey shot the covers for both the UK and US releases of *Out Of Our Heads.*

AFTERMATH

UK Decca, April 1966.

MOTHER'S LITTLE HELPER/STUPID GIRL/LADY JANE/UNDER MY THUMB/DONCHA BOTHER ME/GOIN' HOME//FLIGHT 505/ HIGH AND DRY/OUT OF TIME/IT'S NOT EASY/I AM WAITING/ TAKE IT OR LEAVE IT/THINK/WHAT TO DO

US, London, July 1966.

PAINT IT BLACK/ STUPID GIRL/LADY JANE/UNDER MY THUMB/DONCHA BOTHER ME/THINK//FLIGHT 505/HIGH AND DRY/IT'S NOT EASY/I AM WAITING/GOIN' HOME

All songs Jagger/Richards

Recorded RCA Studios, Hollywood, December 1965-March 1966. Producer: Andrew Loog Oldham Engineer: Dave Hassinger. Cover photography Guy Webster and Jerrold Schatzberg. US cover photography by Steve Inglis.

A huge milestone for the group. Jagger and Richards could long ago have filled a Stones long player with those "terrible pop songs" Mick and Keith farmed out to others but instead bided their time until they had enough quality material to justify an entire album's worth of original compositions. By the time of *Aftermath* (or *After-Math* as it's rendered on the cover), they had that material. Interestingly, Bill Wyman has said that the songs were intended as a soundtrack to a proposed movie entitled *Back, Behind And In Front*. Had Jagger/Richards raised their game for a movie the way Lennon/McCartney seemed to do with the *A Hard Day's Night* project, The Beatles' own first album of all-

The EPs

EPs (extended play records in 45 rpm format) were a popular way of getting more material out to the audience in the early 1960s. For some bands it was a way of squeezing more juice out of previously released singles, but the Stones released two significant studio mini-albums. Both reached the UK EP No.1 chart slots.

The Rolling Stones

(UK only) Decca, January 1964. Recorded August– November 1963.

YOU BETTER MOVE ON/ POISON IVY/ BYE BYE JOHNNY/ MONEY

Five By Five

(UK only) Decca, August 1964. Recorded at the Chess Studios, Chicago, June 1964

IF YOU NEED ME/ EMPTY HEART/2120 SOUTH MICHIGAN AVENUE/ CONFESSIN' THE BLUES/AROUND AND AROUND

new songs? Possibly, but Richards also said at the time that this was the first time the band had been able to take their time in the studio and, though we are talking relatively here (seven days of sessions), it seems to have made a big difference.

There's certainly a remarkable breadth to it, exemplified by the first three tracks: proceedings open with 'Mother's Little Helper', a strident and sitar-driven denunciation of the type of suburban housewives who are usually

The Transatlantic Split

There were marked differences between the release strategies of the Stones' first UK label, Decca, and their Sixties US label, London. Not only did sleeve designs vary, but also the track listings of apparently synonymous albums, with London jumbling together album tracks with cuts intended for EPs, singles and B-sides. There were even some US albums with no UK equivalents and the issuing in the US of tracks that did not see the light of day in Britain, thus creating collectors' items. Only with *Their Satanic Majesties Request* in 1967 did standardization of content occur, although release dates often still varied. The recent re-mastered ABKCO CD releases of the US album back catalog(ue) has somewhat clouded the historical picture for UK listeners. However, the US-only releases below remain at worst excellent early Stones samplers.

12X5

(US only) London, October 1964

AROUND AND AROUND/CONFESSIN' THE BLUES/EMPTY HEART/TIME IS ON MY SIDE (US VERSION)/GOOD TIMES, BAD TIMES/IT'S ALL OVER NOW//2120 SOUTH MICHIGAN AVENUE/UNDER THE BOARDWALK/CONGRATULATIONS/ GROWN UP WRONG/IF YOU NEED ME/SUSIE Q
A collection of singles, B-sides, EP tracks and a smattering of tracks destined to appear on the second UK LP.

The Rolling Stones, Now!

 (US only) London, February 1965

EVERYBODY NEEDS SOMEBODY TO LOVE/DOWN HOME GIRL/YOU CAN'T CATCH ME/HEART OF STONE/WHAT A SHAME/ I NEED YOU BABY (MONA)///DOWN THE ROAD APIECE/OFF THE HOOK/PAIN IN MY HEART/OH BABY (WE GOT A GOOD THING GOIN')/LITTLE RED ROOSTER/ SURPRISE. SURPRISE
Sort of the equivalent of The Rolling Stones No.2, but with miscellany like a track rescued from UK album-only status ('Mona') and a track from UK single-only status ('Little Red Rooster'). 'Surprise, Surprise' was orignally unique to this album.

December's Children

(US only) London, December 1965. Recorded August 1963-October 1965.

SHE SAID YEAH/TALKIN' 'BOUT YOU/YOU BETTER MOVE ON/LOOK WHAT YOU'VE DONE/THE SINGER NOT THE SONG/(GET YOUR KICKS ON) ROUTE 66 (LIVE)//GET OFF OF MY CLOUD/I'M FREE/AS TEARS GO BY/GOTTA GET AWAY/BLUE TURNS TO GREY/I'M MOVIN' ON (LIVE)
Much the same mixture as before, with the added bizarre touch that each side of mostly great singles, flips and album cuts ends with a worthless live track.

Flowers

(US only) London, July 1967. Recorded December 1965-September 1966.

RUBY TUESDAY/HAVE YOU SEEN YOUR MOTHER BABY, STANDING IN THE SHADOW?/LET'S SPEND THE NIGHT TOGETHER/LADY JANE/OUT OF TIME/MY GIRL//BACKSTREET GIRL/PLEASE GO HOME/MOTHER'S LITTLE HELPER/ TAKE IT OR LEAVE IT/RIDE ON BABY/SITTIN' ON A FENCE
The last of the unique US albums is the most bizarre – a mixture of a non-US release mop-up, a greatest hits, and a collection of songs unavailable anywhere else.

Live Albums I

Live albums are, according to your point of view, an essential part of rock tradition or a fraudulent waste of time. Those who adhere to the former view cite records like James Brown's *Live At The Apollo*, The Who's *Live At Leeds*, Bob Dylan and The Band's *Before The Flood* and Bob Marley and the Wailers' *Live!* as classics every bit as memorable as those acts' best studio albums, ones that capture superbly the way that songs take on a different dimension in front of a heaving mass of appreciative bodies. Those in the latter camp insist that they are essentially a con-job simply because there is no such thing as a genuinely live album: not only is what you hear on the record not what the audience heard on the day due to the necessity to re-mix to avoid a sonic mush but also due to the egotism of musicians who just cannot leave in the inevitable bum notes and inconsistent tempos and insist on going into the studio to paper over the cracks with overdubs.

Up until the nineteenth year of their existence as a recording unit, the Rolling Stones had only released three live albums, one of those in America only. Since then, the floodgates have opened (see pages 178–180).

Got Live If You Want It (EP)

WE WANT THE STONES / EVERYBODY NEEDS SOMEBODY TO LOVE / PAIN IN MY HEART / ROUTE 66 // I'M MOVING ON / I'M ALRIGHT
(UK only) Decca, June 1965.

Recorded live in London, Liverpool and Manchester in March 1965, this cacophanous one-mike-over-the-balcony recording was a damp squib of a farewell to the EP format for the Stones. Some tracks were scattered across US albums.

Got Live If You Want It (LP)

UNDER MY THUMB / GET OFF OF MY CLOUD / LADY JANE / NOT FADE AWAY / I'VE BEEN LOVING YOU TOO LONG / FORTUNE TELLER // THE LAST TIME / 19TH NERVOUS BREAKDOWN / TIME IS ON MY SIDE / I'M ALRIGHT / HAVE YOU SEEN YOUR MOTHER BABY, STANDING IN THE SHADOW? / (I CAN'T GET NO) SATISFACTION
(US only) London, December 1966. Recorded September–October 1966. Cover photography Gered Mankowitz

This album has effectively been re-mixed twice, Andrew Loog Oldham tweaking the original (awful) balances for its 'Eighties CD release. There was further work done for its inclusion in the 2002 remasters series. Despite this restoration work, the sound of a band half-heartedly knocking out music against a tidal wave of teenagers screaming has an intrinsically limited aesthetic appeal.

The tracks 'I've Been Loving You Too Long' and 'Fortune Teller' are studio recordings with crowd noises over-dubbed.

Get Yer Ya-Yas Out

JUMPIN' JACK FLASH / CAROL / STRAY CAT BLUES /
LOVE IN VAIN / MIDNIGHT RAMBLER // SYMPATHY FOR
THE DEVIL / LIVE WITH ME / LITTLE QUEENIE / HONKY
TONK WOMEN / STREET FIGHTING MAN

UK Decca, US London, September 1970. Cover photo
by David Bailey.

Despite its, by mod-
ern standards, low
fidelity, this is the
Stones live album
you should buy if you
must own one. The
band often sizzle in
performances from
Baltimore and New
York's Madison Square
Garden on their '69
comeback tour, with
'Midnight Rambler'
a dramatic set piece
rather than the subtle
groove of its origi-
nal incarnation.

**Originally the cover concept
was shot by Michael Berkofsky,
but was reshot by Bailey five
months later.**

**Pre-printed live-show
fliers in the manner of
Alphonse Mucha were
issued for the '69 US
tour, celebrated in the
Get Yer Ya-Yas Out
album.**

anti-drugs but who have their own legal fix in
the shape of stress pills. This then gives way to
the rockin' put-down of a lover 'Stupid Girl'
which itself makes way for 'Lady Jane', a tender song of devotion couched in Chaucerian
English and decorated with dulcimer and harpsichord. Elsewhere we find dark pop ('Under
My Thumb'), blues ('Doncha Bother Me',
'Goin' Home'), country ('High and Dry') and
Indian-style drone ('I Am Waiting'). Though
'Goin' Home' remains the longest studio track
the Stones have released, the extravaganza on
the album is really 'Out Of Time', which gives
an epic setting to the spite Jagger directs at
women for a lot of the record.

Though the achievement of Jagger and
Richards was unequivocal, Jones achieves his
own kind of triumph, providing the cherry on
the cake of his colleagues' compositions with a
variety of new and exotic instruments, contributing marimbas, dulcimer, sitar and keyboards
to the record. Jagger's alleged misogyny grates
on some modern ears but in 1966 that refusal
to follow moon-June pop convention was yet
another aspect of the Stones that made them
cutting edge.

BETWEEN THE BUTTONS

UK, Decca, January 1967

YESTERDAY'S PAPERS/MY OBSESSION/BACK STREET GIRL/
CONNECTION/SHE SMILED SWEETLY/COOL, CALM AND
COLLECTED//ALL SOLD OUT/PLEASE GO HOME/WHO'S
BEEN SLEEPING HERE?/COMPLICATED/MISS AMANDA JONES/
SOMETHING HAPPENED TO ME YESTERDAY

US, London, February 1967

LET'S SPEND THE NIGHT TOGETHER/ YESTERDAY'S PAPERS/ RUBY TUESDAY/CONNECTION/SHE SMILED SWEETLY/COOL, CALM AND COLLECTED//ALL SOLD OUT/MY OBSESSION/ WHO'S BEEN SLEEPING HERE?/COMPLICATED/MISS AMANDA JONES/SOMETHING HAPPENED TO ME YESTERDAY

All songs by Jagger/Richards
Recorded RCA Studios, Hollywood, Olympic Studios, London August-November 1966 . Producer: Andrew Loog Oldham. Engineers: Dave Hassinger (RCA), Glyn Johns (Olympic). Cover photo by Gered Mankowitz, rear design by Charlie Watts.

Gered Mankowitz was a favourite Stones (and The Who) photographer.

Though *Aftermath* had seen the Stones finally record without feeling the dread hand of the clock ticking on the wall above them, it is actually *Between The Buttons* that they felt was their first album recorded as a suite of songs rather than being merely assembled. It was also the first album they made when they weren't either on the road or had just come off it. Although started at RCA studios, it was completed back in their home country at Olympic.

The album was the first to sound lush: whatever the quality of the Stones' previous long players, they had suffered from a slight tinniness. Yet it's a very strange album, muted and mannered in a way that was almost the very opposite of their public image. The album is never spoken of as being a highlight of the Stones canon and Jagger always dismisses it almost completely whenever its raised. However, it's not a poor album – it just seems to meander somewhat aimlessly. Characteristic is the track 'My Obsession', with its almost irritating repetitive structure, lack of any real hook and peculiar ending wherein Charlie bashes uncertainly on a cymbal, as though he hasn't realized that all his colleagues have already finished. Yet there is some genuinely good stuff here. It opens strongly with 'Yesterday's Papers', the closest that the album gets to an iconic track. The pastoral and sophisticated 'Back Street Girl' is a sort of *Lady Chatterley's Lover* with the genders reversed with Brian providing French café ambience via the accordion. 'Miss Amanda Jones' is an endearingly affectionate rocker that gently mocks debutantes. 'All Sold Out' is a highly melodic examination of an unhealthy relationship. Additionally, 'Complicated' and 'Something Happened To Me Yesterday' are interestingly lyrically for their references to their drug consumption (and would have been hostages to fortune had not the authorities been so terminally unhip as to fail to recognize them as such). However, much of the album seems like a loop of aimless, circular melodies that are undermined further by a complete lack of grit.

Oldham asked Watts to do some drawings for the sleeve and told him the title would be between the buttons (i.e. of Charlie's coat on the cover photograph). Watts' misunderstanding gave the album its title.

THEIR SATANIC MAJESTIES REQUEST

UK Decca, US London, December 1967

SING THIS ALL TOGETHER / CITADEL / IN ANOTHER LAND / 2000 MAN / SING THIS ALL TOGETHER (SEE WHAT HAPPENS)// SHE'S A RAINBOW / THE LANTERN / GOMPER / 2000 LIGHT YEARS FROM HOME / ON WITH THE SHOW
Recorded Olympic Studios, London, February-October 1967. Produced by the Rolling Stones. Engineers: Glyn Johns, Eddie Kramer. Cover art and photography by Michael Cooper, Tony Meeviwiffen.

The original lenticular 3-D Michael Cooper photograph was meant to cover the entire front sleeve but proved too expensive.

Satanic Majesties reveals a band trying to accommodate a zeitgeist which wasn't really their thing. The previous June the appearance of the album *Sgt. Pepper's Lonely Hearts Club Band* by The Beatles had seemed to rewrite all the rules of popular music and affirm that it was as valid as classical music. Peace and love sentiments were in the air and musical and cultural exotica were all the rage. All these things influenced the style of *Satanic Majesties*, as most certainly did LSD. It's a matter of opinion whether any of these influences were beneficial.

Like its predecessor, it's an album whose songs generally make one have to wrack one's brains to recall how they go when looking at their titles. Though the songs are often strong, they – as does much of non-Western music – feel unresolved. Its attempts at a communality that was the spirit of the season are also never quite convincing: the Stones have always been more comfortable with *hauteur* and contempt than generosity. However, the album is rarely less than interesting and often brilliant. Jones possibly plays no guitar at all on the record but really goes to town on instruments never heard in Stones music before and unlikely ever to be heard in it again, tackling flute, trumpet and, especially, mellotron, to frequently dazzling effect. 'Citadel' (hard-rocking psychedelia), 'In Another Land' (gentle psychedelia), '2,000 Man' (wonderfully melodic nerd's anthem) and 'She's A Rainbow' (the aural equivalent of a kaleidoscope) are all great songs. None of the tracks are terrible except the reprise of 'Sing This Song Together', a jam that the band mistakenly imagine will be more listenable than most jams because it features unusual instruments.

You certainly wouldn't want all Stones albums to sound like this but you're also glad that it's in the back catalogue.

Two titles were discarded for the record, 'Cosmic Christmas' and 'Her Satanic Majesty Requests', the latter a pun on the British passport legend ("Her Britannic Majesty's Secretary of State Requests and Requires in the Name of Her Majesty all those whom it may concern to allow the bearer to pass freely without let or hindrance, and to afford the bearer such assistance and protection as may be necessary") which Decca refused to countenance.

BEGGARS BANQUET

UK Decca, US London, December 1968.

SYMPATHY FOR THE DEVIL / NO EXPECTATIONS / DEAR DOCTOR / PARACHUTE WOMAN / JIG-SAW PUZZLE // STREET FIGHTING MAN / PRODIGAL SON / STRAY CAT BLUES / FACTORY GIRL / SALT OF THE EARTH
Recorded Olympic Studios, London, February-July 1968. Producer: Jimmy Miller. Engineers: Glyn Johns, Eddie Kramer, Alan O'Duffy. Cover design Tom Wilkes, photography Michael Joseph (original and current CD photography by Barry Feinstein, see page 74).

Beggars Banquet was the first Stones album produced by a 'real' producer, Jimmy Miller. Richards said that one of Miller's contributions to *Beggars Banquet* was to "make a nondescript number into something". This might sound like sacrilege to the album's many fans but one can see what the guitarist means. Large parts of the record are about texture and incremental effect. Witness 'No Expectations', a ballad which at the beginning sounds watery, almost colourless. However, the pathos grows with each verse as a careful build up of vocal and instrumentation takes place until, when Nicky Hopkins' piano emerges, it's enough to break the listener's heart. 'Dear Doctor' and 'Parachute Woman' exhibit similar superficial slightness but genuine depth can be perceived in the texture. Or is it the other way around?

The most startling thing about *Beggar's Banquet* – the title a suggestion by Christopher Gibbs – is the fact that it is an utter departure from everything the Stones had recorded before, except 'Little Red Rooster'. Those (including the Stones themselves) who talk about it marking a return to the Stones' roots as they impatiently threw aside the elaborate clothing of the psychedelic era they had tried their best to pretend to feel comfortable wearing are slightly wide of the mark. Yes, the blues is the touchstone here but it's a different form of blues to the type they had purveyed before. In its subtlety, its maturity, its rejection of pop flash in favour of intricate layering and virtuoso playing and its predominately acoustic ambience, this is as removed from previous Stones music as could be imagined. The point is, their fans had grown up with them and had more mature tastes that were able to accommodate such sophistication.

'Sympathy For The Devil' – the Stones bad-boy chic given mythic status – is naturally the highlight but the growling jailbait anthem 'Stray Cat Blues', the beautiful 'No Expectations', the delightful country blues cover 'Prodigal Son' (fabulous acoustic guitar picking) and the stately proletarian anthem 'Salt Of the Earth' also delight the senses.

LET IT BLEED

UK, Decca, December 1969, US London, November 1969.

GIMME SHELTER /LOVE IN VAIN / COUNTRY HONK / LIVE WITH ME / LET IT BLEED // MIDNIGHT RAMBLER / YOU GOT THE SILVER / MONKEY MAN / YOU CAN'T ALWAYS GET WHAT YOU WANT

Recorded Olympic Studios, London, Sunset Recorders, LA, Elektra Studios, LA, February-October 1969. Producer: Jimmy Miller. Engineers: Glyn Johns, George Chkiantz. Cover design by Robert Brownjohn, Victor Kahn (cake by Delia Smith).

The sleeve for *Let It Bleed*, featuring a grotesque cake, was designed by Robert Brownjohn, a man who had a few years before rejected Keith Richards' art portfolio. How times had changed, as the Stones closed out the Sixties as five of the most important men on the planet in their influence on (if only as behavioural permission-granters by example) the generation that would be taking power when they finished their degrees. The band – or its songwriters – certainly lived up to that power, although not with manifestoes for a better society but with a collection of songs that, in the main, self-consciously bolstered their collective reputation as enemies of orthodox society.

Though Mick Taylor plays on two tracks ('Country Honk' and 'Live With Me'), this was the second album in a row effectively made by a four-man Stones. Jones was still around but only just clinging onto life, let alone the band he had formed. Belying their reduced personnel resources, *Let It Bleed* was a grand-sounding record, with high production values and plenty of augmentation by outside instrumentalists. The cocking of snooks at society's mores has dated this album somewhat, now

that those mores don't prevail too much. In fact, they often seem to be skirting a parody of their bad boy image (the buffoonish title track, the affectedly yobbish 'Live With Me', whose boast "I got nasty habits" is then somewhat undermined by the following revelation of alleged debauchery: "I take tea at three") and sometimes in ways that have dated horribly (the virtual rapist-celebrating 'Midnight Rambler', fine bluesy groove though that track has). But 'Monkey Man' has a pleasing sheen, 'You Got The Silver' is disarming and the album is begun and ended by two utter classics. The first, 'Gimme Shelter', is a brutal and gigantic extrapolation of the blues, aflame with apocalyptic imagery and slashes of mouth harp that sound bigger than life. The second is the lengthy song of heartache 'You Can't Always Get What You Want', whose political relevance might be entirely phoney but which boasts an amazing arrangement that switches from the choral to the rockin'.

STICKY FINGERS

Rolling Stones Records, April 1971.

BROWN SUGAR /SWAY / WILD HORSES / CAN'T YOU HEAR ME KNOCKING / YOU GOTTA MOVE // BITCH / I GOT THE BLUES / SISTER MORPHINE / DEAD FLOWERS / MOONLIGHT MILE
Recorded Olympic Studios, London, Muscle Shoals, Alabama, Stargroves, Trident Studios, London, March 1969-January 1971. Producer: Jimmy Miller. Engineers: Glyn Johns, Andy Johns, Chris Kimsey, Jimmy Johnson. Cover art by Andy Warhol.

There is something sonically about *Sticky Fingers* – the album that inaugurated the

Mick Taylor era - that sounds slightly 'off'. Not maladroit as such, but somehow fatigued, slurred. There is most certainly an energy on tracks like 'Brown Sugar', 'Bitch' and 'Can't You Hear Me Knocking' but – and this description can be applied to just about all of the Stones music of the next few years – it's an energy shot through with lethargy or perhaps exhaustion, the self-consciously high spirits of somebody forcing it. No doubt the Stones didn't necessarily feel that way when they recorded the material (although many was the recording session in the early Seventies attended by a Richards with strangely pin-point pupils) but this was a juncture in the band's career where their music seemed to become infected by their decadence and indulgence, the *ennui* induced by fulfilled artistic ambition and the effects of drink, drugs and late nights. Many classic records it produced too – including this one.

Though nominally Mick Taylor's first complete Stones studio album, an indication that its recording was a protracted affair is provided by the fact that some material here dates from as far back as March 1969 (i.e.before Taylor joined). The songs encapsulate the Stones during this period: decadent artists whose every appetite in life was easily sated. References to hard drugs and kinky sex abound (at a time when that was still shocking). Though 'Brown Sugar' is a quintessential Stones rocker, this is another album where the acoustic predominates over the electric, albeit less so than on *Beggars Banquet*, and an album where there are as many slowies as fast 'uns. In the former category are 'Wild Horses', a sweet ballad about Richards' regret at leaving his newly-born son filtered through Jagger's feelings about a comatose Faithfull, 'I Got The Blues', a song almost as generic as its title suggests but miraculously rescued by some superb horn arrangements and a deliciously shrieking organ interlude, and the haunting beseechment for pain relief 'Sister Morphine'. The up-tempo numbers include 'Bitch' (not another misogynistic Jagger song, love being the bitch concerned), which boasts a rousing saxophone and trumpet riff, and the raggedly majestic epic 'Can't You Hear Me Knocking'. A couple of the songs – the sleepy 'Sway' and the lonesome 'Moonlight Mile' – were more Taylor/Jagger collaborations than anything to do with Richards, who departed the sessions early.

EXILE ON MAIN ST.

Rolling Stones Records, May 1972.

ROCKS OFF / RIP THIS JOINT / SHAKE YOUR HIPS / CASINO BOOGIE / TUMBLING DICE // SWEET VIRGINIA / TORN AND FRAYED / SWEET BLACK ANGEL / LOVING CUP // HAPPY / TURD ON THE RUN / VENTILATOR BLUES / JUST WANNA SEE HIS FACE /LET IT LOOSE // ALL DOWN THE LINE / STOP BREAKING DOWN / SHINE A LIGHT / SOUL SURVIVOR

Recorded Stargroves, Olympic Studios, London, Villa Nellcote, Sunset Sound, LA, March 1970-February 1971. Producer: Jimmy Miller. Engineers: Andy Johns, Glyn Johns, Joe Zagarino. Cover art by Robert Frank.

Robert Frank's striking freak-show collage was almost as shocking as his film, *Cocksucker Blues*.

This 1972 effort – the only double studio album of the Stones' career – is either a slovenly, lazily low-fi record that shows a complete contempt for their audience or a bleary masterpiece, depending on the listener. Though *Sticky Fingers'* music exhibited a frayed quality, it was still a glossily engineered album. The fact that *Exile* was a record that was half recorded in the guitarist's basement was compounded by the fact that it was mixed in a rush to be ready for a tour. To probably the majority at the time of its release (when the album received mostly negative reviews) these were aural deficiencies that were an insult to the songs, let alone the audience. The case can certainly be made that the maladroit recording and production reduced the tracks to glorified demo tape status and that the considerations of the people who would be paying good money for the album were not given a thought – in other words, true decadence.

Over the years, attitudes have changed. Just as The Clash's debut sounded exquisitely menacing partly because of its incompetent mix, so the dank, murky ambience of *Exile* contributed to many people's appreciation of the record. It is now generally considered to be the finest release to which the band have put their name.

It's certainly a better record than first meets the ear, although doesn't have an unequivocal classic or signature song like 'Gimme Shelter' or 'Brown Sugar'. It's more a mood piece, each successive song helping bore it into the listener's affections. Special mention should go to the sleazy 'Turd On The Run', 'Rip This Joint' (breakneck Fifties retro), 'Casino Boogie' (tight funk groove with tender references to Blanca Jagger's pregnancy), the countrified 'Sweet Virginia', the half-horny, half tender, alternately subdued and dramatic 'Loving Cup' and the big production soul number 'Let It Loose'.

Critic Robert Christgau has described this work as a "fagged-out masterpiece" and said that though it was "barely afloat in its own drudgery, it rocks with extra power and concentration as a result." An interesting contrast with this appraisal – and one that sums up the divisions about *Exile On Main St.* – is this observation from Steve Taylor from the 1970s book *The Rock Primer*: "... frankly I'm undecided. It's a muddy album, an ill-defined mix of sliding guitars, thudding bass and cash-register piano jangles which seems suffused with contempt for the listener - an impression strengthened by the cover, with its gloomy collage, its cellotaped freehand annotations and its contemptuously vulgar catalogue number [COC 69100]."

The Glimmer Twins are as divided as the critics. Along with *Beggar's Banquet*, Richards has named *Exile* as his favourite Stones album. Jagger on the other hand has said, "I don't particularly think it's a great album."

GOAT'S HEAD SOUP

Rolling Stones Records, August 1973 (UK), September 1973 (US).

DANCING WITH MR. D. / 100 YEARS AGO / COMING DOWN AGAIN / DOO DOO DOO DOO DOO (HEARTBREAKER) / ANGIE // SILVER TRAIN / HIDE YOUR LOVE / WINTER / CAN YOU HEAR THE MUSIC / STAR STAR

Recorded Dynamic Sound, Jamaica, Village Recorders, LA, Olympic Studios, London, Island Studios, London, November 1972-July 1973. Producer: Jimmy Miller. Engineers: Andy Johns, Bob Fraboni, Baker Bigsby, Howard Kilgour, Carlton Lee. Cover photography by David Bailey.

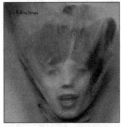

Bailey's front cover shot of Mick was as pure as his portrait of Keith on the back was charred.

Curiously, as though they were aware of the deficiencies of some of the material on *Goat's Head Soup* (named after a national dish in Jamaica, where some of it was recorded), the Stones shoved most of the chaff onto side two of the original vinyl record: the leaden 'Silver Train' – which should have been consigned to a siding instead of being allowed to masquerade as railworthy – 'Hide Your Love' (a jam passed off as a song), 'Winter' and 'Can You Hear The Music' (well-intentioned attempts at atmospheric songs hampered by melodic mediocrity). Only 'Star Star' – the one traditional Stones rocker on the side – is above average. However, on side one are some brilliant tracks which served to prove that, when they tried, the Stones were still the best band in the world. 'Dancing With Mr D' might be the depiction of menace of 'Sympathy For The Devil' reduced to parody but it is still fun in its pulpy way. The super-slick, horn-charged soul protest song 'Doo Doo Doo Doo Doo (Heartbreaker)' and the melancholic '100 Years Ago' ("Don't you think it's sometimes wise not to grow up?") are both superb. 'Angie' is simply lovely.

All of this cut no ice with Lester Bangs who, reviewing the album for *Creem*, fulminated, "Just because the Stones have abdicated their responsibilities is no reason we have to sit still for this shit! ... Unless we get the Rolling Stones off their asses IT'S THE END OF ROCK 'N' ROLL!" With expectations like that on the band's shoulders, their music was hardly likely to be reviewed on its own merits. Still, there was a danger sign present in the form of Keith's vocal showcase 'Coming Down Again'. While quite sumptuous, it is an indulged man's whinge, him complaining to epic backing that his missus didn't like it when he slept with someone else and that he didn't have any drugs.

The album, incidentally, is probably Taylor's high water mark, his classy, virtuoso playing – often with a wah-wah pedal – to be discerned at every turn.

The front cover featured a camp-looking head shot of Jagger and the back a distressed looking Richards visage, both taken by David Bailey, who had also shot the sleeve of the UK version of *Out Of Our Heads* (used on *December's Children* in the States).

IT'S ONLY ROCK 'N' ROLL

Rolling Stones Records, October 1974.

IF YOU CAN'T ROCK ME / AIN'T TOO PROUD TO BEG /IT'S ONLY ROCK 'N' ROLL (BUT I LIKE IT) / TILL THE NEXT GOODBYE / TIME WAITS FOR NO ONE // LUXURY / DANCE LITTLE SISTER / IF YOU REALLY WANT TO BE MY FRIEND / SHORT AND CURLIES / FINGERPRINT FILE

Recorded Musicland, Munich, Stargroves, Island Studios, London. Produced by The Glimmer Twins. Engineers: Andy Johns, Keith Harwood, George Chkiantz. Cover art by Guy Peelaert.

The Stones were presumably hoping for something sensational when they commissioned pop artist Guy Peelaert to paint the cover of their new album, such as the pictures he had previously rendered of them in Nazi uniforms and women's clothing surrounded by very underage girls in an attempt to capture their social outlaw image. However, his picture for *It's Only Rock 'N' Roll* – the Stones as god-like figures in ancient Rome being adored by the crowds – was pretty but somewhat tame. Some thought the same of the contents.

The first thing that one notices about this album is its muddy mix. Having dispensed with the services of Jimmy Miller, the Glimmer Twins proved not quite adequate to the task of producers on their debut turn at the controls. However, persevering with that maladroit production reveals a strong collection.

The group can be forgiven for being taken aback by some of the lukewarm reviews. Unlike on much of *Goat's Head Soup*, they are genuinely trying to make great art. 'Time Waits For No-One' is a deep rumination on the effects of ageing with suitably epic backing. 'Fingerprint File' addresses the ramifications of governments using technology to keep tabs on its citizens, the funky rhythm track and wah-wah guitar creating an appropriately suspense movie-like accompaniment. 'Ain't Too Proud To Beg' pays respectful tribute to The Temptations. There are also a pair of lovely ballads: 'Till The Next Goodbye' details the pain of separation to a swelling melody while 'If You Really Want To Be My Friend' reveals some of the unforeseen complexities of being in a relationship, namely that being in love doesn't preclude missing the freedom one used to have ("Let me live it up like I used to do."). 'Short And Curlies' ("She's got you by the balls," runs its classy refrain) is filler but at the same time very enjoyable, while 'Luxury' is according to some a rock-reggae fusion and to others a ham-fisted attempt at reggae, but everyone agrees that it is very easy on the ear.

BLACK AND BLUE

Rolling Stones Records, April 1976.

HOT STUFF / HAND OF FATE / CHERRY OH BABY / MEMORY MOTEL // HEY NEGRITA / MELODY / FOOL TO CRY / CRAZY MAMA

Recorded Rotterdam, Musicland, Munich, Mkountain Recfording, Montreux, Atlantic Studios, NY. Producers: The Glimmer Twins. Engineers: Keith Harwood, Lew Hahn, Glyn Johns. Cover photography by Hiro.

The Music

Metamorphosis

ABKCO (US), Decca (UK), June 1975

ORIGINAL UK TRACKLISTING: OUT OF TIME / DON'T LIE TO ME / SOME THINGS JUST STICK IN YOUR MIND / EACH AND EVERYDAY OF THE YEAR / HEART OF STONE / I'D MUCH RATHER BE WITH THE BOYS / (WALKIN' THRU THE) SLEEPY CITY / WE'RE WASTIN' TIME / TRY A LITTLE HARDER / I DON'T KNOW WHY / IF YOU LET ME / JIVING SISTER FANNY / DOWNTOWN SUZIE / FAMILY / MEMO FROM TURNER / I'M GOING DOWN

ORIGINAL US TRACKLISTING: OUT OF TIME / DON'T LIE TO ME / EACH AND EVERYDAY OF THE YEAR / HEART OF STONE / I'D MUCH RATHER BE WITH THE BOYS / (WALKIN' THRU THE) SLEEPY CITY / TRY A LITTLE HARDER / I DON'T KNOW WHY / IF YOU LET ME / JIVING SISTER FANNY / DOWNTOWN SUZIE / FAMILY / MEMO FROM TURNER / I'M GOING DOWN

Metamorphosis was a contractual obligation to Allen Klein, comprised of outtakes. Klein rejected many of the suggestions for the project from Bill Wyman (always the band's archivist). Many have noted that Klein seemed to reject cover versions in favour of Jagger/Richards tunes that would yield him publishing royalties. As a consequence of this approach, a lot of the tracks here aren't actually Rolling Stones material but merely key members of the Stones and session musicians recording tracks designed as demos for other artists. Even with the genuine Stones material, there are no hidden classics unearthed, despite the presence of some material recorded in the band's peak years. 'Family', for instance, is a dark tale of incest and disfunctionality that is less impressive than its *Beggar's Banquet* vintage would lead one to assume. Nonetheless, the album is always quite interesting, featuring alternate versions of 'Out Of Time', 'Heart Of Stone' and 'Memo From Turner', Bill Wyman's other Stones composition (the Jagger-sung Mockney 'Downtown Suzie'), a haunted Stevie Wonder cover from the *Let It Bleed* sessions ('I Don't Know Why'), the only song ever credited to 'Oldham/Richards' ('I'd Much Rather Be With The Boys') and a few of those – actually quite good – "terrible pop songs" Mick and Keith were writing in the mid-Sixties (the 'Downtown'-like '(Walkin' Thru the) Sleepy City' and the *mariachi*-inflected 'Each And Every Day Of The Year' among the best). Treat it as an official bootleg and you won't be disappointed.

At about the same time (May UK, June US) Rolling Stones Records released *Made in the Shade*, a greatest hits (since leaving Decca) collection.

Mick Taylor's sudden departure left the band in a quandary. Their solution of combining auditions for his replacement with sessions for their next album was not viewed as an ingenious idea by everyone. In some quarters it was interpreted as yet another example of the band's contempt for fans whom they very often seemed no longer to inhabit the same planet as. Whichever of the two it was, it was a *modus operandum* that led to an interesting variety of guitar styles, from Ronnie Wood's cawing to Harvey Mandel's smoothness. More surprisingly, the album was not a falling-back on by-numbers Stones music but a genuinely daring exercise, with the Stones exploring every musical style imaginable, from funk to reggae to ballad – everything except that quintessential riff-driven, rockin' Stones sound,

one track excepted. Far from this adventurism being appreciated, *Black And Blue* attracted critical brickbats, often from the same people who'd had problems with the previous two albums' generic Stones approach. The fact that it was comprised of an ostensibly parsimonious eight tracks (in fact, all of the songs were of above average length, leading to a standard playing time) didn't help matters either.

Side one of the vinyl record was just about dispensable. 'Hot Stuff' sees the band try to get funky in a world address (Jagger telling the citizens of London, New York and Jamaica, "Shape up", 'You're tough" and "You're hot" respectively) to boring effect. Equally tedious is the clumsy reggae cover 'Cherry Oh Baby'. Meanwhile 'Hand Of Fate' and 'Memory Hotel' are two failed attempts at epics . Side two of the record, however, constituted the best Stones album side for years. 'Hey, Negrita' is a street tableau with a riff that could dice potatoes and sees a Jagger in top vocal form. Jagger's is also delightful in his duet with Billy Preston, 'Melody', a jazzy piano piece with call-and-response and scat vocalizing. The gossamer virtues of 'Fool To Cry' are considerable. The record climaxes with the big and brutal 'Crazy Mama', which is the riff-based, rockin' Stones formula taken to the nth degree.

SOME GIRLS

Rolling Stones Records, June 1978

MISS YOU / WHEN THE WHIP COMES DOWN / JUST MY IMAGINATION (RUNNING AWAY WITH ME) / SOME GIRLS / LIES // FAR AWAY EYES / RESPECTABLE / BEFORE THEY MAKE ME RUN / BEAST OF BURDEN / SHATTERED
Recorded Pathé-Marconi, Paris, October 1977-February 1978. Producers: The Glimmer Twins. Engineer: Chris Kimsey. Cover art by Peter Corrison.

Actresses Lucille Ball and Raquel Welch took exception to their inclusion on the cover, which was inspired by adverts for wigs in black magazines.
.

In the time since their last studio album, the musical world had shifted on its axis. Whatever the Stones' denials, *Some Girls* was surely an album that would never have taken the form it did without that seismic shock to their systems engendered by being told by younger musicians that they were not the epitome of the rebel but old, conformist and elitist. On this album, they were trying to prove themselves, and it shows. Jagger even began to address the establishment status that the Stones hadn't known they possessed in the first verse of 'Respectable', before chickening out and using the rest of the song to slag off his estranged missus.

It's a fun record, with a good-naturedness unusual for the Stones. The music is more brittle and bright than before, as though the departure of Mick Taylor caused the Stones to lose a certain amount of 'bottom'. However, there also is an overall feeling of sprightliness, as though the music itself, not just the recently reformed Richards, was shrugging off a drug torpor. Charlie Watts is on blistering form throughout. With Jagger playing more and more guitar, the album is veritably and delightfully buried under interlocking, overlapping fretwork.

'Miss You', in which the Stones effortlessly embraced the voguish disco, was a deserved world-wide hit single but was only one of a whole host of gems. The brutal 'When The Whip Comes Down' only has in common with the more thoughtful preceding opener the rendering of fine detail of New York life - a strand running throughout the album. The cover of The Temptations' 'Just My Imagination', is achingly tender. The album's title track is perhaps less enlightened (the line "Black girls just wanna get fucked all night" causing complaints), but who can fail to forgive this in the face of a wall of divinely intermeshed guitars, cheeky schoolboy innuendo and Sugar Blue's show stealing mouth harp. 'Far Away Eyes' is a hilariously shit-kicking country croon. Keith's 'Before They Make Me Run' adds further to the overall reflective feel: his moving account of his retreat from the lovelessness of the junkie lifestyle is carried on a classic Richards riff. The riff of 'Beast of Burden', is even better, a lilting lick for a gorgeous melody. After so many fine tunes, the closing 'Shattered' comes as a shock at first, being more based around rhythm, but this rap number about the perils of high society Big Apple life is funny, clever and disarmingly confessional. Ironically, only 'Lies' – in which the band try to out-punk the punks – doesn't work.

EMOTIONAL RESCUE

Rolling Stones Records, June 1980

DANCE (PT. 1) / SUMMER ROMANCE / SEND IT TO ME / LET ME GO / INDIAN GIRL // WHERE THE BOYS GO / DOWN IN THE HOLE / EMOTIONAL RESCUE / SHE'S SO COLD / ALL ABOUT YOU

Recorded Wally Heider's Studio, LA, Compass Point, Bahamas, Pathé-Marconi, Paris, Electric Lady, NY, August 1978-April 1980. Producers: The Glimmer Twins, Chris Kimsey. Engineer: Chris Kimsey. Cover art by Peter Corriston, Roy Adzak.

After the artistic triumph of *Some Girls*, it is unforgivable that the Stones fell back into bad habits for *Emotional Rescue*, which was largely comprised of leftover tracks from its predecessor. An utterly lazy record which doesn't even manage to pick the best of the material in the vault, it sold more copies than any previous Stones album.

Having said that, *Emotional Rescue* possesses significant virtues. They were in fine form on several tracks. 'Down In the Hole' is a fabulous, eerie number, 'Send It To Me' a delightful lovelorn reggae with some of Mick's best singing for years, and 'She's So Cold' incontrovertible proof that the band can pull off a high-quality archetypal Stones rocker when they try. However, some tracks were featureless and flat ('Summer Romance', 'Let Me Go') and the affectedness yobbishness of others ('Where The Boys Go') was embarrassing for men in their late thirties. Even though some tracks were fairly experimental (the falsettovocaled dance-oriented title track, the semi-political 'Indian Girl' and the funky 'Dance Pt 1)' they were also a bit boring.

The front cover featuring thermal images of the band members was awful.

TATTOO YOU

Rolling Stones Records, August 1981.

START ME UP / HANG FIRE / SLAVE / LITTLE T & A / BLACK LIMOUSINE / NEIGHBOURS // WORRIED ABOUT YOU / TOPS HEAVEN / NO USE IN CRYING / WAITING ON A FRIEND
Recorded Compass Point, Bahamas, Pathé-Marconi, Paris, Electric Lady, NY, Atlantic Studios, NY, 1972–June 1981. Producers: The Glimmer Twins, Chris Kimsey. Engineeers: Chris Kimsey, Barry Sage.

On one level, a bizarre album: Mick Taylor and Wayne Perkins must have both been laughing down their sleeves as this hodge-podge of material from the vaults was received as a great return to form. Either that or fuming over their disingenuous lack of credits. However, the band creating a spanking new Rolling Stones album with virtually nobody but its lead singer having to lift a finger actually fulfilled a long held dream of Stones aficionados who knew that there were many Stones tracks in the vaults that were rumoured to be close to or even matching their normal standards.

In a sense the album was cumulatively what you would expect an album created out of such methods to be: *Tattoo You* contained some gems but other tracks that weren't really fit to occupy space on *bona fide* Rolling Stones prod-

uct. In the latter category comes 'Hang Fire', a pedestrian boogie number with buffoonish comments about UK inertia guaranteed not to go down well in a country suffering record unemployment and 'Neighbours', a track whose cacophonously loud drum track (courtesy of the utterly unsubtle Bob Clearmountian) renders it tiresome indeed. In point of fact, only 'Start Me Up' and the slinky 'Slave' from the first, rock side of the album escaped the sin of being either boring or generic, but the merits of those tracks are considerable.

The second, ballad side, however, was far superior: five highly respectable tracks – albeit of varying vintage – whose unacknowledged highpoint is the ultra-delicate 'Heaven'. 'No Use In Crying' is a high-gloss venomous kiss-off to a lover. 'Worried About You' is a *Black And Blue* outtake with Wayne Perkins playing a mellifluous solo. Mick Taylor appears on casting couch story 'Tops' and the courtly, sweet 'Waiting On A Friend', the latter also boasting Latin-esque rhythms and a warm sax solo.

Album Sleeves

The Stones contracting David Bailey – epitome of the Swinging Sixties photographer – for *Out Of Our Heads* and *Get Yer Ya-Yas Out* displayed a determination to be as hip with their album cover art as their music, as did the 3-D sleeve of Satanic Majesties and the engagement of cult rock artist Guy Peelaert for *It's Only Rock 'N' Roll*. By the time of Forty Licks, though, things had just been reduced to the corporate logo.

Live Albums II

It is now inconceivable for the Stones to close a tour without subsequently issuing a live album. What with the slowdown in their productivity on the studio album front, this has created something of an imbalance: during the Nineties, they actually released more live albums than studio efforts. However, only the biggest aficionados of the in-concert aural document would suggest that the latter-day live albums are anything other than methods by which to mop up the dollars of satisfied concert goers requiring a souvenir of their experience.

Love You Live

INTRO (FANFARE FOR THE COMMON MAN) / HONKY TONK WOMEN / IF YOU CAN'T ROCK ME / GET OFF OF MY CLOUD / HAPPY // HOT STUFF / STAR STAR / TUMBLING DICE / FINGER- PRINT FILE / YOU GOTTA MOVE // YOU CAN'T ALWAYS GET WHAT YOU WANT / MANNISH BOY / CRACKIN' UP / LITTLE RED ROOSTER / AROUND AND AROUND // IT'S ONLY ROCK 'N' ROLL / BROWN SUGAR / JUMPIN' JACK FLASH / SYMPATHY FOR THE DEVIL
Rolling Stones Records, September 1977

Warhol complained that Jagger had scrawled the lettering across his original design.

Though a contractual obligation, *Love You Live*'s release had a poignancy because with the Toronto drug bust hanging over Richards this could conceivably have been the final Stones product ever. Once removed from that concern, it's chiefly interesting for the way these mature men revisit the blues songs they had played when younger on the four tracks from the El Mocambo club performance.

Still Life

INTRO: TAKE THE 'A' TRAIN / UNDER MY THUMB / LET'S SPEND THE NIGHT TOGETHER / SHATTERED / TWENTY FLIGHT ROCK / GOING TO A GO-GO // LET ME GO / TIME IS ON MY SIDE / JUST MY IMAGINATION (RUNNING AWAY WITH ME) / START ME UP / (I CAN'T GET NO) SATISFACTION / OUTRO: STAR SPAN- GLED BANNER
Rolling Stones Records, June 1982

A record of the band's 1981 American tour, *Still Life* is fairly lacklustre and the sound of Jagger speaking to the crowd in what he imagines is an American accent is toe-curling. However, it does contain a sweet version of 'Time Is On My Side' plus, interestingly, a rendtion of Eddie Cochran's 'Twenty Flight Rock', the only instance of the band releasing a version of a Fifties rock 'n' roll standard.

Sleeve design was derived from the elaborate 1981 tour stage sets designed by Kazuhide Yamazaki.

Flashpoint

CONTINENTAL DRIFT (INTRO) / START ME UP / SAD SAD SAD / MISS YOU / ROCK AND A HARD PLACE / RUBY TUESDAY / YOU CAN'T ALWAYS GET WHAT YOU WANT / FACTORY GIRL / CAN'T BE SEEN / LITTLE RED ROOSTER / PAINT IT BLACK / SYMPATHY FOR THE DEVIL / BROWN SUGAR / JUMPIN' JACK FLASH / (I CAN'T GET NO) SATISFACTION / HIGHWIRE / SEX DRIVE

Virgin, April 1991

Recorded over 1989-90, the album is slightly note-worthy because the band have a crack at stuff rarely given a live outing like 'Ruby Tuesday', 'Factory Girl' and 'Little Red Rooster' (the latter sees Eric Clapton guesting). By now, the Stones were possibly becoming conscious of the milking-it cloud hanging over their live releases, which might explain why they included amongst the perfunctory you-had-to-be-there live songs two new studio tacks, 'Sex Drive' and the anti-arms industry 'Highwire'. The result? Er, you probably had to be there.

One of the most uninspired Stones covers of all time, though some might unkindly suggest this reflected the contents.

Stripped

STREET FIGHTING MAN / LIKE A ROLLING STONE / NOT FADE AWAY / SHINE A LIGHT / THE SPIDER AND THE FLY / I'M FREE / WILD HORSES / LET IT BLEED / DEAD FLOWERS / SLIPPING AWAY / ANGIE / LOVE IN VAIN / SWEET VIRGINIA / LITTLE BABY

Virgin, November 1995

Perhaps guessing that the gap between Voodoo Lounge and the next album would be another long one and perhaps realising that yet another straight-forward post-tour live album would not be enough to satisfy either their fans or their own artistic palettes, the Stones began putting together a new record while still on the road. This one would be a hybrid unique in their catalogue: some of the tracks were recorded at their smaller concerts on the tour but others were laid down at rehearsals and not augmented with overdubs, making them neither live nor studio tracks. Its an interesting failed experiment, although the version of Dylan's 'Like A Rolling Stone' is not only pointless (you can't match perfection) but is smart-assedly post-modern.

A cool response to the 'unplugged' fad at the turn of the century.

The Music

Live Albums II *(continued)*

The Rolling Stones Rock And Roll Circus

ENTRY OF THE GLADIATORS / SONG FOR JEFFREY / A QUICK ONE, WHILE HE'S AWAY / OVER THE WAVES / AIN'T THAT A LOT OF LOVE / SOMETHING BETTER / YER BLUES / WHOLE LOTTA YOKO / JUMPIN' JACK FLASH / PARACHUTE WOMAN / NO EXPECTATIONS / YOU CAN'T ALWAYS GET WHAT YOU WANT / SYMPATHY FOR THE DEVIL / SALT OF THE EARTH

ABKCO, October 1996

Sanctioned by Klein, rather than the Stones, this 1996 audio album, though good stuff, is also available in video and DVD releases which – as they provide both visuals and sound of the same event – makes it redundant. The releases retained the original circus poster concept.

No Security

YOU GOT ME ROCKING / GIMME SHELTER / FLIP THE SWITCH / MEMORY MOTEL / CORINNA / SAINT OF ME / WAITING ON A FRIEND / SISTER MORPHINE / LIVE WITH ME / RESPECTABLE / THIEF IN THE NIGHT / THE LAST TIME / OUT OF CONTROL

November 1998

This assemblage of tracks recorded in concert on the *Bridges To Babylon* tour features songs that have never or rarely appeared on Stones live releases.

Perhaps we're supposed to feel grateful but by this point most were beyond caring – apart of course from the millions who bought it, and the two Stones fanatics pictured on the cover.

Live Licks

BROWN SUGAR / STREET FIGHTING MAN / PAINT IT BLACK / YOU CAN'T ALWAYS GET WHAT YOU WANT / IT'S ONLY ROCK 'N ROLL (BUT I LIKE IT) / ANGIE / HONKY TONK WOMEN / HAPPY /GIMME SHELTER / (I CAN'T GET NO) SATISFACTION / NEIGHBOURS / MONKEY MAN / ROCKS OFF / CAN'T YOU HEAR ME KNOCKING / THAT'S HOW STRONG MY LOVE IS / THE NEARNESS OF YOU / BEAST OF BURDEN / WHEN THE WHIP COMES DOWN / ROCK ME, BABY / YOU DON'T HAVE TO MEAN IT / WORRIED ABOUT YOU / EVERYBODY NEEDS SOMEBODY TO LOVE

November 2004

As if to add insult to injury of the fact that their 2002 world tour had no new album to accompany it, this document of that tour is a double live CD no less – just what the world wasn't waiting for come 2004. For those who could still muster a passing interest – yes, it sold, but how often is it brought out of the CD jewel case? – the first disc was made up of hits, the second of stuff less used to stage outings – including, bizarrely, a rendition of Hoagy Carmichael's 'The Nearness Of You'.

UNDERCOVER

Rolling Stones Records, November 1983

UNDERCOVER (OF THE NIGHT) / SHE WAS HOT / TIE YOU UP (THE PAIN OF LOVE) / WANNA HOLD YOU / FEEL ON BABY // TOO MUCH BLOOD / PRETTY BEAT UP / TOO TOUGH / ALL THE WAY DOWN / IT MUST BE HELL
Recorded Pathé-Marconi, Paris, The Hit Factory, NY.Producers: The Glimmer Twins, Chris Kimsey. Engineer: Chris Kimsey.

Whoa! The Stones get very naughty with a visual pun – peel off the stickers and see what you get ...

Things look bad after the quality opener 'Undercover (Of The Night)' when that fine single is followed by something called 'She Was Hot', an exercise in the generic which is almost beyond belief in its cliché-squared formula of Keith's most hackneyed Chuck Berry retreads crossed with Mick's most wince-inducing leering old roué songwords. That Keith's vocal showcase 'Wanna Hold You' is just an echo of his hardly awe-inspiring *Tattoo You* track 'Little T&A' is also another bad portent. More grating overgrown adolescence informs both the cover art – you get to see a naked woman's bits if you peel off strategically placed stickers – and the horribly titled tracks 'Tie You Up (The Pain Of Love)' and 'All The Way Down' (as in: "She went ..."). Yet even they have a sort of dirty momentum, the same kind of bristling, mean-spirited energy that informs the rest of an album that turns out to be surprisingly enjoyable.

'Feel On Baby' is a nice shimmering reggae. 'Pretty Beat Up' is a brood over lost love with some fine parping sax. The closing 'It Must Be Hell' initially repels because of its use of the riff of *Exile*'s 'Soul Survivor' but there is no getting round the fact that the strident, choppy guitar work and the Kalashnikov-like chorus are extremely catchy. The centrepiece of the album is 'Too Much Blood', a lengthy, leisurely rumination on the violence of Western culture (they're against it, incidentally). It carries a great, elongated, slow brass refrain. The verses are spoken word. The second one, in which Jagger drops his American accent in favour of his Mockney is actually funny, him extolling the virtues of films like *Officer And A Gentleman* as against the demerits of *Texas Chainsaw Massacre* ("'orrible, wasn't it?")

The absence of that fat, rich tone which had informed much of *Tattoo You* comes as a shock at first, but in retrospect we know that that *Tattoo You* sound was an illusion, an artificially achieved throwback to the Mick Taylor era. It was now clear The Rolling Stone sound with Ronnie Wood in the band would be that thinner, sharper, often vibrato-inflected sound first heard on *Some Girls*. Once having got used to the fact, it is easier to enjoy *Undercover* – while at the same time hoping that future Stones releases will be informed by more of a humanity.

DIRTY WORK

Rolling Stones Records/CBS March 1986.

ONE HIT (TO THE BODY) / FIGHT / HARLEM SHUFFLE / HOLD BACK / TOO RUDE // WINNING UGLY / BACK TO ZERO / DIRTY WORK / HAD IT WITH YOU / SLEEP TONIGHT
Recorded Pathé-Marconi, Paris, RPM, NY, January–October 1985. Producers: The Glimmer Twins, Steve Lillywhite. Engineer: David Jerden.

The 1980s were the era of click-track dictated metronomic drum patterns that were themselves mixed up absurdly high. The Stones submitted to this trend by employing Steve Lillywhite – then an archetypal modern producer – to helm *Dirty Work*. The results were predictable: an album that could have been – despite the internal band bickering and bitty recording process – quite solid instead quickly ending up a cacophonous relic of its era.

True, not even Lillywhite's production can ruin the fantastic opening rocker 'One Hit (To The Body)', an intriguing mix of acoustic and electric with a Jimmy Page solo. Also on the plus side, 'Back To Zero' is a protest song (written with keyboardist Chuck Leavell) in which Jagger and Richards take to task the politicians who play with the lives of the world's population with their war games. Watts' drums are mercifully left alone by Lillywhite as he lays down a fine groove while some squalling sax mixed way down in the mix contributes to the air of stone-cold funk.

In fairness, also, no production method in the world could salvage the tuneless, yowling 'Fight', in which Richards' vents his frustration with Jagger (who bizarrely invests his full emotion in the vocal track). Nor 'Winning Ugly', about doing anything to ensure victory. The latter track is relatively cleverly constructed but utterly empty.

'Harlem Shuffle' is fun if treated as merely an album track instead of its totally underserved lead-off single status. It's possible that there are good songs underneath the deafeningly mixed drums of 'Hold Back' and the title track but frankly not only is it exhausting listening to them but what can be heard of Jagger's vocal behind the fusillade is so tiresomely mannered in its permanently exclamatory tone that one doesn't feel inclined to bother finding out.

The closing, 'Sleep Tonight' is a lullaby sung by Richards (one of two Richards vocal show-cases, the other being the good-ish reggae cover 'Too Rude') and though Wood plays drums and does so badly, even if Watts had been behind the kit Lillywhite would probably still have managed to find a way to make the drums so horribly intrusive as to spoil a sweet song.

The Stones' nadir.

STEEL WHEELS

CBS September 1989.

SAD SAD SAD / MIXED EMOTIONS / TERRIFYING / HOLD ON TO YOUR HAT / HEARTS FOR SALE / BLINDED BY LOVE // ROCK AND A HARD PLACE / CAN'T BE SEEN / ALMOST

HEAR YOU SIGH / CONTINENTAL DRIFT / BREAK THE SPELL / SLIPPING AWAY
Recorded Air Studios, Montserrat, Olympic Studios, London. Producers: The Glimmer Twins, Chris Kimsey. Engineer: Christopher Marc Potter. Sleeve design by Karl Hyde and Rick Smith.

After the honest and confessional flavour of Jagger's solo *Primitive Cool* album, how depressing that the next Stones song the world would hear – 'Mixed Emotions', the lead-off single from this album – should start with the line, "Button your lip baby". It seemed to illustrate a depressing truth, namely that writing songs for the Stones was now a matter of Jagger fulfilling a role. 'Mixed Emotions' – quite the most uninteresting song ever chosen for a Stones single thus far – was the epitome of generic tired old R&B plastered with lyrics that were simply bad boy slogans, if shot through with a little token vulnerability.

The album's production is credited to 'Chris Kimsey and the Glimmer Twins'. It's as though each wanted to blame the other for the awful ringing, irritating mix, with Watts' drums – unbelievably – testing one's patience almost from the get-go. The whole of the original side one of vinyl can be written off as an extremely unsteady warm-up for the second side, although the country song 'Blinded By Love' – which has a weirdly old fashioned, corn-poke feel – is mildly engaging. 'Rock And A Hard Place' is almost a very good song, despite its overly shrill blasts of horn. Keith's vocal showcase 'Can't Be Seen' is quite sweet if over-long. The closest the album comes to greatness is the pretty 'Almost Hear You Sigh', whose one-third credit for Steve Jordan – Richards' co-writer on his solo albums – indicates that it originated outside of these sessions. The most interesting track by far is 'Continental Drift'. The band's nostalgic reunion with the Joujouka Pipers results in a highly intriguing aural landscape, the massed beaten drums creating a sweeping tribal flavour. The lyric is suitably surreal ("Love comes at the speed of light".) It's not a great track but is very good and, more importantly, adventurous. Unfortunately, the following track, 'Break The Spell', can't help but sound almost comically bog standard after it. The closer is 'Slipping Away', the sort of meandering, whining ballad Richards would come to specialize in. What a way to commemorate your quarter century of making albums – with a turkey.

VOODOO LOUNGE

Virgin July 1994.

LOVE IS STRONG / YOU GOT ME ROCKING / SPARKS WILL FLY / THE WORST / NEW FACES / MOON IS UP / OUT OF TEARS / I GO WILD / BRAND NEW CAR / SWEETHEARTS TOGETHER / SUCK ON THE JUGULAR / BLINDED BY RAINBOWS / BABY BREAK IT DOWN / THRU AND THRU / MEAN DISPOSITION
Recorded September 1993-April 1994. Producers: Don Was and the Glimmer Twins.

Rocking used to come effortlessly to The Rolling Stones. Now, it is something at which they have to snatch, usually vainly so. Proof of this

The Music

is provided by many tracks on *Voodoo Lounge* but none more so than 'Sparks Will Fly', which huffs and puffs and crashes and snarls but is boring and much ado about nothing.

But it's not just the uptempo stuff that is pedestrian. The ballads here are also underwhelming. Keith's vocal 'The Worst' is a fair take at the self-pitying country genre ("I'm the worst kind of guy for you to be around" he says, as a pedal steel whines in the background) but it's fleeting and his vocal lacks power. 'New Faces' is almost a throwback to 'Sixties Stones pop, with its saccharin melody and harpsichord and harmonium decoration but it doesn't even match up to (alleged) throwaways like 'The Singer Not The Song'. 'Out Of Tears' threatens to become a great Stones ballad in places but despite pleasing passages it never takes off. 'Sweethearts Together' sees Mick and Keith aping John and Paul's Everly Brothers-style acoustic duet on *Let It Be*'s 'Two Of Us'. It's a nice idea but doesn't sound as good in reality as it does on paper. 'Blinded By Rainbows' is quite a thoughtful song about the self-doubt that a terrorist might experience but the chorus isn't rousing enough to make it truly moving.

This litany of mediocrity is almost unbroken but not quite. 'Brand New Car' is simply garbage, like something a teenager just learning to write songs would toss in the dustbin as too

lyrically banal and melodically pedestrian for public exposure.

In short, an album whose chord changes, riffs and lyrics are stuff the artists could have devised in their sleep. Almost everything is competent but nothing is ever special. There are literally no flashes of brilliance, no dazzling melodies or passages of instrumentation.

Meanwhile, 'Suck On The Jugular' highlights a fault of the album's production: its potentially interesting brass sections are strangely muted while the drums – as elsewhere - are mixed too high: Don Was, co-producing with the Glimmers, doesn't make the drums as deafening as Lillywhite did on *Dirty Work* but they are always slightly above the threshold of comfort. Bizarrely, at the time of writing, Jagger and Richards appear to have decided that the disappointing Was will be their permanent production collaborator.

BRIDGES TO BABYLON

Virgin September 1997.

FLIP THE SWITCH / ANYBODY SEEN MY BABY? / LOW DOWN / ALREADY OVER ME / GUNFACE / YOU DON'T HAVE TO MEAN IT / OUT OF CONTROL / SAINT OF ME / MIGHT AS WELL GET JUICED / ALWAYS SUFFERING / TOO TIGHT / THIEF IN THE NIGHT / HOW CAN I STOP

Recorded February–July 1997. Producers: Don Was and the Glimmer Twins.

Charlie Watts' rapid-fire drum intro on the opener 'Flip The Switch' immediately gets the toes tapping and the listener anticipating a good time. Within a minute or so, the listener's feet start to wiggle less and the grin fades from

his face as he realises the track is a big, loud, tuneless nothing. The only way *Bridges To Babylon* manages to distinguish itself aesthetically from its mediocre predecessor is because amongst the nondescript majority, it contains a couple of songs that constitute flashes of the band's old brilliance.

The problem is not merely the songs. There is also the bewildering insistence on sticking with Don Was as co-producer. 'Thief In The Night', one of the Richards vocals, actually has some interesting coiling acoustic guitar work going on in the background but, typical of Was, it's mixed much lower than a weird effect running throughout the song that makes listening like trying to hear an old vinyl record through a blunt stylus.

It's not that the Stones don't try hard in places. 'Might As Well Get Juiced' sees Jagger almost desperately striving to keep up with the young things via his collaboration with the Dust Brothers. The track – a paean to the glories of escaping the travails of life through alcoholic oblivion – has a vaguely interesting sonic texture but underneath the mangled vocals and abrasive modern effects there doesn't seem to be a substantial song. 'Anybody Seen My Baby?' is quite an impressive smoky ballad but the gloss was knocked off it when it was decided that Jagger had unconsciously ripped off the melody of a k d lang song and the band had to cede

her royalties. In any case, once you hear one chorus, you've heard enough. The closer 'How Can I Stop' starts well with some pretty electric guitar work and equally attractive soul vocal harmonies but then descends into something more objectionably easy listening than anything the band have yet recorded – before a late flourish where some very sophisticated guitar and smoky sax rescue it from being soporific.

There are two genuinely great tracks. 'Already Over Me' is a simply gorgeous ballad. 'You Don't Have To Mean It' is a lovely, brass-riffed reggae worthy of Aswad with piano work from Clinton Clifford that is such a rippling, receding affair that it seems like an exquisite mirage. Only these tracks can have given knowledgeable long-term Stones fans hope for the future.

A BIGGER BANG

Virgin September 2005.

ROUGH JUSTICE / LET ME DOWN SLOW / IT WON'T TAKE LONG / RAIN FALL DOWN / STREETS OF LOVE / BACK OF MY HAND / SHE SAW ME COMING / BIGGEST MISTAKE / THIS PLACE IS EMPTY / OH NO, NOT YOU AGAIN / DANGEROUS BEAUTY / LAUGH, I NEARLY DIED / SWEET NEO CON / LOOK WHAT THE CAT DRAGGED IN / DRIVING TOO FAST / INFAMY Recorded November 2004-June 2005. Producers: Don Was and the Glimmer Twins.

What was remarkable about the ludicrously over-the-top praise that greeted this album's release was the fact that so many of those who praised it went, in doing so, out of their way to deny that they had fallen into the same trap of so many critics in the past of hailing a

The Music

return to form that on reflection turned out to have been a false Stones dawn.

Just one listen to the new album confirmed that the critics who praised it were talking nonsense in their claims of artistic renaissance. The trick is to use the *It's Only Rock 'N' Roll* litmus test: ask yourself if the new album is even as good as that respectable but broadly derided 1974 album. The answer here is: nothing like as.

Opener 'Rough Justice', praised by some as a high octane rocker, is actually yawnsome rock *ordinaire* which by the end of the first chorus has you shouting "Yadda-yadda-yadda-enough already!". A breakneck tempo and one supposedly endearingly incorrigible couplet (Mick mentions he was once his lady's rooster and then asks, "Now am I just one of your cocks?") does not a classic rocker make. Tracks like this and 'Oh No Not You Again' are lazy exercises, their clipped, jerky melodies – so clipped as to almost not constitute melodies but barked phrases strung together – are easy to write and to put featureless, hard rock instrumentation behind. The hope is that given a fast tempo, the listener will be fooled into thinking this is primal rock energy in the classic Stones style rather than a mockery of the Stones' tradition of never sacrificing good tunes for rock roar. Too many Stones songs today are in this vein. That they are capable of more if they try is illustrated by some of the other material on the album.

'Rain Fall Down' has a great swirling guitar riff and an interesting poverty tableaux, a couple making "sweet love" in a filthy flat while the heavens open. The groove is slinky and funky and the vocal goes in places into a double-time that is almost rap, only much more tuneful. 'Streets Of Love' is a reasonably moving audience singalong. Though critics seemed inordinately impressed by 'Back Of My Hand' – as though the world should be grateful that the Stones should deign to perform a 12-bar blues like it was old times - it can't be denied that there is a real, static-flaring rawness about this that is pleasing. It sits somewhere between the excellence of 'Little Red Rooster' and the generic tedium of 'Black Limousine'. 'Biggest Mistake' is one of what seems an unusual number of songs about a failed love affair (Mick and Jerry?) To a classy musical backdrop, Jagger acknowledges he has treated a woman badly and made a huge error in walking out on her. It takes one aback, so lacking in 'side' or irony does it seem. 'Laugh I Nearly Died' covers similar territory in its detailing a man's lonely global wanderings with a velvety electric guitar riff and a neon-lit ambience. One again Keith grabs the closing track for a vocal in the shape of 'Infamy' (as in: "You've got it ..."). It might sound good if it weren't for the way the drumming is mixed to temples-pounding levels.

Overall, an album that does prove the band

aren't yet dead, or their inspiration completely exhausted but profound questions still remain about consistency and choice of producer.

Compilations

Though there have always been plenty of Rolling Stones compilation albums since the 1966 release of *big hits (high tide and green grass)*, a collection of Stones hits with a slight variation in track listing either side of the Atlantic to reflect different single releases in the UK and US, up until the 2002 release of *Forty Licks*, they had always been bitty affairs, lacking completeness either due to their release date or because they concentrated either on the Decca years or the post-Decca years but never both. *Forty Licks* has really

made all the previous compilations except *The London Years* redundant, unless you are hunting for rarities rather than a greatest hits for a pleasant car journey.

THE ROLLING STONES SINGLES COLLECTION – THE LONDON YEARS

COME ON / I WANT TO BE LOVED / I WANNA BE YOUR MAN / STONED / NOT FADE AWAY / LITTLE BY LITTLE / IT'S ALL OVER NOW / GOOD TIMES, BAD TIMES / TELL ME / I JUST WANT TO MAKE LOVE TO YOU / TIME IS ON MY SIDE/ CONGRATULATIONS / LITTLE RED ROOSTER / OFF THE HOOK / HEART OF STONE / WHAT A SHAME / THE LAST TIME / PLAY WITH FIRE / (I CAN'T GET NO) SATISFACTION/ THE UNDER ASSISTANT WEST COAST PROMOTION MAN/ THE SPIDER AND THE FLY / GET OFF OF MY CLOUD / I'M FREE / THE SINGER NOT THE SONG / AS TEARS GO BY / GOTTA GET AWAY / 19TH NERVOUS BREAKDOWN / SAD DAY / PAINT IT BLACK / STUPID GIRL / LONG LONG WHILE/ MOTHER'S LITTLE HELPER / LADY JANE / HAVE YOU SEEN YOUR MOTHER, BABY, STANDING IN THE SHADOW?/ WHO'S DRIVING YOUR PLANE / LET'S SPEND THE NIGHT TOGETHER / RUBY TUESDAY / WE LOVE YOU / DANDELION/ SHE'S A RAINBOW / 2000 LIGHT YEARS FROM HOME / IN ANOTHER LAND / THE LANTERN / JUMPIN' JACK FLASH / CHILD OF THE MOON / STREET FIGHTING MAN / NO EXPECTATIONS / SURPRISE SURPRISE / HONKY TONK WOMEN / YOU CAN'T ALWAYS GET WHAT YOU WANT / MEMO FROM TURNER / BROWN SUGAR / WILD HORSES / I DON'T KNOW WHY / TRY A LITTLE HARDER / OUT OF TIME / JIVING SISTER FANNY SYMPATHY FOR THE DEVIL
Released August 1989

A mopping up of (supposedly) all Stones singles and B-sides during their tenure with London and Decca. There are a couple of omissions and incorrect uses of album rather than single mixes. There are also anomalies

such as Jagger's solo single 'Memo From Turner' (frankly welcome) and the inclusion of post-Decca tracks like 'Brown Sugar' on the grounds (that were no doubt thrashed out between lawyers) that they were recorded before the advent of Rolling Stones Records, as well as stretching-it-a-bit inclusions ('Sympathy For The Devil', because it was used as the B-side of a reissue of 'Honky Tonk Women'). Nonetheless, this is a highly useful piece of product. Aesthetically, it's magnificent, and proves that so good were the band in the period covered that their B-sides were often as unforgettable as their hit sides.

FORTY LICKS

STREET FIGHTING MAN/GIMME SHELTER/(I CAN'T GET NO) SATISFACTION/THE LAST TIME/JUMPIN' JACK FLASH/YOU CAN'T ALWAYS GET WHAT YOU WANT/19TH NERVOUS BREAKDOWN/UNDER MY THUMB/NOT FADE AWAY/HAVE YOU SEEN YOUR MOTHER BABY, STANDING IN THE SHADOW?/ SYMPATHY FOR THE DEVIL/MOTHER'S LITTLE HELPER/GET OFF OF MY CLOUD/WILD HORSES/RUBY TUESDAY/PAINT IT BLACK/HONKY TONK WOMEN/IT'S ALL OVER NOW/LET'S SPEND THE NIGHT TOGETHER/START ME UP/BROWN SUGAR/ MISS YOU/BEAST OF BURDEN/DON'T STOP/HAPPY/ANGIE/ YOU GOT ME ROCKING/SHATTERED/FOOL TO CRY/LOVE IS STRONG/MIXED EMOTIONS/KEYS TO YOUR LOVE/ANYBODY SEEN MY BABY?/STEALING MY HEART/TUMBLING DICE/ UNDERCOVER (OF THE NIGHT)/EMOTIONAL RESCUE/IT'S ONLY ROCK 'N' ROLL/LOSING MY TOUCH

Released September 2002

The *rapprochement* between Allen Klein and his ex-charges that led to this album almost came too late: in a day and age where technology allows the public to burn their own compilations, many had presumably already allowed themselves the hitherto unknown pleasure of hearing, say, 'Wild Horses' cheek-by-jowl with 'Ruby Tuesday'. *Forty Licks* makes no claims for comprehensiveness – no 'Come On' or 'I Wanna Be Your Man' or 'We Love You', for instance – and its sequencing makes one wonder whether the group were nervous that the arc of their creative decline would be a little too clear for comfort if they had stuck to the chronology. Still, it is good to see the entire span of the band's career represented on a commercially-released audio product for the

first time. As a way of either keeping the fans waiting for a new studio album happy or enticing those who already owned the rest of the contents several times over into shelling out for it, the Stones included on *Forty Licks* four new songs, all decent, the best of which being 'Keys To Your Love' a pretty ballad with nice Jagger falsetto on the title phrase. Another of them – 'Losing My Touch' yet another morose Keith-sung ballad – closed the album. This was an unwise move: for conceptual reasons, they should have let 'It's Only Rock 'N' Roll' fulfil that function.

RARITIES 1971-2003

FANCY MAN BLUES/TUMBLING DICE (LIVE)/WILD HORSES (LIVE STRIPPED VERSION)/BEAST OF BURDEN (LIVE)/ANYWAY YOU LOOK AT IT/IF I WAS A DANCER (DANCE PT. 2)/MISS YOU (DANCE VERSION)/WISH I'D NEVER MET YOU/I JUST WANNA MAKE LOVE TO YOU (LIVE)/MIXED EMOTIONS (12" VERSION)/THROUGH THE LONELY NIGHTS/LIVE WITH ME (LIVE)/LET IT ROCK/HARLEM SHUFFLE (NY MIX)/MANNISH BOY (LIVE)/THRU AND THRU (LIVE)

Released November 2005

Released unexpectedly (so unexpectedly that it necessitated a hasty rewrite of the rarities section in this book's 'Stonesology'), this album was a joint enterprise between the Stones and Starbucks, the coffee chain having got in on classic rock rarities previously with a Bob Dylan set. This release is less intriguing than it at first sounds, covering only previously released material, and even then material starting from '71 (i.e. not long before the Stones were past their peak). It's also conceptually inconsistent (the unplugged 'Wild Horses' and the live 'Mannish Boy' have already appeared on non-compilation Stones albums, thus making them not rare at all). Much of the rest of the material is comprised of hardly earth-shattering latter-day live Stones performances. However, the album is worthwhile for the inclusion of three noteworthy tracks never previously issued on a UK or US album. 'Let It Rock' was an additional track on the B-side of the UK 'Brown Sugar' single when such 'maxi-singles' were fashionable. (Though this live rendition of the Chuck Berry classic recorded at Leeds University had never appeared on a UK or US album, it did turn up on the Spanish version of *Sticky Fingers* in place of the supposedly outrageous 'Sister Morphine'). 'Through The Lonely Nights' was the B-side to the UK and US single 'It's Only Rock 'N' Roll'. Originating in Jamaica in 1972, it's rumoured to feature Jimmy Page. 'Miss You (Dance Version)' originated back in the days of vinyl (remember that?) when 12-inch singles were all the rage and allowed artists to issue – usually, it must be said, artistically worthless – extended versions or mixes of songs. The Stones' 'Miss You' 12-inch single is actually an interesting alternate to the 7-inch/album version, containing more of Sugar Blue's exquisite harp playing over a loop of the *Some Girls* highlight.

The Rest of the Best

A special mention for this 1984 vinyl box set from Polygram Germany which rounds up every non-album track ever released by the Stones, including the UK EPs, as well as both sides of Jagger's 'Memo From Turner' single. (Some editions even featured a bonus single of 'Cocksucker Blues'.) A superb mopping up exercise, it would be wonderful to see this reissued on CD.

"... the way they walk and the way they talk and the songs they sing, all become part of some long, mean reach for the jugular."

Pete Hamill, *New York Post*, 1965.

50 Great Stones Songs

This selection is not intended to be definitive, but does reflect the sheer range and invention of the Stones, from the covers of the early years and the masterpieces of the late Sixties and Seventies, to the only occasional classic of the last decade or so.

1. COME ON

AVAILABLE ON CD ON *THE ROLLING STONES SINGLES COLLECTION - THE LONDON YEARS*
Recorded May 1963

The inclusion of The Rolling Stones' debut single in this list will cause many to splutter in amazement, not least of those people being Mick Jagger and Keith Richards. "Very, very pop" and "Our first compromise" Richards has said of it. "It was shit," Jagger stated. They are wrong. 'Come On' sums up everything that was great about The Rolling Stones in their first incarnation as a R&B covers band. This latter category was one containing dozens upon dozens of groups. The only way to stand out from the crowd in such circumstances was to give your cover versions an individuality.

The individuality with 'Come On' started with the choice of song – everyone else covering a Chuck Berry track would have plumped for 'Johnny B Goode', 'Roll Over Beethoven' or any of his other over-familiar hits, not this relative obscurity – and continued with the way they rendered it. Though the song featured a catalogue of grievances about pro-

letarian life that echoed his own 'Too Much Monkey Business', Berry's rendition of it had been more soothing than seething. His delivery was laid back and augmented by female vocals and the guitars and saxophone backing was almost gentle. The Stones took the song to its logical conclusion. Jagger's delivery of the lyric is infuriated. As he spits out the details of his woes – his stalled car, his unemployed status, his irritation at the wrong number on his telephone line, all salt in the wound of the fact that he has recently been dumped – the listener believes him. This is even despite the fact that the Stones tone down the original lyric, substituting "Stupid guy" for "Stupid jerk" in reference to the incorrect dialler. Meanwhile, the band provide musical accompaniment that cranks up the drama as much as Jagger's vocal: Watts and Wyman quickening the tempo, Jones blasting train-whistle notes on the mouth harp, and Richards' stabbing brutal rhythm guitar. In this reinvention of a song by one of R&B's masters, the Stones were revealing the very originality of vision that would see them shortly leave their fellow cover version bands in the dust by graduating to writing their own material.

For the record, this author is not alone in considering 'Come On' high-class. "I think it's brilliant," Ronnie Wood has said.

2. I NEED YOU BABY (MONA)

AVAILABLE ON CD ON *THE ROLLING STONES, NOW!*
Recorded January 1964

Though the Stones' debut album was rock-solid, it takes something more than not having a duff track in sight to make a classic album. A great band understands that there is something more to the artform of creating a long player than just slapping ten or twelve top quality tracks on a record. In addition to song quality control there is the issue of variety of tone, that final little effort of thought, the absence of which can take the edge off an album and consign it the ranks of the merely very good. Though the Stones had assembled a dozen top-notch recordings to put on their debut long player, the overall soundscape would have sounded slightly unvaried without this track.

This song of worship to a desirable female was written and first performed by Bo Diddley and known as and referred to more by its parenthesised title than 'I Need You Baby'. Diddley's main trademark was the rat-tat-tat-tat-tat-tat-tat − or 'shave-and-a-haircut-two-bits' − rhythm. It can be heard on the Stones' 'Mona', but in utterly strange form. Jones' guitar was treated with so much reverb that it makes the entire track shimmer. Aligned

with a slightly languid air and oodles of tribal percussion, it makes for an almost surreal concoction. Along with the lazy sensuality of 'I'm A King Bee', this ghostly ambience − coming in the middle of a set of hard-tooled metallic precision − shoves the album outside of the parameters the listeners had been assuming and, merely in the action of doing that, confers an even higher status on the album than the already elevated one it would possess.

Many had tried and failed to replicate Diddley's imprimatur. This track was just about the only attempt the gunslinger (see page 24) was impressed by. As Richards observed, "Diddley himself was astounded, saying that Brian was the only cat he knew who'd worked out the secret of it."

3. TIME IS ON MY SIDE

AVAILABLE ON CD ON *BIG HITS (HIGH TIDE AND GREEN GRASS)* AND *HOT ROCKS*
Recorded November 1964.

A smouldering declaration of love to a feckless partner, this song was written for jazz trombonist Kai Winding, although the Stones probably heard the version released as a B-side by Irma Thomas. It was composed by Norman Meade - not Meade/Norman as the publishing credits often render it - a prolific songsmith also known as Jerry Ragavoy and responsible for, among other hits, 'Anytime You Want Me' and 'Piece Of My Heart'. The Stones' version is better-known to US audiences, having been a hit there but never seeing a UK single release. There are in fact two studio versions by the Stones. The one under discussion is not the US single version (also to be found on CD on the US *12x5* album) but the version from the Stones' second UK LP, recorded five months later. The *12x5* take is good, with a more prominent organ part from Ian Stewart, but it is a bit more clipped both musically and vocally.

The *No.2* version certainly sounds like a later version in that both Jagger and the group have learnt how to tease out the poignancy of the material. Things are clearly on a higher level right from the beginning as heart-tugging guitar lines appear on a bed of subtle organ. When singing the song's title refrain, Jagger stretches out the word 'Time' over multiple syllables to exquisite effect, while the band cause the instrumentation to lilt beautifully behind him. Equally wonderful is the spoken word middle eight where Jagger tells his lover that his devotion can outlast her wanderlust, his defiance counterpointed by spiky guitar work. And when Jagger – returning to singing – enunciates the line, "I got the real love, the kind that you need", it's just about time for the listener to reach for a handkerchief. Even the way the song is faded away on the last notes, despite its 'real' ending, somehow seems an additional stroke of the genius-like manipulation of emotions that has attended the entire affair.

Note: though this is not the single version, it is, bizarrely, the one that appears on the first release of the *London Years* singles collection. This was corrected on the 2002 remaster.

4. IT'S ALL OVER NOW

AVAILABLE ON CD ON *THE ROLLING STONES SINGLES COLLECTION - THE LONDON YEARS*
Recorded June 1964

Bobby Womack is a man who has continually popped up in the Stones' story almost since their inception. His first link with them came through this song – a triumphalist denunciation of a discarded unfaithful lover – which he wrote for his band The Valentinos. Released as a single Stateside in 1964, its fortunes were probably hurt by the decision of the Stones to cover it. Womack was initially upset but found his irritation somewhat alleviated when he got his first set of royalties. "When I saw the first cheque, I was shocked," he said. "It was huge." He would subsequently become a good mate of the band.

Oldham may have considered the reinvention of 'Not Fade Away' to effectively constitute the inaugural Jagger/Richards original, but this track is really the first Rolling Stones recording to sound what we now consider to be 'Stonesey'. It was the American DJ Murray the K – the self-proclaimed 'Fifth Beatle' – who suggested to the band that they record it. The Stones set about the task with relish. It seems bizarre now but at the time more than one reviewer suggested the track had a country & western ambience. Wyman responded that this was not intentional and that it was probably due to its twelve-string guitar. From today's perspective its reverberating, floorboard-rattling riff, rousing chorus, yowling ambience

The Music

and anthemic flavour are quintessential Rolling Stones. As is the hint of outrage: its lyric contained the phrase "half-assed games", which caused some US radio stations to censor it.

5. (I CAN'T GET NO) SATISFACTION

AVAILABLE ON CD ON *THE ROLLING STONES SINGLES COLLECTION - THE LONDON YEARS*
Recorded May 1965

No matter how close to genius songwriters are – and Jagger and Richards have come closer more times than most – they do not always have the requisite judgement to ensure the optimum fulfilment of their visions. Had Keith Richards had his way, 'Satisfaction' would not be a roaring fuzztone rocker and a magnificent articulation of the disaffected Sixties gestalt, but a Stax-style soul workout with a parping brass section.

On 10 May 1965, the Stones entered Chess studios and laid down a new track. Sounding like nothing spectacular, they re-recorded it two days later at RCA, changing its tempo, stripping it of its Jones-played harmonica and adding a guitar riff played through a fuzz-box.

Dave Hassinger, engineer on the RCA re-recording, recalls, "When they did 'Satisfaction', [even with fuzzbox] Keith had a very thin sound on the guitar. What I did with that is fatten it up 'cos he was playing a saxophone line really and to me it needed more of a broader tone to it. Sounded very tinny. I just went out and tinkered with their amps because I didn't want to be overbearing. I added a lot of bottom end to it. You really just change the curve of the sound. We were mixing it down in a big mixdown room at RCA and I had too much vocal and Mick would just say, 'Less vocal'. I had to run through it about five or six times 'til I had the vocal where he wanted it. I thought, 'Well, gee, nobody's gonna even hear the lyric.' But it turned out to be perfect." Asked whether he wondered whether this song would be too far-out for audiences of the day, he says, "Oh no, I thought that was incredible. Not only that, but from the time we recorded it to the time it went on the air was very quick. When I first heard it on the air, I thought, 'That's a smash'." He then adds a comment that could have come straight from the mouth of Keith Richards: "Sometimes you've gotta back away from something to get a better look at it and when you're working in the studio and you're working long hours like we did, it's hard to see it unless you get away for a day or two and then listen to it."

When Jagger and Richards were outvoted by the other Stones about releasing the new 'Satisfaction' as a single, Richards wasn't happy: for him, it was a demo for his soul vision, the fuzzbox a weedy approximation of the horn sections he wanted. To everyone else on the planet, the fuzztone riff – which roared out of the speakers like a clarion call of the generation for whom it seemed an anthem – was the most galvanizing thing about a magnificent and flawless record.

6. THE SINGER NOT THE SONG

AVAILABLE ON CD ON *DECEMBER'S CHILDREN*

Recorded July-September 1965

Journalist James Hector has opined of this B-side to 'Get Off Of My Cloud' that it is "commonly cited as one of the worst Jagger/Richards songs ever to have been blessed with an official release". Oh really? Would that some of the crap that the Stones have blessed with an official release in the last decade-and-a-half possess even half of the simple charms of this number.

Of course, had The Beatles written it, it would have been considered – despite its slight naiveté – to sum up their charm. For the Stones to write anything tender always carried to some – illogically – the whiff of compromise. An objective look at the track reveals it to be quietly inventive. A song of devotion, it couches its pledges of love in something other than banalities which, lest we forget, were still the bedrock of the lexicon of ballad lyrics in 1965. Structurally, it's quite intriguing, with an unexpected half-line thrown in like a melodic hiccup in the middle of each verse ("You just say so").

The song gave its title to an interesting 1973 'non-fiction novel' by J Marks which alternated straight biography of The Rolling Stones (if that is what you can call the likes of a phone call to Alexis Korner transcribed verbatim, including the line going dead) with the adventures of a transvestite following the Stones on the road.

7. GET OFF OF MY CLOUD

AVAILABLE ON CD ON *THE ROLLING STONES SINGLES COLLECTION - THE LONDON YEARS*

Recorded September 1965

Yet another example of how wrong an artist can be about his own work. "I never dug it as a record," Richards once sniffed. "The chorus was a nice idea but we rushed it as the follow-up. We were in LA, and it was time for another single. But how do you follow 'Satisfaction'? Actually, what I wanted was to do it slow like a Lee Dorsey thing. We rocked it up. I thought it was one of Andrew's worst productions." Hardly the kind of endorsement to make those who have never heard the track seek it out. In fact, 'Get Off Of My Cloud' is a classic.

> ROLLING STONES — GET OFF OF MY CLOUD (Gideon, BMI)—Another wild, far out beat number which will have no trouble topping their "Satisfaction" smash. Rocks all the way with exciting vocal work. Flip: "I'm Free" (Gideon, BMI). London 9792

Richards' comments bring up an issue about the act of creation that doesn't get as much attention as perhaps it ought: sometimes an artist creates not because he is inspired but because he has to. It's called hackery. Does the fact that an artist is responding to the demands of the market/his record company/his publishers/the necessity to acquire some quick cash make the end result intrinsically less worthy than if he had simply been chasing his muse? Not if the end result is a great song/book/play etc. Paul McCartney had a word for songs created in such circumstances: "Work" songs. He has also pointed out that several Beatles numbers considered to be classics were written in this manner.

The "work" song with which the Stones followed up 'Satisfaction' – itself a record that had turned them from a pop group into a phenomenon – had a melody written by Richards and a lyric devised by Jagger. The latter's words were really a quite shameless retread of the lyric to 'Satisfaction': where the former had blasted disc jockeys' inanities, intrusive advertising and not being able to get laid, this one took aim at neighbours who complained about noise, traffic wardens and cheerful purveyors of news about special offers. As protest, of course, it's hardly 'The Lonesome Death of Hattie Carroll' – and many perfectly reasonable people would actually have sympathy for the neighbour driven to distraction by Jagger's hi-fi – but that's not really the point: in a society so accustomed to false politeness and deferential attitudes, the very way the Stones articulated their grievances – bellowed and unapologetic – was a thrilling act of rebellion in itself. That Jagger's lyric is in double-time only adds to the sense of righteousness. The air-punching, call-and-response chorus is intoxicating stuff. Musically, the track is almost chaotic. We will never know how Keith's original vision differs from what is here – a concoction with some nicely and inexplicably liquidey guitar lines and rapid-fire drum interjections – but we can happily settle for what we have, a resplendent *blitzkrieg*.

8. GOTTA GET AWAY

AVAILABLE ON CD ON *OUT OF OUR HEADS (UK EDITION)*
Recorded July-September 1965

'Gotta Get Away' demonstrates how arbitrary the process can be of a song becoming perceived as iconic and a classic. Had that unholy, sloppy mess 'Tumbling Dice' not been released as a single, would it enjoy a status as an instantly recognizable Stones song and be a staple of their live set? Meanwhile there are plenty of songs in the band's catalogue that never became iconic but are genuinely high quality. Witness this lyrically fascinating and musically crisp and imaginative peach hidden on the Stones' third UK album.

It's a song that almost certainly has its roots in Jagger's tempestuous relationship with Chrissie Shrimpton. If it had once been love, their affair had already deteriorated by this point into spite and mutual mock violence. Jagger began writing about their squabbles, hence the torrent of Stones songs putting down the female to whom it is addressed in 1965/66/67. Though Jagger/Richards songs of malice like 'Under My Thumb', 'Stupid Girl' and 'Yesterday's Papers' are more celebrated, this track is a gem of the genre but little recognized.

The music is mid-tempo, understated, trebly, easy on the ear and non-intrusive without being featureless but it is really the lyric and Jagger's delivery of it that makes the song. Jagger sounds almost sad as he catalogues his grievances against his lover but then rises to a crescendo as he declares that he can't stand to see her face. The "Gotta-gotta-gotta get-away!" refrain – which constitutes the chorus – is impressive, Jagger executing a machine-gun delivery of what is actually a bit of a tongue twister.

Even Jagger and Richards have probably barely given this track a thought from the moment they recorded it. At the time of writing, it has never been performed onstage by the Stones.

9. BLUE TURNS TO GREY

AVAILABLE ON CD ON *DECEMBER'S CHILDREN*
Recorded July-September 1965

The fact that Jagger vented his spleen against Chrissie Shrimpton as their relationship went through its long, painful disintegration disguises the fact that he wrote as many songs of devotion and tenderness in this period as he did put-downs, several of them hidden on B-sides ('The Singer Not The Song', 'Sad Day', 'Long Long While'). Perhaps we can even read something into the fact that this song – written in the second person – depicts a man trying in vain to convince himself that he doesn't care that his partner has deserted him, only to have the realization of the fact that he does, raining on his parade, or turning his blue skies to grey as the lyric puts it.

Like 'Gotta Get Away', the fact that this has never been played on stage by the Stones indicates that the band didn't think much of it, something only apparently confirmed by the fact that they never sanctioned its release in their home country: this track was actually unknown

in Britain until given its first release on that controversial 1971 compilation *Stone Age*.

They demoed it in July 1964, apparently to try to get other people to record it. In this they were highly successful: the Mighty Avengers, Dick and Dee, and Cliff Richard all put out versions, and the latter took it to No.15 in the UK chart in early 1966. However, the fact that a full year after that London-recorded demo the band laid down a version at RCA indicates they didn't think it was completely worthless.

It's a pretty little creation. The melody is a turning, winding thing and the guitar figures are folk-rock-like in their chiming quality. A lovely little strummed flourish on the guitar heralds each chorus. The permanent air of melancholy is almost overdone – Jagger's emoting double-tracked on the choruses – but no less moving for it.

10. 19th NERVOUS BREAKDOWN

AVAILABLE ON CD ON *THE ROLLING STONES SINGLES COLLECTION – THE LONDON YEARS*
Recorded December 1965

This song starts with its narrator telling a woman that she is the kind of person one meets at dismal parties typified by a type of loud and hyperactive group of which she is the sort to be the centre.

Many must have been the teen – or indeed adult – in 1966 who, upon hearing that opening verse, thought "Whaaaat?" Though people had come to expect such stuff from Bob Dylan – who had recently introduced himself to the kids by

crossing over from the folk ghetto – this was simply not the material of which pop records were
considered to be made at the time. Just about
everything about '19th Nervous Breakdown'
is unusual-verging-on-revolutionary. It begins
with the conversational style of the words and
the subject matter (parties were almost always
portrayed as glamorous and exciting in song,
not meeting grounds for the unhappy).

Things only get more radical from there. Verse
two is Freudian, talking of a childhood of the
person being addressed of material wealth and
kindness but with no real love from or sense of
responsibility on the part of her parents, who
were also careless with their money. The third
verse alludes to LSD. The chorus meanwhile
– in which the narrator heralds his addressee's
latest breakdown and informs her how many
this is now – is a taunt, nothing less.

The music shows similar disdain for the norm.
There was some controversy at the time of the
record's release about how murky the Stones' sin-

gles were becoming (apparently Oldham nixed a
mix that gave Jagger's vocal greater delineation).
The way the instrumental opening features a conventionally tringing electric guitar that is shoved
aside by another more distorted one is the tip of
the iceberg of this aural whirlwind. Bill Wyman
adds the *coup de gràce* to the delicious discor-
dance with a series of bass runs at the close that
sound like the bubbles emerging from a deep-sea
diver's helmet as he attempts to come to the surface of the song's very, very muddy waters.

11. PAINT IT BLACK

AVAILABLE ON CD ON *THE ROLLING STONES SINGLES
COLLECTION - THE LONDON YEARS*
Recorded March 1966

Bill Wyman provided some melodic inspiration for this raga rock number by mocking
the cheesy organ runs Eric Easton had once
professionally played in cinema pits. The others took up his theme. Wyman also showed an
ingenuity rivalling Brian Jones' by playing the
organ pedals with his fists at double time to
create a second bass riff. The contribution of
Jones to the proceedings gives further credence
to the idea of a full group credit being the just
publishing arrangement: it was his sitar playing
that made the record fit in perfectly with the
times, in which Western youth (or perhaps those
members of it who happened to be pop stars)
were looking to the East for both philosophical
wisdom and new sounds. No doubt seasoned
sitar players would laugh at Jones' technique,
him spurning the languid, wandering, authen-

tic approach for something altogether more Western in its urgency and rigidity. Nonetheless, it worked beautifully. Or as he explained it himself, "On 'Paint It Black', I used a flattened third in fret position. The sound you get from a sitar is a basic blues pattern, which results in the flattening of the third and seventh as a result of the super-imposition of primitive Eastern pentatonic scales on the well-known Western diatonic." Of course.

Charlie joins in the spirit, his two-beat – and his drums treated to sound dead – adding to the mysterious Eastern air. Mick and Keith of course are hardly idle. The vocal melody is a haunting affair, and Mick's lyric sees him portraying a man who sees no meaning in life now that his lover is gone – the implication is that she is dead. Jagger cleverly abandons his usual street vernacular, using words like "darkness" and "foresee" to chime with the mythic mood.

To this day, many reference books refer to this song as 'Paint It, Black' because of how it was originally rendered on the record label. Those looking for hidden meanings were barking up the wrong tree. "Don't ask me what the comma in the title is for – that's Decca's" Richards shrugged.

12. LONG, LONG WHILE

AVAILABLE ON CD ON *THE ROLLING STONES SINGLES COLLECTION - THE LONDON YEARS*
Recorded March 1966

What impresses most about The Rolling Stones' Sixties catalogue is the sheer abundance of it.

As Bono said to Jagger in a scene from the 2001 documentary *Being Mick*, "How did you write so many songs?" So prolific were they, that Jagger and Richards and their colleagues can barely remember some of the material which in those days – Jagger revealed to Bono – they often wrote on their way to the studio. The interesting thing about this material is that there was no common thread to it. If every album made sounded different to its predecessor and every single seemed to break new artistic ground, what could it be said gave the group responsible a sonic imprimatur? Even The Beatles – also artistically restless and eclectic – at least retained a trademark on their every record in the form of their distinctive harmonies. The answer is: there was no Stones imprimatur in the Sixties except sheer quality.

As with several tracks on this list, the Stones have never played 'Long, Long While' – the B-side of 'Paint It Black' in the UK – on stage. They would probably respond with blank looks if asked about it. Only those who have written umpteen classic songs can possess such a large psychological comfort zone as to not even think about material to which they – Jagger's comments about quick turnarounds notwithstanding – applied their time and craft.

'Long, Long While' is a gorgeous song. It is unusual in the Stones canon, not because of its tenderness (there are plenty such songs in their catalogue, whatever their detractors might say) but because of its unequivocal apologeticness. What other Rolling Stones numbers feature lines like "I was wrong girl, and you were

The Music

right"? Musically, it's a soul ballad with a heavy emphasis on sonorous piano, played by Jack Nitzsche, complemented by organ from Ian Stewart. The whole effect is so blissful that – had it not been impossible to release, at least in the UK, at this stage of their career for image reasons – it's not stretching it to say that this could have been a Sixties equivalent of 'Angie', scaling the charts with the assistance of people who would not normally touch the Stones' product.

13. STUPID GIRL

AVAILABLE ON CD ON *THE ROLLING STONES SINGLES COLLECTION – THE LONDON YEARS* AND *AFTERMATH*
Recorded March 1966

The lyric of 'Stupid Girl' is impressively colloquial. It is also in its way quietly revolutionary. When Jagger remarks, "She bitches 'bout things that she's never seen", he is talking the language of the street. It's certainly a long way from Elvis Presley – who was colloquial but in a watered-down way – let alone Frank Sinatra. Watts helps get things underway with a drum roll and then proceeds to deploy an almost marching beat, which virtually makes it seem like Jagger's humiliation of his estranged lover is being paraded before the world (which in a way it is, although Jagger never identified its subject as an individual). When Jagger says that the titular girl is the *worst* thing in this *world* the stressed words are punched home with parallel guitar bashes. Rarely has vituperativeness been so attractive.

14. LADY JANE

AVAILABLE ON CD ON *THE ROLLING STONES SINGLES COLLECTION – THE LONDON YEARS* AND *AFTERMATH*
Recorded March 1966

At a time when The Rolling Stones were considered an undisciplined rabble by much of 'decent' society, they recorded a song which proved just how efficient and musically intelligent they were. To get an indication of what a perfectly sustained exercise this song is, contrast it to Queen's 'Lazing On A Sunday Afternoon'. A track from their 1975 album *A Night At The Opera*, it is a very impressive pastiche of 1930s pop records – until the instrumental break, where Brian May storms in with a hard rock guitar solo. No such conceptual sloppiness here. While this is not necessarily authentic to the Elizabethan period it alludes to, everything 'rock' is set aside for its duration (unless we are to consider acoustic guitar rock instrumentation). The dulcimer – a sort of precursor to the guitar dating from the Middle Ages – is naturally played by Brian Jones. Jack Nitzsche supplied the harpsichord, introduced in the instrumental break to emphasise the antediluvian nature.

The conceit of antiquity is superbly sustained by the lyric. One can even imagine Mick Jagger, of all people, on bended knee as he explains his situation successively to Lady Jane, Lady Anne and Sweet Marie. Courtly phrases like "Your servant am I and will humbly remain" litter the song. Just in case we mistake *politesse* for tenderness, Jagger's kiss-off for both Sweet Marie and us accurately reflects the mercenary that attended marriage in the period he is alluding to when he explains of his final choice of Lady Jane that her station's right and life is secure with her.

15. OUT OF TIME

AVAILABLE ON CD ON *AFTERMATH*
Recorded March 1966

The aspiration of Andrew Loog Oldham to make Mick Jagger and Keith Richards the equal of Lennon & McCartney in the stakes of farming out compositions to other artists was never quite fulfilled. Though the likes of Gene Pitney, Cliff Richard and, er, George Bean did consider some of their compositions potential hits, the number of Jagger/Richards songs recorded by performers other than the Stones is dwarfed by the number of non-Beatles songs bearing the names of John and Paul. This was more to do with the Stones songs being of a certain type than with quality. Frank Sinatra could see himself singing 'Something' in a way he never could, say, 'You Got The Silver'.

One of the few Jagger/Richards songs to become a *bona fide* hit for a third party was 'Out Of Time', originally recorded by the Stones for *Aftermath* but re-recorded (probably without the Stones behind Mick) as a demo for Chris Farlowe, a British blues singer similar to Eric Burdon and Stevie Winwood in his gritty authenticity. The combination of Farlowe's passionate vocals, Jagger's elegantly venomous lyric and the song's fine melody couldn't really fail. Farlowe's 'Out Of Time' – produced by

Jagger – became a UK No.1 in Summer 1966. By then, the Stones' own version of the song had appeared on their first album to be completely written by the group's songwriting axis. It was even better than Farlowe's much-loved rendition. Theirs is of a length that Farlowe would not have attempted on a single and that is its – rather ugly – strength. Because of its length, it feels unpitying and relentless, the ultimate exultation in the rejection of a would-be returning lover.

The main musical feature is the marimbas, a percussion instrument (hit with mallets) similar to the xylophone but pitched an octave lower. Such a relatively dainty instrument is ostensibly incongruous in the context of such a malicious number, but Jones – for it is, naturally, he – uses them in such a way as to create a sort of jaunty menace. (The perky "bop, bop" backing vocals assist the overall tone of gleeful vengeance in a similar way.) The leisurely pace as Jagger variously informs his lover she is "out of touch", "out of time", "obsolete", etc. only adds to the general mercilessness.

16. LET'S SPEND THE NIGHT TOGETHER

AVAILABLE ON CD ON *THE ROLLING STONES SINGLES COLLECTION - THE LONDON YEARS*
Recorded November 1966

To today's generation of kids – who can see sex mentioned and depicted in the mainstream media every hour of every day should they be so inclined – it is difficult to convey how

shocking this record was in 1967.

Sex was a subject still surrounded by taboo. It was only seven years since D H Lawrence's *Lady Chatterley's Lover* had been put on trial for obscenity, and although the publishers won the case the fact that it had reached court indicated the mindset of the generation who held the strings of power. (As did the comments of the trial judge who – in a comment one would think had come straight out of a *Monty Python* sketch had that show existed at the time – remarked, "Is it a book you would even wish your wife or your servants to read?") The theatre was surrounded by absurd censorship presided over by the grandly-titled Lord Chamberlain, and would be until 1968.

A BBC Variety Programmes *Policy Guide* booklet distributed to Writers and Producers stated, "There is an absolute ban upon the following: Jokes about lavatories; Effeminacy in men; Immorality of any kind; Suggestive references to Honeymoon couples; Chambermaids; Fig-leaves; Prostitution; Ladies' underwear, e.g.'winter draws on'; Animal habits, e.g. rabbits; Lodgers; Commercial travellers. Extreme care should be taken in dealing with references to or jokes about Pre-natal Influences (e.g. 'His mother was frightened by a donkey'); Marital infidelity. Good taste and decency are the obvious governing considerations. The vulgar use of such words as 'basket' must also be avoided."

In this ridiculously buttoned-up media climate, 'Let's Spend The Night Together' was like an atom bomb. A single that was unusually piano-heavy for a Stones number, its keyboard work for many people might as well have been the type heard in a bordello. The title – and chorus refrain – was the sort of thing that led to "Did-he-just-say-what-I-thought-he-said?" incredulity. While it is true that the kids were newly-confident about sex after the introduction of the Pill, it was still so unfamiliar to hear on the airwaves even this cleaned-up language of the street as to cause a jolt.

The melody was written by Richards on piano. The lyric actually doesn't exhibit the predatory sentiment suggested by the title but is characterized more by yearning. In fact, the statements of the narrator are the kind normally heard in conventional love songs ("This doesn't happen to me every day") and it is only the chorus phrase and the line where Jagger promises to satisfy the every need of the woman he's addressing that suggests a more base motive.

17. YESTERDAY'S PAPERS

AVAILABLE ON CD ON *BETWEEN THE BUTTONS*
Recorded August-December 1966

The opening track of the UK version of *Between The Buttons* marked a bit of a milestone for Jagger: the first time he had written 100% of a Stones composition. He had long had a gift for penning above-par songwords, of course, but being skilled in that area can be as much a consequence of practice as inspiration – after all, the full-time lyricist has nothing else to do. Now that Jagger had a melody under his belt, he could begin to plausibly consider himself on the same composing plateau as Richards.

A percussive rumbling intro suddenly gives way to a gentle backing. A cooing Jagger posits the question of who wants yesterday papers, a metaphor for former partner, and viciously concludes, "Nobody in the world". The utter brutality against such a sweet backing – which becomes even more decorative as his colleagues start producing feminine backing vocals – is startling. As Jagger continues the abuse, confessing that it's very hard to be satisfied with one girl in a world of millions of them, Jones – apparently oblivious of what he's being a party to – continues playing utterly gentle patterns on marimbas.

18. RUBY TUESDAY

AVAILABLE ON CD ON *THE ROLLING STONES SINGLES COLLECTION - THE LONDON YEARS*
Recorded November 1966

If there was ever a Rolling Stones song that merited the inclusion of Brian Jones in the writers' credits, 'Ruby Tuesday' would seem to be it.

Despite the fact that he could effortlessly learn to play any variety of instrument and that he wrote the soundtrack to the movie *Mord Und Totschlag*, everyone involved with the Stones has expressed scepticism that Jones would ever have actually been able to master the knack of putting a vocal melody line to a chord sequence. Yet according to Richards employee Tony Sanchez, 'Ruby Tuesday' was something devised by Richards in collaboration not with Jagger but with Jones. This idea is only given more credence by Jagger having said of it, "I think that's a wonderful song. It's just a nice melody, really. And a lovely lyric. Neither of which I wrote, but I always enjoy singing it."

Even if he did not co-write it, Jones would still be largely responsible for its brilliance. Just as his sitar playing had made 'Paint it Black' the haunting work it was, so his recorder and piano ensured that 'Ruby Tuesday' was an utterly beautiful and pastoral recording. Although a cousin of 'Lady Jane' in its olde-worlde flavour, it is incongruously a farewell to a groupie.

Jagger drew back at doing the logical thing and purging the song of double-negatives and his voice of American inflections, thus creating a stylistic inconsistency which weakens it slightly. Nonetheless, there is still enough in the way of courtly phrases and delicate enunciation to mark it out as something very different to what was considered ordinary Stones – or rock – fare. A normal rock bass sound would not have been appropriate to the soundscape so Richards and Wyman provided a deep, almost buzzing accompaniment on double bass with, Wyman recalled, "me selecting the notes and Keith bowing the strings."

In what is an exquisite track, the best is saved for last as Jones provides a close in which he is playing piano and recorder in tandem. The latter instrument is then employed on its own to create a delightful wisp of a coda.

19. WE LOVE YOU

AVAILABLE ON CD ON *THE ROLLING STONES SINGLES COLLECTION - THE LONDON YEARS*
Recorded June-July 1967

The mellotron was all the rage in 1967. Though now it seems positively quaint, this instrument was then what had until recently been the stuff of science fiction tableaux. Essentially a precursor of the synthesizer or sampler, it consisted of keys which when pressed would play several seconds of a recording of a musical instrument. In this manner, musicians who understood notes and keys but had no facility on a particular instrument – usually nonstringed ones – could employ the sound of that instrument without having to bring in a session musician. Predictably, The Beatles were pop pioneers in the use of this new-fangled (and very expensive) device, using it to create the flute sound on their 1967 track 'Strawberry Fields Forever'. The Stones were close behind The Beatles (also predictable, some would unkindly assert). It was Brian Jones who was

the Stone who took interest in it. This was ironic, in light of the fact that he could be posited as a living, breathing mellotron himself: such was his facility with instruments that one apparently disbelieving internet site erroneously has him pioneering the mellotron's use by "the flute track on... 'Ruby Tuesday'." Jones used mellotron on 'We Love You' to create an Arabian brass effect which – as his playing on 'Paint It Black' and 'Ruby Tuesday' had – simply made the record.

The lyric was the Stones' message of defiance to the authorities, refracted through the prism of the then in-vogue Flower Power vocabulary. Still at the time unsure whether they would be going back to prison, Jagger yowled at the powers-that-be, "You will never win" and – to the group's fans – the title phrase. Somehow, though, the intended 'love and peace' vibe didn't come across. As rock critic Greil Marcus put it about this track, "The Stones' sullenness prevailed even when they affected optimism". Nonetheless, it was a psychedelic epic that, as Robert Christgau, another rock critic, said, was the "only time the Stones trounced *Sgt. Pepper* good." Nicky Hopkins provides a dark, rippling piano motif while behind him an indefatigable Jones creates vistas of sand dunes and Bedouins. Though he was playing a series of tape loops, the idea that anyone could replicate what he produced on this track is, for George Chkiantz, who engineered it, absurd. Relying as it did on a pinch wheel that went down when a key was pressed and held back as it was by the delay while the relevant tape started moving across the head and by variable speed depending on how many keys were pressed, it was a cumbersome affair to play anything that was not a simple progression. "For him to play this part he had to be anticipating the beat by a variable amount," said Chkiantz. "How the hell he got his head into that has always been one of the amazing things in life to me."

20. IN ANOTHER LAND

AVAILABLE ON CD ON *THEIR SATANIC MAJESTIES REQUEST*
Recorded July 1967

Bill Wyman recorded this song on a day that only he and Watts of the band were able to make it to the studio, thus effectively delivering Jagger and Richards a *fait-accompli*. Hitherto, he had got used to having to give his songs to the likes of The End, so proprietorial had Jagger and Richards come to be about the original numbers on Stones records. Engineer Glyn Johns had suggested that they use the downtime that day to demo any new songs Wyman had. (The Stones would have had to pay for the studio time anyway.) Wyman had in fact been working on something that he later described as "kind of spacy", which of course was the 'in' sound at that point in pop history. Johns almost tricked the Glimmer Twins into acknowledging its quality: he played it to them the next day and waited for their enthusiastic response before telling them it was Bill.

In some senses, it's not really a Stones track at all: the only contribution of Jagger was the backing vocals he (with Richards) overdubbed

at a later date and, although Richards can be heard on acoustic guitar, so can the Small Faces' Steve Marriott, roped in from a session in the next studio. Marriott and his colleague Ronnie Lane beefed up Wyman's voice, which he was so insecure about that he asked it to be treated with a tremolo effect – which was fortuitous because the weird result chimed with the song's surreal ambience. Nicky Hopkins plays harpsichord and piano and Ian Stewart contributes organ to a track that has a slightly Elizabethan undertow, but thoroughly space-age imagery. The lyric is simply brilliant, describing a blissful tableau shattered when a man realizes he is just dreaming, the latter rude realization perfectly captured when the song leaps into the chorus ("Then I awoke – is this some kind of joke!") It then turns out that the narrator has awoken into another dream, which is once again shattered.

It was a recurring grievance of Wyman that his songs were never given space on Stones albums. This track – the best thing on *Satanic Majesties* – shows that this was a legitimate grievance.

21. JUMPIN' JACK FLASH

AVAILABLE ON CD ON *THE ROLLING STONES SINGLES COLLECTION - THE LONDON YEARS*
Recorded March-April 1968

Recalling a day in 1968, Bill Wyman has said that he, Jones and Watts found themselves alone in the Stones' rehearsal studio. Waiting for the Glimmer Twins to arrive, Wyman

sat down at the piano and began "messing about". Jones and Watts began joining in on the dark riff he started producing from the keys. The trio vamped on the riff for around twenty minutes. Wyman: "Mick and Keith came in and we stopped and they said, 'Hey, that sounded really good, carry on, what is it?' And then the next day we recorded it and Mick wrote great lyrics to it and it turned out to be a really good single."

That fine riff was turned via Richards' skilled hands – and laterally-thinking brain – into something remarkable. He played an acoustic Gibson Hummingbird tuned to open E for a ringing sustain and employed a capo for additional tightness. Overlaid on that was another guitar tuned Nashville-style, something Richards had learnt from a musician in George Jones' band when the Stones had played on the same bill in San Antonio in 1964. Both acoustics were played through the extension speaker of a Philips cassette recorder. So was born 'Jumpin' Jack Flash's air of murky menace.

Jagger's lyric was inspired by a somewhat unlikely source, a gardener named Jack employed by Richards, whose massive feet clumping on the driveway of his home woke Jagger up one morning. From the instantly coined Jumpin' Jack, it was then a short step to Jumpin' Jack Flash, but a somewhat greater leap had to be made for the song-words' demonic ambience. Jagger's lyric begins with a dramatic conversational gambit as he reveals he was born in a crossfire hurricane and reaches its devilish apotheosis with the

immortal line "I was raised by a toothless bearded hag". The reaction of Mrs Eva Jagger of Dartford to this last tribute is unrecorded.

22. SYMPATHY FOR THE DEVIL

AVAILABLE ON CD ON *BEGGAR'S BANQUET*
Recorded June 1968

The Master and Margarita is a novel by pre-war Russian dissident Mikhail Bulgakov which, in 1968, had recently been published in an English translation. The book concerns a visit to present-day Moscow by a physical incarnation of the Devil. Marianne Faithfull read it and enjoyed it and, as often happens in relationships, passed it on to her partner. As often doesn't happen, the partner proceeded to base a classic rock song on it.

The material in one sense was ideal for a man who was considered Public Enemy No.1.

Though Jagger never really sought to be a spokesman or a figurehead for his generation, he certainly often succumbed to the temptation of exulting in the 'outlaw' status that had been conferred upon him. What could enable him to do that more than assuming the persona of Satan in a lyric? He brings it off very well, spurning the type of crass sloganeering that would soon come to characterise a new form of music called 'heavy metal' for a subtler approach, depicting an articulate but chilling Beelzebub.

The aural backdrop to this matter-of-fact confession of ultimate evil changed massively in the studio. The band went through arrangements ranging from folky to samba-esque before settling on the familiar one that begins as a slow blues and builds into a sinister, fiery crescendo, accompanied by the sort of demented, insistent "Whoo-whoo!" chanting that one could imagine is heard around a pentagram.

The highlights of the song are Richards' electric guitar solos. Though acclaimed as a supreme rhythm player, Richards has never been known as a virtuoso in the style of contemporaries like Jeff Beck or Eric Clapton. For that reason, the level he rises to here is astounding. He peels off two lengthy breaks that are not only wonderfully fluid but also achieve an amazing razor-edged menace: he sounds like he's playing on strings made out of barbed wire. So uncharacteristically expert is his playing, in fact, that if we hadn't seen him doing it in Jean-Luc Godard's documentary of the recording of the song, we would probably

have assumed that it wasn't his handiwork, but the contribution of a sessioner.

Spooky footnote: as the Stones' finished the final take of 'Sympathy For The Devil', the studio caught fire and had to be evacuated.

23. STRAY CAT BLUES

AVAILABLE ON CD ON *BEGGAR'S BANQUET*
Recorded March-May 1968

The Velvet Underground – a New York group of the late Sixties who had then released two low-fi albums that had disappeared without trace – hardly sound like the kind of people to have been an influence on the world's second-most-successful band in 1968. Though they had procured a fame of sorts amongst the type of circles in which the Stones moved, at that point the Velvets hadn't achieved the cachet of being massively influential on subsequent generations of musicians, something that itself would have to be their consolation for never having a hit album or single to their name by the time of their 1970 split. The world was completely ignorant of the fact that the Stones were even aware of the Velvet Underground until Jagger blew the gaffe on the band in a 1977 interview with the journalist Nick Kent. When the subject turned to Velvet's leader Lou Reed (by way of punk), Jagger said, "I mean, even we've been influenced by the Velvet Underground..." Kent was incredulous. Jagger insisted it was true: "I'll tell you exactly what we pinched from him too. You know 'Stray Cat Blues'? The whole sound and the way it's paced, we pinched from the very first Velvet Underground album. You know, the sound on 'Heroin'. Honest to God, we did!"

Returning to the aforesaid third track on *Beggar's Banquet* with fresh ears after reading that, you can see what Jagger means. 'Heroin' and 'Stray Cat Blues' begin with similar guitar figures. There is also a certain similarity in the subterranean tone of the recordings. However, a band as adroit and talented as The Rolling Stones know the difference between inspiration and imitation, and the similarities end there. 'Heroin' was a ground-breaking discussion of drug addiction in pop, whose scuzzy atmosphere was somewhat undermined by a banal lyric. It also suffered in places from a slight tinniness. No such gap between ambition and achievement afflicted 'Stray Cat Blues'. It is a track precisely as lecherous, decadent and sinister as it's meant to be. Jagger invites a girl into his bed, dismissing the fact that she is underage with the shrugged line "I don't want your I.D." Behind him the band render magnificently a superior version of the style of music soon to be known as 'heavy metal', with growling guitar work from Richards and with Watts and Wyman providing an absolutely cavernous bottom end. Jagger himself would probably find the song morally dubious today – it's doubtful he would welcome an older man taking sexual interest in a fifteen-year-old daughter of his – but what price hostages to fortune when you have an image of a social outlaw to maintain?

24. HONKY TONK WOMEN

AVAILABLE ON CD ON *THE ROLLING STONES SINGLES COLLECTION - THE LONDON YEARS*
Recorded May-June 1969

Though, in 1968, Keith Richards was inspired by the sight on a Brazilian ranch of black cowboys riding on beautiful quarter horses to come up with a country ditty, by the time it saw release as a single in July of the following year, the ditty had mutated into something altogether different. In fact, the slinky, electric rock number into which the music had transmogrified was so far removed from the guitarist's original vision that he felt compelled to record 'Country Honk', another version closer to what he had originally wanted.

The dedication the band were able to display in perfecting this song was a massive contrast to the rushed recording schedules to which they'd been subjected only three or four years before, and underlined their rock aristocracy status. Recalled Vic Smith, who engineered much of its recording at Olympic, "We had to go through the process of completely re-recording the track five times. Glyn [Johns] created the very first backing track, then I joined." After completing that recording, which took several weeks, Smith and the Stones worked on *Let It Bleed* tracks. Another full version of 'Honky Tonk Women' was then cut, which took several more weeks. Having mixed that, the Stones decided to record the song again but this time completely live. Another recording was attempted after that. Smith: "Then later on during the *Let it Bleed* album recordings we attempted the fifth version. We actually went back to the original bass and drum track and then we rebuilt that again to form the final single." Right at the end of this tortuous process, Mick Taylor played his first Stones session, and graced the track with some serpentine guitar work that twined beautifully with Richards'. By coincidence, a link to the original Brazilian ranch concept was retained when they decided to use an introduction employing a cowbell (played by Jimmy Miller) an instrument originally designed to go round the necks of cattle.

While the music was honed to perfection, the title phrase – which doesn't actually make sense in the context of the song's erotic travelogue lyric – was not. As Richards explained, "A lot of times you're fooling with what you consider to be just working titles or even working hooks, and then you realize there's nothing else that's going to slip in there and fit in the same way. So you're left with this fairly inane phrase."

Despite the impressively booming drum track on the finished recording, the single features a surprisingly maladroit mix with the brass section on the instrumental break barely audible, although – judging by the outtakes that have leaked out – the decision to mix Ian Stewart's leaden piano work to inaudibility was a wise one.

25. GIMME SHELTER

AVAILABLE ON CD ON *LET IT BLEED*
Recorded February-November 1969

In 2002, a panel of critics and musicians contacted by Britain's Uncut magazine declared 'Gimme Shelter' (sometimes rendered as 'Gimmie Shelter' on album sleeves) the greatest original Rolling Stones song of all time. The poll was right. Other recordings by the band have more of a feeling of the Grand Statement that one associates with opuses (e.g. 'Satisfaction', 'You Can't Always Get What You Want', 'It's Only Rock 'N' Roll') but 'Gimme Shelter' takes the accolade of top Stones track through sheer musical magnificence.

Because Jagger and Richards have never spoken publicly about the affair between Jagger and Pallenberg that threatened to destroy both their friendship and the Rolling Stones, the supposition that the lyric of 'Gimme Shelter' – which was Richards' – was prompted by his feelings of pain and betrayal over it remains precisely that. However, the visions Richards dredged from his psyche certainly do seem inordinately tormented (he talks of a storm threatening his very life and a fire sweeping through the streets). Even though his depression seems somewhat over the top in the way he extrapolates an entire global malaise from it ("Rape, murder it's just a shot away!"), it is by this method that an artist makes his viewpoint universal, not specific to his own domestic travails. It's also an interesting contrast to Jagger's own chosen method of exploring the faults in his relationships in song hitherto: acidic put-downs. Also an interesting contrast is the note of hope on which the song ends where it is suggested that love is just a kiss away. If the song is about what we think it is about and Jagger knew this, psychologically it just boggles the mind as to how he must have felt as he – brilliantly – bellowed the lyric.

The music accompanying this lyric is what Led Zeppelin's music always promised to be but never was: 'Cosmic Blues', a gargantuan, speeded-up version of Muddy Waters and Howlin' Wolf (though some musicologists insist that Richards' guitar picking here is a slowed-down generic Chuck Berry riff). A guiro or 'scraper', and a eerily cooing female voice sets the tone in the beginning before the track explodes into an apocalyptic soundscape made all the more menacing by massively amplified and distorted blasts of mouth harp. Once again, Richards' ever-inventive mind was the source for the novel sounds. Having discovered that some rather second-rate Triumph transistorized amplifiers sourced for the group by Ian Stewart produced an intriguing atmospheric effect – what Chkiantz described as an "amazing crunch" – just before overheating, the group set about abusing them until the optimum distortion was reached. Similar ingenuity was the cause of the lacerating power of the mouth harp blasts, with the band overdriving an old Dynacord tape-loop machine, then for good measure putting the results through limiters.

The track – recorded in Blighty – would have sounded fine just with Jagger's vocal but, directly before their 1969 US tour, the group decided to utilize the magnificent banshee voice of soul singer Merry Clayton for backups and a chorus on her own and thereby lifted the song from the merely superb into the immortal.

26. YOU GOT THE SILVER

AVAILABLE ON CD ON *LET IT BLEED*
Recorded February 1969

Though he had made solo vocal contributions to previous Stones tracks, 'Something Happened To Me Yesterday' and 'Salt Of The Earth', 'You Got The Silver' was the first recorded Stones song that Keith Richards sang in toto. Though a Jagger vocal exists, it seems only right, considering this track's genesis, that it was decided to leave it in the can and give Keith his first full turn in the vocal spotlight. Originally called 'You Got Some Silver Now', this is another song that one suspects (but cannot prove) originated in the fallout from the affair between Pallenberg and Jagger. This one is as small-scale and introspective as 'Gimme Shelter' is gigantic and projected. Marianne Faithfull recalled first hearing it when Richards played it to an audience of four while sitting on the four-poster bed of Robert Fraser. It's a song almost of worship, but that doesn't prevent the narrator from imploring the object of his devotion to stop hurting him. The vulnerability is extremely affecting.

The song begins with a rustic and mellow ambience, with Richards' pleasantly reedy voice set against acoustic guitar, pedal steel and small flecks of crow's-call electric guitar. A glossy sheen is then added by the discreet introduction of Nicky Hopkins' organ. By the third verse, the mood has changed. The track jumps into a medium-fast rock tempo at the same time as Richards begins to sound angry rather than worshipful, demanding to know what is the laughing quality in his lover's smile. "I don't care, no, I don't care!" he yells before revealing that the last declaration is denial by admitting his woman's love just leaves him blind.

'You Got The Silver' saw one of the only contributions on the *Let It Bleed* album of Brian Jones, who for some reason decided to play autoharp with his car keys. Jones was probably unaware of the irony this injected into the song's recording: the ghost of his love affair with Pallenberg, which Richards had in a way ended, entering into Richards' dissection of the way his own relationship with Pallenberg was itself now being threatened by a third party.

27. YOU CAN'T ALWAYS GET WHAT YOU WANT

AVAILABLE ON CD ON *LET IT BLEED*
Recorded November 1968–August 1969

'You Can't Always Get What You Want' closed the album that 'Gimme Shelter' opened, making for surely the most stunning pair of bookends rock music has ever seen.

Though it was the first *Let It Bleed* track worked on in the studio, "You Can't Always Get What You Want' would take many months to complete and would be subjected to numerous rethinks and overdubs that transformed it from the relatively simple recording it was at the beginning.

The lyric is opaque but the second verse, in which Jagger (whose song this mainly is) talks of going down to a demonstration to avoid

blowing a fuse, seems a quite clear reference to the '68 protests that Jagger had participated in outside the American embassy in London over the Vietnam War. The rest of the verses – which switch between second and third person perspectives – talk about a woman making her connection, getting her prescription filled by the narrator and being practiced at the art of deception. Marianne Faithfull's assertion that this song documented Jagger's torment at the way she was descending into heroin addiction seems quite plausible. Less plausible is the Shakesperian-couplet profundity many attribute to the chorus refrain, wherein it is stated that while getting what one wants is not always possible, "You might find you get what you need". Wiser instead to treat it – and the song – as an impressionistic examination of resignation.

At the session, Al Kooper mentioned to Jagger that he heard in his head a horn chart for the song and said he'd be happy to contribute it if the Stones wanted. The band would take him up on his offer but not until they had taken the extraordinary step of overdubbing onto the song the massed voices of the London Bach Choir, who supplied a sweet introduction in the form of an *a cappella* rendition of the chorus, as well as other angelic colourings. When he was flown the tape, Kooper recorded three saxes, two trumpets and a French horn onto it but wasn't completely happy with the results. He was therefore pleased when the band decided to retain only his French horn part (played by himself), which added an exquisite seam of melancholy.

The track made its debut on the b-side of 'Honky Tonk Women', *sans* the *a cappella* intro for reasons of space. The full version on *Let It Bleed* deserved every second of its 7 minutes and 28 seconds playing time.

28. BROWN SUGAR

AVAILABLE ON CD ON *STICKY FINGERS*
Recorded December 1969

Like its parent album *Sticky Fingers*, the timbre of 'Brown Sugar' is a slurred one, as if the slightly dragged rhythm were designed to describe the wiped-out sensation just prior to leaving an all-night party. It's there in the first moment with the simple but effective riff which sounds like its been truncated and could have done with another take and is there at the end when the song threatens to become leaden by seeming to last one bar too long. In between there is superb, high-octane rock, but exhaustion always seems just below the surface.

The number – riff and all – originated with Jagger. Stranded in Australia filming *Ned Kelly* and with lots of time on his hands between takes, Jagger began composing a song that depicted sex between slaves and their masters and featured a chorus that was an unmistakable reference to cunnilingus. ('Black Pussy' was a working title.) Richards also later said, "The lyrics were partially inspired by a black backing singer we knew in LA called Claudia Linnear." By 1995, Jagger was admitting that he could never write such an un-PC song again.

The song was originally recorded in December

1969 at Muscle Shoals Studio, Alabama, when the group were on tour. Not convinced about that take, partly because of a chaotic and accident-prone recording process, the band cut it again in Olympic a year to the month later. In the end, the Olympic version was rejected because of the uniquely musty and rhythmic quality of the first recording. The highpoints of a bravura performance are Bobby Keys' sax solo and the middle eight ("I bet your mama was a tent show queen, etc.") where an already infectious song explodes into a joyous crescendo.

29. CAN'T YOU HEAR ME KNOCKING

AVAILABLE ON CD ON *STICKY FINGERS*
Recorded March-May 1970

Just as a song with an extended improvised coda sprawled across a vast section of *Aftermath* ('Goin' Home'), so *Sticky Fingers* featured a "They kept the tapes rolling" track in the shape of 'Can't You Hear Me Knocking'. The card inset from the original *Sticky Fingers* album carried a rather nervous caveat (presumably from the record company) pointing out that the distortion on the guitars was actually intended. It's hard to imagine Stones fans nurtured on the sonic murk of tracks like '19th Nervous Breakdown' and 'Jumpin' Jack Flash' returning their albums in outrage to their retailer on the ground that it didn't sound as well-groomed as the latest Simon & Garfunkel LP, but 'Can't You Hear Me Knocking' certainly features more than a bit of distortion. It boasts the monster, frayed Richards riff-of-all-time, one seemingly cranked up to eleven (although in fact Mick Taylor revealed it was played through a modest amp, probably a Fender Twin Reverb, but treated with Revox echo by Miller). Despite its distressed nature, there is something grand, almost regal, about this riff. This impression is assisted by the almost strutting gait Watts gives the proceedings.

After 2:45 of Jagger calling up to a lover's window like some ragged-assed Romeo variant ("You've got cocaine eyes" is an example of his modern-day beseeching-to-balcony dialogue), a wash of congas materializes, which acts as a bridge from this archetypal Stones anthem into a Santana-type Latin percussive 'blow'.

The instrumental coda (perhaps 'second act' would be a better term, as we are talking of a section longer than what had preceded it) feels in a way like a different song. Because it has no musical motifs or themes that featured in the 'first act', it feels like something artificially grafted on. However, one gets over that initially jarring fact because of the quality of what it contains: rapidly tapped bongos, Bobby Keyes' saxophone appearing and receding to the horizon like a desert hallucination,

Carlos Santana-esque guitar runs from Taylor, Watts' ride cymbal tinkling like a trebly pacemaker, and Billy Preston's organ just audible below the sonic surface, like waves lapping on a shore that's just out of sight.

30. SWEET VIRGINIA

AVAILABLE ON CD ON *EXILE ON MAIN ST.*
Recorded June 1970–March 1972

It's Mick Jagger's misfortune to be skilled on an instrument for which plaudits do not profusely flow, the harmonica. His talent on the instrument is proven forever on the opening to this lazy sojourn down Country Road when he blows an utterly lovely, mellow sequence. In fact, it's initially quite a shock the way the song switches from that blissful opening and apparently enthusiastically authentic country vibe into a chorus that ridicules the genre – and its demographic – by culminating in the (admittedly laugh-out-loud funny) line "Got to scrape the shit right off your shoes".

Another *Exile* song that secretly originated in Britain, it still has that musty feeling that you imagine existed in Richards' Nellcote basement. It also possesses a certain joyousness, helped in no small measure by the massed singing of the chorus (including by female voices) and Bobby Keys' wonderful, restrained sax solo.

It's now an irrelevance, except as an historical footnote, but this song originally kicked off side two of the original vinyl of *Exile*, a mellow side that Richards explained was designed to be listened to late at night.

31. TURD ON THE RUN

AVAILABLE ON CD ON *EXILE ON MAIN ST.*
Recorded June 1971-March 1972

'Turd On The Run' sums up the impressionistic nature of the qualities of *Exile*. The song feels like a fragment, a sort of middle part of a trilogy, not unpleasant on the ear but missing a sense of significance. Yet as one becomes more familiar with it, one looks forward to various of its contents: its fine bluesy groove, its urgent, double-time vocal delivery, its sweaty desperation, its greasy mouth harp, its clanging guitar riff, its nicely-judged overlaying of double vocals to emphasize the dramatic moments, and its hilarious lyric depicting a man trying literally to hold onto his lover ("I reached for your lapel but it weren't sewn on so grand"). The song, like so many others on *Exile*, is more than the sum of its parts – as indeed is the entire album.

32. LET IT LOOSE

AVAILABLE ON CD ON *EXILE ON MAIN ST.*
Recorded October 1970-March 1972

The sonic murkiness attending much of *Exile On Main St.* should not be overstated. None of it is clean-cut as such, but there is plenty of aural (and, indeed, moral) brightness shining through the gloom. 'Let It Loose' is a case in point. An exercise in gospel music, it is actually quite breathtaking – considering its surroundings and its own less-than-pristine state – just how rich this track is. And how beautiful.

The lyric starts out in the second person with a verse that sounds like the warnings Jagger's friends were then giving him about Bianca and then switches to the first person (although not necessarily a different subject: "bit off more than I can chew".) There seems to be a reference to Bianca's pregnancy and the birth of his daughter Jade with a line about a female delivering right on time but frankly such are Jagger's slovenly vocal stylings, which he has always seemed to think are part of the bad boy persona, that it's impossible to decipher the general meaning. Having said that, he sings with real passion in this song.

The instrumentation and vocal back-ups here are a real feast. Nicky Hopkins gets proceedings underway with a mellotron playing a surreal strings part. The voices of Tamiya Lynn, Shirley Goodman, Dr. John, Clydie King, Venetta Field & Joe Green – added at the mixing stage at Sunset Sound studio – often shadow Jagger's, male and female alternating throughout, helping to create a wonderful mosaic. The Stones are superbly disciplined for the song's duration, never ever succumbing to the temptation to prove they're a rock guitar band but instead, in the two instrumental passages, allowing an exquisite brass section to do its work, with Hopkins twinkling on piano behind them.

So absorbing is all this that it's a shock at the end of 'Let It Loose' to discover that this song has lasted nearly five and a half minutes.

33. SHINE A LIGHT

AVAILABLE ON CD ON *EXILE ON MAIN ST.*
Recorded March 1969-March 1972

An edition of the 1970s Marvel comic *Shang-Chi: Master Of Kung Fu* saw the titular martial arts expert quote a line from this composition:

"Make every song your favourite tune."

"Confucius?" wondered the addressee, of the source.

"No, Mick Jagger," responded Shang-Chi.

There's certainly a touch of Zen about 'Shine a Light' – or is it just compassion, the unadulterated presence of which on a Stones record is so relatively rare as to make us sometimes unable to recognise it? The narrator is showing an affecting tenderness to the (presumably) woman he is addressing. In the first verse, he talks of seeing her stretched out in a room with a number in what seems like another reference to Bianca's pregnancy. He displays concern for her when her late night friends have left as a cold dawn breaks. The choruses feature that Confucius-like pearl of wisdom. It's actually preceded by the mention of the good Lord, part of the gospel underpinning of the track.

The music is gorgeous. Though Taylor's lead lines go hither and thither, they don't seem intrusive, nor does the drumming, which – for all the criticisms of this album's mix – is wonderfully subtle, Watts dampened so as not to spoil the beatific mood.

Just to hammer home both the beatific and celestial air, Jagger talks of angels beating their wings in time, simultaneous with which – sublimely – a female choir punches in. This passage in particular is made all the more poignant by the rumour that this song may have started out as being a valediction to the recently-deceased Brian Jones. A heavenly track, in both senses of the word.

34. DOO DOO DOO DOO DOO (HEARTBREAKER)

AVAILABLE ON CD ON *GOAT'S HEAD SOUP*
November 1972-June 1973

Though they were considered the spokesmen for their generation in the Sixties, how many protest songs did the Stones write in that disaffected decade? If we define a protest song as a composition which unequivocally complains about a specific injustice, the answer is none. There is an argument for saying that the first track they ever released which came close to being a conventional protest song was 'Sweet Black Angel', the *Exile* cut that paid tribute to American black rights activist Angela Davis. That latter song had its heart in the right place but was a little too opaque to be effective – few would know what its subject was if Jagger hadn't explained it in interviews. 'Doo Doo Doo Doo Doo (Heartbreaker)' was the second Rolling Stones protest song and, despite its vaguely silly title, a pretty decent number on that level. Because its target is scattershot and not really political – who could really not be opposed to dealers selling smack to 10-year-old girls and trigger-happy cops? – it's really a 'safe' protest song. There also arises the issue of culpability in one of the issues addressed.

Joe Strummer of The Clash, in reference to the drug allusions that had littered Stones lyrics as far back as 1966, once said that the Stones were responsible for killing people by saying drugs were cool. Even so, the song is genuinely moving. Additionally, on another level – a sheer musical one – it's brilliant.

The Stones are taking their cue for this track not from Bob Dylan's acoustic broadsides but from funkier protest antecedents like The Temptations' 1970 hit 'Ball Of Confusion' and Marvin Gaye's 'What's Goin' On' (1971). The song starts with a space-age keyboard sound, courtesy of Billy Preston. The second chorus features a gorgeous sweeping horn section and segues into some equally expansive and strikingly pretty soul vocal decorations courtesy of Jagger, Richards and Taylor, before an instrumental break in which Taylor treats us to some appropriately lachrymose electric guitar work. In the fade, brass, clavinet and vocal lines meld to glorious effect.

35. ANGIE

AVAILABLE ON CD ON *GOAT'S HEAD SOUP*
Recorded November 1972–June 1973

The issue of who inspired this song is really as irrelevant as the fact that Paul McCartney began writing 'Hey Jude' as 'Hey Jules' as a fleeting idea to comfort John Lennon's son Julian over his parents' divorce. Just as McCartney merely used that swiftly-abandoned idea as a springboard to a track that was about something else entirely, so the Stones took

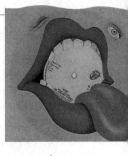

the name Angie – either from Angela Bowie, wife of Mick's good friend David Bowie, or from Keith Richards' daughter Angela – and used that to write a quite amazingly convincing song about a couple driven to separation by poverty.

Richards devised the chord structure and put the word 'Angie' to it. Jagger then added a lyric, and it was his idea to add strings to the result. Mick Taylor provides an utterly lovely acoustic guitar introduction which has us ready to have our hearts broken even before, first, Nicky Hopkins' elegant piano and then Jagger's tender vocal appear over the horizon. As often happens, Jagger's singing skirts parody in places through its self-consciousness but not so much that he turns us off as he begins recounting the tale of a couple who are gradually realising that their love is doomed. One critic memorably described the vista Jagger conjured as "patchouli-scented squalor" and you can see what he means. Jagger emotes to the titular girl that with neither loving in their souls nor money in their coats, it is time they said goodbye. That, and the vintage of the song, puts into one's head a picture of a pair of twenty-somethings caught in that strange overhang of the Sixties that was the early Seventies, the verities of the hippies and the counterculture now seeming not quite so concrete as the world rolled on with them having made no discernible impact on it. The musical accompaniment is perfectly complementary, although the sweeping orchestral strings are not any more emotionally devastating than Hopkins' utterly beautiful piano break. Just to twist the knife in our hearts further, Jagger wraps up – to the background of a swirl of strings – by telling Angie, "They can't say we never tried."

At the time, NME critic Nick Kent dismissed 'Angie' as "a dire mistake on as many levels as you care to mention" and "atrocious". One can understand the mentality behind that comment: ballads were tainted with the sexlessness and lack of grit in popular music before rock, therefore this was selling out or somehow retrograde. However, 'Angie' can now be re-evaluated – removed from any socio-political significance it may have once had – as nothing less than one of rock music's greatest ballads.

For the record, when Richards' daughter Dandelion aka Angela got married in 1998, she was led down the aisle by her dad to the strains of this song.

36. IT'S ONLY ROCK 'N ROLL (BUT I LIKE IT)

AVAILABLE ON CD ON *IT'S ONLY ROCK 'N' ROLL*
Recorded July 1973–February 1974

It seems symbolic that this song was a composing collaboration between Jagger and the man who would eventually replace Taylor in The Rolling Stones, Ronnie Wood, then guitarist of The Faces. It in fact featured only Jagger from the then-line-up of the band on the basic track, The Faces' Kenney Jones providing the drums, Willie Weeks the bass, and Ian McLagan the keyboards (later replaced by Ian Stewart). Richards

overdubbed some guitar parts but Taylor doesn't appear on the finished record. Recalls George Chkiantz, "I got called up at 11:30 at night by Mick saying, 'We need an engineer and we need one now. It's all hot – can you come round to Ronnie Wood's house?' So I drove myself round there and found this studio in the bottom and we got together the basic track."

Like 'Brown Sugar', the inaugural recording – or at least its basic elements – was retained because its attractively wasted ambience was considered unimprovable. The lyric is in the long tradition of songs like Danny and the Juniors' 'Rock And Roll Is Here To Stay', The Showmen's 'It Will Stand' and about a dozen of Chuck Berry numbers, i.e. songs declaring the validity of rock in the face of an attitude (usually from parents) that declared it trash not far above the level of cavemen bashing rocks together. Only Jagger was insisting on the medium's worth not to Joe and Eva Jagger but to – we suspect – his wife. Bianca never did think much of the rock 'n' roll lifestyle, and possibly rock itself. If indeed the refrain is Mick's justification to a spouse who thought the whole profession juvenile, how ironic that Bianca should have brought about yet another iconic Stones anthem: no Stones concert would now be complete without this message of defiance. Also ironic is that Mick Taylor dismissed it as an attempt to "write something in the classic Stones style". A further irony is that the song is only rock 'n' roll in the widest sense: by 1974, all white popular music had come to be termed 'rock' – even mid-tempo tracks like this.

37. TILL THE NEXT GOODBYE

AVAILABLE ON CD ON *IT'S ONLY ROCK 'N' ROLL*
January-May 1974

The final Stones track on which Mick Taylor recorded parts has a chorus where the narrator insists he will be thinking of the person to whom he is saying goodbye. Not only is that an almost eerie coincidence, the song constitutes a hell of an epitaph for the guitarist.

Some have suggested this track is a throwaway. Wrong. It would be a throwaway in lesser hands. In the Stones' hands, it is an exercise in superb craftsmanship. The song calculatedly opens with an emotive acoustic guitar figure, moves into a manipulative Jagger vocal that sees him inject the right amount of cracked-voice emotion as he offers to take his lover out to dinner before their latest separation, which conversation is interlaced quite cynically with Latinesque acoustic guitar to ratchet up the emotion and leads into a chorus decorated at the crucial juncture with a meaningful piano glissando. Utter cliché it might sound on paper, but the Stones were something other than mere rock mortals and, with their hands on the tiller, all these ingredients become examples of a perfectly reasonable – admirable, even – means to an end of creating a convincing ballad. (As if to ram home the quasi-generic nature of this exercise in balladry, Nicky Hopkins almost cheekily ends it with a piano triplet.)

Such is the affecting cumulative effect of those adroitly-judged sound elements that it is not even undermined by the fact that Jagger seems to be talking about an extra-marital conquest from the French Quarter. As if it needed it, Taylor ups the emotional ante with slide guitar, which of course always sounds like weeping.

38. HEY NEGRITA

AVAILABLE ON CD ON *BLACK AND BLUE*
Recorded April 1975-February 1976

"Inspiration by Ron Wood" reads the addendum to this song's publishing credit of "Jagger/Richards". An identical 'explanation' of Wood's contribution was tacked on to 'It's Only Rock 'N' Roll'. "There were a lot of 'inspired' days like that," Wood later sardonically remarked.

Wood's 'inspiration' here seems to have been the utterly splendid gilded-splinters riff, as close as any guitarist has ever come to making his instrument sound like a fistful of razor blades.

Not that the rest of the band are exactly maladroit. Watts' drumming – as it is on everything else on *Black And Blue* – is big and brutal, ramming home every musical point with a sort of haughty malevolence. Jagger's lyric, meanwhile, is wonderful. The title refrain was inspired by something shouted admiringly at his wife in reference – from what one can gather – to her Latinesque beauty, Jagger paints a picture of a poor man soliciting a lady whose price turns out to be higher than he can afford, which arouses considerable anger in said lady. The manner in which Jagger relays this exchange is part of the track's considerable strength. Jagger has never had a conventionally great singing voice but with a certain style of song – one that lends itself to playful or buffoonish vocal stylings – he excels. He whoops, yodels and growls for all he's worth on this gritty comedy. The way he enunciates the woman's threat to tan his ha-a-de is delightful.

39. MELODY

AVAILABLE ON CD ON *BLACK AND BLUE*
Recorded January 1975-February 1976

American rock critic Robert Christgau was one of the minority of reviewers to see the considerable merits of *Black And Blue* (although his album grading of A-minus was pushing it a bit). In his review, he commented that the record was "More blatantly imitative of black-music rhythms and styles than any Stones album since *December's Children*". Indeed, here was a Stones first: a jazz track. Clearly times had changed since the early days of the "Rollin' Stones" when they had to pretend to be a jazz band even though they hated the music because jazz clubs would not book R&B groups.

Once again, we have an "inspiration by" credit on this alleged Jagger/Richards track. The inspiring individual was Billy Preston, a supremely gifted black keyboardist who hailed from Houston, Texas. Though a few years younger than Jagger and Richards, Preston had been a veteran of the music business considerably longer than they. A true prodigy, he was playing keyboards for Mahalia Jackson at the age of ten. Though he had a string of solo albums to his name from 1963 onwards (and would have several Seventies hits, including two US No.1s), he is probably best known as a session musician. Preston was also widely-loved for his infectious and gregarious personality, though sadly he died in June 2006.

Preston's elegant electric piano contributions to both sides of The Beatles' 1969 'Get Back'/'Don't Let Me Down' single earned him a unique accolade: the only person with whom The Beatles ever shared billing on a record label on an official release. Speaking of the Fab Four, perhaps the hero/anti-hero divide between The Beatles and the Stones was right after all: the moral gap between The Beatles' generous (even unnecessary) credit for Preston and the Stones lack thereof is quite marked.

'Melody' is a piano ballad with a vocal duet between Jagger and Preston. The two trade lines in a story about a man abandoned by a freeloading lover, lines which impressively use the idiom of the jazz song (the man talks of looking for the woman like a mustard for a ham). Though Preston had the technically superior singing voice, Jagger acquits himself very well, this being one of those quasi-comedy numbers to which his talent is best suited. As usual, he really exults in one particular line, this one being the promise to roast the feckless lady alive. The icing on the cake is the brass section towards the end, one that definitely does have that swing.

40. CRAZY MAMA

AVAILABLE ON CD ON *BLACK AND BLUE*
Recorded January-November 1975

Rod Stewart was once rendered into a state of apoplexy when a journalist said of his 1978 single 'Hot Legs' that it was a "Stones-type boogie". "Why is it Stones boogie music?" Stewart erupted. "Why the Stones all the time? Is that the only other band you can compare it to? That's not a yardstick for everybody to measure up against, surely?" Well, yes, Rod, but like it or not, the term "Stones-type" has become a convenient form of shorthand to describe a particular variety of music and 'Hot Legs' fitted that description perfectly (even if it was a rather clunky and hackneyed example of it.) Basically, we are talking about a staccato, usually raspy guitar riff, a dense rhythm track, a melody that vaguely or overtly sounds like somebody's national anthem and a tempo that is not necessarily fast but is usually one meriting the adjective swaggering, or at least strutting. To be precise, it was the style in which The Rolling Stones played during the Mick Taylor years. (The preceding years were marked more by no style other than eclecticism and the succeeding ones by a brittler, thinner tone.) They would never really return to it, post-Taylor. How appropriate then that 'Crazy Mama' sees the Stones saying goodbye to that sound in style, for this is that "Stones-type boogie" taken to the absolute limit.

The vignette described in the lyric sounds like it is set in a neighbourhood to which you would not want to pay a nocturnal visit. The instrumentation, like so much of *Black And Blue*, uses open spaces and a prominent rhythm track (on which Richards plays bass) to create something gargantuan-sounding. Richards comes up with an archetypal scruffy riff, which is then joined by a sort of harmony riff, also played by Richards. The brutality of Watts' drumming on this album is particularly apt here. Mick, naturally, tackles with relish lines about such things as busting knees with bullets. The result is like the band's trademark sound magnified several times – "Stones-type boogie" to the nth degree.

41. MISS YOU

AVAILABLE ON CD ON *SOME GIRLS*
Recorded December 1977

How startling is the introduction to this record. After a lifetime of playing mostly Check Berry-derived R&B and rock 'n' roll, the Stones decided to have a go at an exercise in the disco medium that came to prominence in the late Seventies. They mastered it effortlessly, as indicated by an opening that – instead of cacophonously trying to impress with its authenticity – is jaw-dropping in its calmly understated nature.

Musically, 'Miss You' started life with a bass riff supplied by Billy Preston, who picked up Wyman's instrument and started vamping on it after a recording session. Wyman developed it from there. Preston also suggested a four-on-the-floor bass drum part to Jagger, who was writing the song during the band's ill-fated venture to Toronto in 1977.

What is particularly remarkable is that, although the track doesn't feel in any way inauthentic, the band take precisely what they need from disco and spurn its faults. Though the '70s disco genre produced many brilliant records, its major deficiency was that it was overbearing in its relentless buoyancy and suffocating in its insistence on filling up every spare second with sound (even if those sounds were often utterly infectious). In short, you wouldn't want to listen to a whole album of it. By speeding and slowing for emotional emphasis and dropping out instruments when they feel it necessary, the Stones allow this song to breathe. It is also unusually slow for a disco record. However, though the pace is stately and the band take their time getting across their message – alternating verses with lengthy cooing falsetto passages – the song is by no means without passion. And that's passion, not horniness: this is a Jagger that we rarely see, vulnerable, confessing unequivocally his love to his absent partner, admitting he is lying to himself by pretending there's anybody else for him, even going so far as to ridicule (hilariously) the *machismo* of a friend who rings him and offers to bring some chicks round.

Very unusually, the song's riff is not played on guitar but electric piano (by Ian McLagan).

The riff is repeated at various points by Jagger's falsetto, Sugar Blue's brilliant harmonica and Keith's and Ronnie's chanted back-up vocals.

Jagger's vocals are amongst the finest of his career: swooping and fluttering to meet the emotional requirements of the lyric. Behind him the band are stunning, sounding almost like another group in their temporary setting aside of the rocking Stones style for a tight, gleaming, utterly-of-its-time dance floor confection. Wyman's funky, endlessly interesting basslines are particularly impressive.

Slick, modern, youthfully energetic, this was a Rolling Stones for a new age, and its brilliance is such that it is undiminished by the fact that they subsequently fell back on bad habits.

42. RESPECTABLE

AVAILABLE ON CD ON *SOME GIRLS*
Recorded October 1977-March 1978

In this song's opening couplet Jagger declares with heavy irony that the Stones are now respected in society and no longer worry about the way they were once perceived. This leads into a verse that sarcastically declares, "We're so respectable". It was of course his riposte to the likes of Malcolm McLaren, Johnny Rotten, Joe Strummer and multitudinous other punk icons who had declared that the Stones were

Establishment. It was the only musical statement the band made about the unexpected flank on which this rash of detractors had attacked them. Unless of course, we count the fact that the album this number resided on features a primal rock energy that hadn't been seen much on Stones albums for several years.

It's rather a shame that Jagger didn't sustain the original subject of the song and instead switched in the second verse to bad boy sloganeering (or is that conceptual?) which seemed to take in Margaret Trudeau (presumably the target for comments about the easiest lay on the White House lawn) and Bianca (ditto for comments inviting someone to take his wife away permanently).

The promotional film for this track featured the Stones kicking their way through the walls of a house, something as ostentatiously punk as the suspiciously newly-short haircut Jagger was to be seen sporting in it.

Jagger plays guitar on a Stones track for one of the first times here.

43. BEFORE THEY MAKE ME RUN

AVAILABLE ON CD ON *SOME GIRLS*
Recorded March 1978

Those detecting a timbre to 'Before They Make Me Run' which seems slightly different to the rest of the *Some Girls* album would be correct. It was the only track not to be mixed by Chris Kimsey, courtesy of a decision by Richards – who sings it – to employ Dave Jordan (who

helped mix *Love You Live*) to record it in Jagger's and Wyman's absences. Consequently, we have a track that doesn't quite chime with the bright and brittle tenor of its surroundings but instead has some of that lethargic-but-in-a-good-way ambience of the Stones circa 1971-74. In one way, though, the song does fit in with the rest of the record, its reflective tone giving it something in common with *Some Girls*' generally thoughtful tone. At the time of its writing, Richards had yet to hear that he was not going to face drug trafficking, rather than possession, charges and had determined to kick the heroin habit that he had had for the better part of a decade. No doubt the fact that his bail conditions stipulated continued drug treatment played its part, as did the fact that if he could tell a judge in future that he had cleaned up it might lead to a lenient sentence; but – listening to the lyric of this song – there can be no doubting the sincerity of his increasing disgust with smack and the underworld those in its thrall necessarily sink into. When he talks of waving goodbye to another good friend, he is speaking from bitter, bitter experience – and possibly imagining the ghosts of drug casualty friends and acquaintances like Gram Parsons and Jimi Hendrix hovering over his shoulder as his pen traced the lyric. Meanwhile, the essential shallowness of the friendships forged in the drug *demi-monde* – dealers ostensibly glad to see you but in reality only interested in your money – is summed up in a reference to there not being a dry eye in the house as he leaves town. No wonder he adds, "Gonna find my way to heaven, 'cos I did my time in hell". The chorus – in which he announces he's had fun but that he's determined to walk before anyone makes him run - manages to be almost anthemic at the same time as it's humble. This is far from the braggadocio of a lot of Stones songs, or the glorification of drugs of *Sticky Fingers* and *Exile On Main St.*

What was it that someone once said about growing up in public?

44. BEAST OF BURDEN

AVAILABLE ON CD ON *SOME GIRLS*
Recorded October 1977-March 1978

If the sales potential had not been diluted by it being the second, not the lead-off, US single from *Some Girls*, 'Beast Of Burden' could conceivably have made No.1 in the States, such is its prettiness, catchiness and vulnerability. (*Some Girls*, incidentally, was the first Rolling Stones album to yield three singles in one country, 'Shattered' following 'Beast Of Burden' in America.)

Richards provided the melody and Jagger the lyric of this song. Some of Richards' comments indicate that he actually provided Jagger with the words of the chorus and certainly some have interpreted the song's sentiments as Richards' message to Pallenberg, from whom he would soon become permanently estranged. Jagger possibly trivialized whatever message Richards may have intended with the falsetto section in which he sings "You're a pretty, pretty, pretty, pretty, pretty girl". However

such is the beauty of the number that this slightly silly part comes across as endearing rather than irritating. The listener can forgive just about anything when confronted with a track that is heart-rending from its opening moment: the lurching guitar line that sees it spring to life yanks the strings of the ticker before Jagger has even opened his mouth.

Mid-tempo rather than slow, it had actually started out at a faster clip, but when the group began to play it in a mellower vein – albeit retaining electric instrumentation – they nailed it in one take. The result was a sweet contrast to the sometimes exhausting punk frenzy of some of the rest of the album. As Richards put it, "After all the faster numbers on *Some Girls*, everybody settled down and enjoyed the slow one."

45. DOWN IN THE HOLE

AVAILABLE ON CD ON *EMOTIONAL RESCUE*
Recorded June-October 1979

This Jagger/Richards song apparently had a major Ron Wood input. It was by far the best track on a very lazy album.

Though essentially a blues number, the Stones were by now far too infused with commercialism to render it as a bog-standard 12-bar. Dispensing with the tradition of the repetition of every second line and absolutely cramming the track with diverting instrumentation, they make something new and vital of a now archaic form. Sugar Blue – who helped make 'Miss You' such a great record

– makes a very welcome return, this time staying mostly in the background but adding a crucial tone of foreboding to a song that sees the narrator almost taunting somebody down on their luck.

Lines about bartering for nylons in the American Zone seem to place the song in a smouldering, devastated Berlin immediately after the end of World War II. Appropriately, the guitar lines are like twining wisps of smoke from exploded shells. Jagger's drama-teasing singing – apart from one unfortunate moment when he slips into his Mockney accent – is very good. The way that he turns a simple line like "Looking for cover and finding out there ain't nowhere to go" into an elongated, hiccupping, switchbacking epic is quite miraculous. As is the revelation by Jagger and Wood in an interview that this magnificently evocative track took a maximum of two takes to perfect.

The song was also released as the B-side to the 'Emotional Rescue' single. Although the latter achieved a respectable chart placing, it did not earn much kudos. A track like 'Down In The Hole' would almost certainly not have generated such a high chart placing if released as a single (mind you, if 'Tumbling Dice' could be a hit, why not?) but it would certainly have, at least temporarily, silenced those who thought the Stones no longer capable of coming up with vital-sounding records.

46. START ME UP

AVAILABLE ON CD ON *TATTOO YOU*
Recorded January 1978-June 1981

Perhaps it would be unkind to say that 'Start Me Up' was rescued from the dustbin, but there is certainly a tinge of that in the way Chris Kimsey fished this out of the middle of a spool of tape long after the band had just about forgotten about it, and suggested to them that it could be turned into something significant. Jagger had a listen to it and agreed. Realizing the power of Richards' riff, he wrote a new lyric to the basic track. The result was a massive world-wide hit, and probably the last iconic Rolling Stones song.

The track had slipped the band's memory because they had started out on a wild-goose chase with its nature early on. By the time that goose chase failed, they simply didn't remember the original, more worthwhile direction. "It was from *Emotional Rescue*," Mick later explained. "It was just sitting there, and no one had taken any notice of it. There were like 40 takes. What happened, I think, is we made it into a reggae song after, like, take 12, and said, 'Well, maybe another time'. I used take two." Richards said, "We ... realized that was what we wanted all along. ... It was just buried in there. Nobody remembered cutting it, nobody remembered doing it... It was like a gift."

Jagger's lyric posits a man and his lover as automobiles, thus creating all sorts of opportunities for car metaphors ("My hands are greasy, she's a mean, mean machine", etc).

Despite the hairy hoof, Microsoft paid an undisclosed sum for the rights to use 'Start Me Up' to launch Windows 95.

The line about the woman being able to make a dead man come heard toward the end probably originates from an obscene ditty called 'Shave 'Em Dry' ("I got something 'tween my legs can make a dead man come,") which, Stanley Booth revealed in his book *Dance With The Devil*, Richards had had on a home-made compilation tape back in 1969.

Since 1989, 'Start Me Up' has often been awarded the accolade of being used to start a Stones concert.

47. HEAVEN

AVAILABLE ON CD ON *TATTOO YOU*
Recorded October 1980-June 1981

What was one of only two songs to be recorded especially for the *Tattoo You* album turned out to be one of its highlights. (And the other, 'Neighbours', its nadir.) Brought into existence by Jagger toying with a chord sequence on

guitar while he, Watts and Wyman awaited the arrival of Richards and Wood, it saw Chris Kimsey contribute some basic piano as he gamely joined in the 'blow'. Kimsey indicated to his assistant that he should record what was happening.

Though what was laid down might originally have been rather slight and threadbare (Richards and Wood never did add a contribution), a certain amount of treatment of the components made it sound substantial indeed. The guitar arpeggios are garnished with sustain to create a dreamy effect. Charlie's tapped-drum edges are also given a little subtle echo. Jagger's vocal – comprising sensual, impressionistic snatches of phrases like "Kissing and running away" – is also awash in reverb. Consequently everything has inexact margins and the elements – including discreet synthesizer from Wyman – meld into one another. The result is an impressionistic paean to lovemaking that is as light as a cloud.

So gossamer is this track, in fact, that 'No Use In Crying' – which sounded so gentle, if bittersweet as the flip of 'Start Me Up' – sounds positively brutal following on its tail on the album.

48. UNDERCOVER OF THE NIGHT

AVAILABLE ON CD ON *UNDERCOVER*
Recorded January-August 1983

Another Stones protest song recorded long after the Stones' supposed years of social relevance. This one concerns the 'disappeared' of Latin America, and the fact that Chile and Argentina were at that time bloodbaths.

Strangely, Jagger – for it is 100 per cent his song, lyric and melody – doesn't mention El Salvador, where America was supporting, training and arming death squads or Nicaragua, where it was trying to overthrow an elected Leftist government using a guerrilla army whose methods were not completely dissimilar from those of the Salvadorean death squads. This is not because Mick is chickening out of criticizing the government of the country that had been the Stones' most lucrative market from the mid-1960s onwards: he's hardly pulling any punches with lines about prostitutes' Johns in bars being American G.I.s on Rest & Recreation from Cuba and Russia. Yet by making the subject so wide as to take in both Chile (a country whose dictator, Pinochet, had been installed by an America that didn't like its elected Marxist leader, Salvador Allende) and Argentina (which had no real history of American interference and whose bloody feuds were homegrown) he's putting out an inchoate message – unless it's, ooh-er, what a bunch of murderous in-fighters Latinos are. Obviously, that's not what Jagger intended – and at least he's not committing the offence of many Leftists at the time of excoriating America for its sins while ignoring those bloodbaths America was not responsible for – but he runs the risk of rendering his commentary without a target. There's also a danger of trivializing the terrible facts he is dealing with. When he curls his lips around the phrase "South Ameerrricah" in

that distinctive drawl, things seem in danger of getting very dodgy for a moment. There is also the unfortunate fact that he seems incapable, even when writing a song of this magnitude and seriousness, of not writing a chorus featuring the word "baby".

The song has an infectious yodelled vocal riff to go beside the muffled machine-gun guitar lick. The musical backdrop is percussion-heavy, the consequence of it initially being worked up by Jagger and Watts, and highly funky. "Mick's calculations about the market," is how Richards dismissed it but the result – given plenty of reverb effects to add to the drama – made it at the time one of the most energetic and worthy Stones single of recent years.

49. ONE HIT (TO THE BODY)

AVAILABLE ON CD ON *DIRTY WORK*
Recorded April-October 1985

On that unfortunate album *Dirty Work*, we get an opener that makes us believe at least temporarily that all is actually well in the Stones camp – and almost as good as ever.

The decision to make the introductory riff an acoustic one puts one in mind of 'Brown Sugar'. The brain behind this idea – and this time he actually got remunerated for his 'inspiration' – was that of Ron Wood. Engineer Dave Jerden recalled, "He was trying to come up with an electric guitar part and it wasn't grooving enough, so he went out and started banging on the acoustic. Woody's really great at coming up with ideas like that." The acoustic riff then melts into an electric riff of some foreboding, a dramatic progression which causes the pulse to quicken in excitement.

The lyric sees Jagger proving that after more sexual conquests then he could ever remember, he can still be physically captivated by a new woman. Because the atmosphere is so dramatic, we can accept this as a bewitched state of mind rather than mere brainless horniness. Jimmy Page is given a 'While My Guitar Gently Weeps' role – i.e. just as The Beatles uniquely handed over a guitar solo to a superstar guest for the only time on that track, the Stones were doing so here. Page doesn't really live up to this privilege – the Led Zeppelin maestro doesn't do anything here that the supposedly non-virtuoso Richards didn't do better in the middle of 'Sympathy For The Devil' – but does provide an interesting contrast to normal Stones fretwork, especially in the manic fade out.

50. ALREADY OVER ME

AVAILABLE ON CD ON *BRIDGES TO BABYLON*
Recorded February-June 1997

This number went through a bit of a wild-goose chase before its style was settled on. Always open as he is to new ideas, Jagger asked producer of the moment Babyface to helm this track on *Bridges To Babylon*. He then found that the modern results weren't working. "It was really my fault – I threw the wrong song at him," he later said. "We went in and wrote the loops and the programs. We got Charlie to play on it. And in the end, I didn't

like the way it was looped." It was decided that, after all that, it would be best served by being rendered as a Stones ballad in the classic tradition. The result is a track to stand beside all but their very greatest slowies.

We know that something special is afoot by the lovely burble of acoustic and electric guitar at the beginning. In fact, this track, though a tender ballad, is awash with guitar. Crucially, the stringed instruments are not strummed but picked, including Wood on haunting dobro and some tumbleweed-connection, wild-west acoustic. There's also a couple of sweet, slow, up-the-neck guitar solos, and some discreet cushioning piano.

The lyric seems to bespeak an aching loneliness behind Jagger's Lothario lifestyle, with him lamenting the way a fling with an exciting-seeming woman has turned into a feeling of being used. The chorus refrain of "What a fool I've been", has a real poignancy. Though nearly five-and-a-half minutes in length, the track in no way outstays its welcome. In the middle of *Bridges To Babylon* – a veritable nothing of an album with nondescript melodies and lyrics and singing that sounds devoid of anything but artifice – it's a small miracle of emotional sincerity and melodic integrity.

"You have to tour. That's really when a band is a band."

Bill Wyman
Miami Herald, 11 June 1978.

Odds & Sods

Like any band comprising such diverse talents, and often contrasting creative ideas, and enjoying such a long lifespan, the individual members of the Stones have become involved in a number of byroads in their careers.

SIDE PROJECTS

BRIAN JONES

The great sadness of Brian Jones' death is that when it happened he was apparently on the verge of making his own music for the first time – that is, music with a vocal melody line as well as chord changes. His fans will have to suffice with his soundtrack to the 1967 film *A Degree of Murder* – available here and there, legally and illegally – and the *Pan Pipes of Joujouka* album. The latter – commercially released in 1971 as an actually quite touching gesture by his ex band-mates on Rolling Stones Records and now available on CD – is a collection of six pieces of music (one of which lasts more than 18 minutes) recorded in Morocco in March 1969 featuring nothing more than percussion, brass and flute. A bold move – and the claims made for the record as the very first world music (i.e. a Westerner giving artistic credence to sound forms not immediately assimilable by those raised on western classical and popular music) are plausible but

frankly, the record does not do justice to Jones' reputation as a musical adventurist. Firstly, because he doesn't play a note on it. Secondly, because the efforts of the 'master musicians of Joujouka' are simply boring. One can imagine that this music would have a throbbing power in the flesh, but on record – emanating from a mere sound system – it is repetitive, samey, monotonous, ululating and inchoate – and one doesn't have to be a "psychic weakling" of Western civilization (to use Jones' phrase from the liner notes) to be of that opinion.

JOHN PHILLIPS: *Pay Pack and Follow (2001)*

The friendship between John Phillips and Mick Jagger is as little known as it seems unlikely. As the artistic force behind The Mamas and The Papas, the organizational brains behind the 1967 Monterey Pop Festival and the composer of Scott McKenzie's 'San Francisco (Be Sure To Wear Some Flowers In Your Hair)', Phillips would seem to be the epitome of the flower power that the Stones tried so unsuccessfuly to get into step with. However, mates they were, even if it was a friendship tested by Phillips'

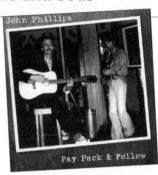

John Phillips

Pay Pack & Follow

fling with Blanca and Jagger's own tryst – it's said in retaliation – with Philips' daughter. The access Phillips enjoyed to the Stones resulted in the music on this album. Richards (credited with Jagger as producer), Jagger (backing vocals and co-writing one song), Ron Wood (on bass) and Mick Taylor all appear. Recorded from 1973 to 1979, it goes without saying that it features some fine playing. It also boasts some decent songs (Phillips had a slew of classics to his name so was not exactly a pygmy to the Stones' giants) as well as a pleasant, easy-rolling production gloss. Sadly for Phillips, he died on the very eve of a release that had been delayed by the tapes being lost.

NICKY HOPKINS, RY COODER, MICK JAGGER, BILL WYMAN, CHARLIE WATTS:
Jamming With Edward (1972)

In April 1969, during the making of the *Let It Bleed* album, Keith Richards failed to turn up for a recording session. Whether the cause was drug fuelled inertia or a disinclination to share the same room as Ry Cooder has not been

firmly established but those present decided to kill time with a blow, or jam. As those present were some of the finest musicians on the planet – Jagger, Watts and Wyman being joined by Ry Cooder, and Nicky Hopkins what resulted, though naturally inchoate – a jam is a collective musical doodle – was also occasionally fascinating. "It was great, it was a really good fun jam," said George Chkiantz, who was engineering that evening and was one of the people who agitated for its release. When Rolling Stones Records did indeed retrieve it from the vaults for commercial release in January 1972, Jagger's sleevenote indicated a somewhat more ambiguous attitude: "It was promptly forgotten (which may have been for the better) until it was unearthed from the family vaults... As it cost about $2.98 to make the record, we thought that a price of $3.98 was appropriate for the finished product. I think that that is about what it is worth. No doubt some stores may even give it away... I hope you spend longer listening to this record than we did making it." Though there are clearly elements of 'Midnight Rambler' in 'The Boudoir Stomp', this – and all other originals – are credited to "Hopkins, Cooder, Watts". Wyman mysteriously only receives a performer's credit. It's not as worthless an artefact as Jagger's fuck-you sleevenote implies but neither does it live up to Chkiantz's enthusiasm. Let's just say that each of these jams are better than 'Sing This All Together (See What Happens)', the rambling psychedelic improvisation that closed side one of *Satanic Majesties*.

BILL WYMAN

MONKEY GRIP (1974); STONE ALONE (1976); GREEN ICE (1981, SOUNDTRACK); BILL WYMAN (1982); DIGITAL DREAMS (1983, SOUNDTRACK); STRUTTIN' OUR STUFF (1998, WITH THE RHYTHM KINGS); ANYWAY THE WIND BLOWS (1999, WITH THE RHYTHM KINGS); GROOVIN' (2000, WITH THE RHYTHM KINGS); DOUBLE BILL (2001, WITH THE RHYTHM KINGS); JUST FOR A THRILL (2005, WITH THE RHYTHM KINGS); BILL WYMAN'S RHYTHM KINGS LIVE (2005)

Though it wasn't his choice, Wyman was the first Stone to release a solo single ('In Another Land'). It was his choice to release a pair of solo albums in the mid-Seventies, making him the first Stone to issue a long-playing effort of his own. *Monkey Grip* and *Stone Alone* were pleasant enough exercises and one could imagine them being worthwhile had the Stones been playing on them and Jagger belting them out. However, Wyman's delivery, and some of the production, was so gentle that, despite the undeniable craftsmanship of his writing, the records lacked sonic impact. Wyman also became the first Stone to have a hit when his delightful '(Si Si) Je Suis Un Rock Star' went No.14 in the UK. Its corresponding album *Bill Wyman* (1982) was again quite good but somehow flat, the presence of another quality single '(A New Fashion') notwithstanding. The salutary fact about Wyman's career is that the most interesting project he has been involved in is one on which he handed his songs over to other people to sing. Producing (and sometimes composing with) UK psychedelic group The End, he managed to create an album – *Introspection* (1968) – that was arguably better than *Satanic Majesties*.

Stone Rock Blues

CAROL – CHUCK BERRY / LOOK WHAT YOU'VE DONE - MUDDY WATERS / LITTLE QUEENIE – CHUCK BERRY / MONA – BO DIDDLEY / YOU BETTER MOVE ON – ARTHUR ALEXANDER / AROUND AND AROUND – CHUCK BERRY / I JUST WANT TO MAKE LOVE TO YOU – MUDDY WATERS LITTLE RED ROOSTER – HOWLIN' WOLF / YOU CAN'T CATCH ME – CHUCK BERRY / NOT FADE AWAY – THE CRICKETS / COME ON – CHUCK BERRY / SUSIE Q – DALE HAWKINS / CRACKIN' UP – BO DIDDLEY / MANNISH BOY – MUDDY WATERS / I'M TALKING ABOUT YOU – CHUCK BERRY / I CAN'T BE SATISFIED – MUDDY WATERS / BYE BYE JOHNNY – CHUCK BERRY / ROLLIN' STONE – MUDDY WATERS (MACA/CHESS; 1994)

An album that rounds up the original and/or definitive versions of several songs made famous by the Stones. The songs that gave the band their name – whether it was 'Mannish Boy' or 'Rollin' Stone' – are also present. The set is restricted to recordings owned by the Chess label, except 'Not Fade Away', originally released on Brunswick. It's also a little heavy on Chuck Berry numbers – but then so were the Stones' early albums and EPs. It's a useful collection that serves to both make an interesting contrast between the Stones' recordings and the originals that inspired them, and to provide a musical education for those curious about the band's roots.

The Music

MICK JAGGER

NED KELLY (1970, SOUNDTRACK, ONE TRACK ONLY);
PERFORMANCE (1970, SOUNDTRACK, ONE TRACK ONLY);
SHE'S THE BOSS (1985); PRIMITIVE COOL (1987); WANDERING
SPIRIT (1993); GODDESS IN THE DOORWAY (2001); ALFIE (2004,
SOUNDTRACK, WITH DAVE STEWART)

Nothing, literally nothing, has caused as much long-running anguish in the Stones camp as the solo career that Mick Jagger embarked on (discounting the 'Memo From Turner' single and 'The Wild Colonial Boy' on the *Ned Kelly* soundtrack album) in 1985. Considering the critical and commercial failure of that career – the sight of his first album adorned with discount stickers not long after its release was a shocking reminder to both him and the public that the Stones' always-high record sales would not necessarily translate to a solo career even for the frontman – Jagger can be forgiven for thinking it was all a waste of time and a massive aggravation. Richards clearly thinks so and described the poor sales as a "dash of cold water" for Jagger. Whatever, the sales level though, Jagger has made some interesting music on his own. *She's The Boss* and *Goddess In The Doorway* are artistically negligible, as is his 1985 cover of 'Dancing In The Street' with David Bowie, but his middle brace of albums are genuinely worthwhile. *Primitive Cool* saw him dropping the posturing that he seems to think must inform all his Stones lyrics these days for an honesty and confessional approach that was quite disarming. Musically, his most successful album was *Wandering Spirit*, which encompassed rock, folk, funk and even a bizarre Irish sea shanty. Whisper it lightly for fear of ridicule but both the latter albums are better than the best Stones albums of the past two decades. Additionally, he and his collaborator Dave Stewart won a Golden Globe for the song 'Old Habits Die Hard', which features on their joint soundtrack to the 2004 remake of the movie *Alfie*.

KEITH RICHARDS

TALK IS CHEAP (1988); LIVE AT THE HOLLYWOOD
PALLADIUM (DEC. 15, 1988) (1991); MAIN OFFENDER (1992)

Though Richards' grudgingly acquiesced to a solo career to fill up the time created by Jagger's solo ventures, he had actually released a record on his own as far back as 1978 when he issued a cover of Chuck Berry's Christmas ditty 'Run Rudolph Run'. He was also the first Stone to tour under his own steam, playing gigs in 1979 with the New Barbarians, which included Ronnie Wood. *Talk Is Cheap* got sycophantic reviews from journalists who had decided to take sides in 'World War III' but was surprisingly less than stellar. Keith of all people should have known not to work with a drummer – Steve Jordan – whose monotonous thumping was not even in the same universe as the ability of the sticksman with whom he usually played. Still, he had little choice: Jordan co-wrote all of the songs with him. Most were okay and there was one great number, the sensual 'Make No Mistake'. The follow-up *Main Offender* was similar fare. Apart from a live album with his backing group the X-Pensive Winos, he has done nothing else on his own, apparently having satisfied any desire or curiosity he had in that direction.

CHARLIE WATTS

LIVE AT FULHAM TOWN HALL (1986); FROM ONE CHARLIE (1991); A TRIBUTE TO CHARLIE PARKER WITH STRINGS (1992) WARM AND TENDER (1993); LONG AGO & FAR AWAY (1996); CHARLIE WATTS/JIM KELTNER PROJECT (2000); WATTS AT SCOTT'S (2004)

With a long tradition of popping up at gigs on the London jazz-club and pub circuit unannounced, and notable side ventures with Rocket '88 (alongside Alexis Korner and Jack Bruce) and his own Big Band, it is still quite a startling fact that since 1986 Charlie Watts has released half a dozen albums under his own name. None have really registered on the public radar. One also assumes that the ever self-effacing Watts was extremely embarrassed that the releases bore his handle rather than those of his collaborators.

As somebody who merely drums on all the releases – all of which contained either classic jazz songs or new songs written by people other than Watts – it's clear that giving him billing was the idea of the relevant record companies. The most interesting release for Stones aficionados was 1991's *From One Charlie*, a tribute to Charlie Parker which came with a facsimile of Watts' 1964 book *Ode To A High Flying Bird*, original copies of which now sell for ridiculous amounts on bibliophilic internet sites.

MICK TAYLOR

MICK TAYLOR (1979); STRANGER IN THIS TOWN (1990); TOO HOT FOR SNAKES (1991, WITH CARLA OLSON); LIVE AT 14 BELOW (1995); A STONES' THROW (1998); KNIGHTS OF THE BLUES TABLE (1997, ONE TRACK ONLY); GUITAR SPEAK III (1991, ONE TRACK ONLY)

The lead guitarist of The Rolling Stones' middle period had big plans when he left the group. However, career disappointments (a highly intriguing partnership with Jack Bruce ultimately led to nothing) and disillusion (he once said that he didn't bother making albums anymore because he received no money from playing on some of the biggest selling albums of all time) have taken their toll. Most of his subsequent releases have been intrinsically dispensable live albums, records with ill-advised cash-in titles like *A Stone's Throw* (in fairness, probably not his idea) and records featuring groan-inducing covers of the hoary likes of 'Jumpin' Jack Flash' and 'Little Red Rooster'. His one real substantial release is 1979's *Mick Taylor*. It's a quietly impressive album. Taylor's guitar work is naturally brilliant. He also turns out to be a unexpectedly good and confident singer. It goes without saying that the album lacks the spark to make it something special – the spark that, say, comes from having the greatest band in the world behind you – but at the same time it's easily a better album than *Emotional Rescue*, released not long afterwards. Interestingly, according to David Dalton's *First Twenty Years* book, one of the tracks on it, 'Leather Jacket', was actually recorded by the Stones during the *Exile* sessions.

RONNIE WOOD

I'VE GOT MY OWN ALBUM TO DO (1974) ; NOW LOOK (1975) MAHONEY'S LAST STAND (1976; SOUNDTRACK; WITH RONNIE LANE); GIMME SOME NECK (1979); 1234 (1981); LIVE AT THE RITZ (1988; WITH BO DIDDLEY); SLIDE ON THIS (1992); SLIDE ON LIVE (1993); LIVE & ECLECTIC (1988); NOT FOR BEGINNERS (2002)

Ronnie Wood has had far the most prolific extra-curricular career of any Rolling Stone. This is partly, of course, because of the fact of his coming late to the fold. His pre-Stones work with The Birds, The Jeff Beck Group, The Creation, The Faces and Rod Stewart is all worth listening to to some degree. He formed a formidable writing partnership with Rod Stewart which graced the latter's solo albums and Faces albums (although the better stuff seemed suspiciously more likely to end up on Stewart's own records). Wood inaugurated his solo career in 1974 with *I've Got My Own Album To Do*. It followed the pattern of his subsequent releases: an impressive array of big name mates (Ian McLagan, Keith Richards), song contributions from superstars (two Jagger/Richards numbers) and a couple of high quality tracks by him was not enough to lift the album out of the merely passable. It is clear by now that Wood can make valuable contributions to ensembles but doesn't quite have the ability to create great art on his own. One looks forward with increasing frustration to the resuscitation of his writing partnership with Rod Stewart that has long been promised. A superb sampling of his entire career is provided by the 2006 compilation *Anthology: The Essential Crossexion*.

STONES RARITIES

FORTUNE TELLER/POISON IVY

The pairing originally intended to constitute the Stones' second single release was eventually abandoned in favour of 'I Wanna Be Your Man' b/w 'Stoned'. They were initially only released on a 1964 BBC *Saturday Club* compilation album, although also appeared in the States on the *More Hot Rocks* best-of, albeit in noticeably different mixes.

TELL ME BABY, HOW MANY TIMES

Recorded in Chicago in 1964, this Big Bill Broonzy song has only turned up on the 1980 German compilation *For Collector's Only* and the *The Rest of the Best* German box-set.

I'VE BEEN LOVING YOU TOO LONG

The Otis Redding classic (written by Redding and Jerry Butler) recorded Los Angeles, May 1965. The album *Got Live If You Want It* (1966) saw it released with crowd noise overdubbed but sole studio version release details as above.

CON LE MIE LACRIME

An Italian language version of 'As Tears Go By' recorded in 1966, it also appeared on the above compilations from the enterprizing Germans.

STREET FIGHTING MAN

Four months before its appearance on *Beggar's Banquet*, this song appeared as a now long-deleted single in America in a provocatively violent picture sleeve. It is discernibly distinct from the album take, with different vocals and more prominent piano.

COCKSUCKER BLUES

The notorious 'fuck-you' to Decca recorded at Olympic in 1970 has, naturally, never been released officially – except by those enterprizing Germans again, who employed it as a 7-inch bonus single with *The Rest Of The Best*. The fact that it quickly ceased to be issued with said box-set indicates m'learned friends may have been in touch.

SWAY

Released as a B-side to the US-only 'Wild Horses' single, this version of the song is longer than the *Sticky Fingers* version.

ALL DOWN THE LINE

B-side to the US single 'Happy'. The take is a different one to the *Exile* version.

NOTE: *Stones rarities have become less rare numerically since the advent of the CD age and the fashion for multiple B-sides to the same single: non-album live versions of Stones chestnuts particularly now proliferate.*

10 UNRELEASED STONES RECORDINGS

1. LITTLE BOY BLUE AND THE BLUE BOYS

Mick Jagger's childhood band recorded themselves on the reel-to-reel tapes people used in those days. A cache of thirteen songs were sold at auction at Sotheby's in 1995 by a former band school friend, with Jagger allegedly the buyer (for £50,000).

2. CURLY CLAYTON SOUND STUDIOS

Three tracks recorded by a bass-less Stones with Tony Chapman on drums in October 1962 at the above-named studio. One of them, 'You Can't Judge A Book By The Cover' was broadcast on radio in 1988.

3. THE IBC DEMOS

The five songs cut under the auspices of Glyn Johns in April 1963. The version of 'Road Runner' here is unexciting – in contrast to the way that The Animals' Hilton Valentine scraped his pick down a guitar string to imitate the titular cartoon animal on their version – but otherwise this recording does lives up to Brian Jones' estimation of it as quintessential Stones. 'Bright Lights Big City', despite its callow Jagger vocal, is nice and smooth (Ian Stewart's piano very audible), 'Beautiful Delilah' sounds like it is being transmitted by telephone but this actually gives it a sort of murky attractiveness while an assured rendition of 'Diddley Daddy' is startlingly gentle with pretty cooing backing vocals.

4. ANDREW'S BLUES

Not exactly artistically impressive, but this 12-bar blues jam from February 1964 boasts a profane lyric depicting Andrew Oldham in obscene situations, and has scurrilous references to the chairman of Decca.

5. HONKY TONK WOMEN – PARIS CUT

An alternative version of the Stones' classic that, as well as boasting audible piano, features an additional verse set on the boulevards of Paris in which Mick suggests he would as soon partake of the erotic delights of sailors as the titular ladies.

6. YOU GOT THE SILVER (JAGGER VOCAL)

Sounding as though it's recorded over a different backing track to the familiar Richards rendition of this song, Jagger's vocal sounds remarkably similar to his colleagues' in terms of which words he stresses and which parts he emotes on.

7. MEMO FROM TURNER (THIRD CUT)

It's not entirely certain whether either of the two commercially-released versions of 'Memo From Turner' are *bona fide* Rolling Stones recordings. A third recording would seem to exist: Al Kooper recalls overdubbing guitar

on an already recorded version in late 1968, one that he says does not sound like either the Jagger or *Metamorphosis* versions.

8. CLAUDINE

Recorded for *Some Girls*, this song, about Claudine Longet who secured an acquittal for killing her partner after claiming that the gun had gone off accidentally, was suppressed for legal reasons, although the uncomfortable fact of a teenage boy dying in Anita Pallenberg's bedroom through a gunshot wound may have had something to do with it.

9. DRIFT AWAY

Recorded at the *It's Only Rock 'N' Roll* sessions, this sweet, respectful version of Dobie Gray's laidback paean to the therapeutic properties of popular music was probably never intended to be anything other than a warm-up. It would make a good album track all the same.

10. RICHARDS' TORONTO RECORDINGS

In mid-March 1977, stranded in Canada following the bust and having been left behind by his colleagues, Richards went into Sounds Interchange Studios in Toronto with Ian Stewart for a very strange recording session. Here, sitting at a piano and with despair evident in his voice, he laid down five country songs taught him by Gram Parsons, one of which – Merle Haggard's 'Sing Me Back Home' – is about a man facing the electric chair.

INFLUENCES

The Rolling Stones emerged unashamedly as blues and R&B aficionados at a time in America when this was seen as solely black or 'race' music and, as far as the older blues musicians were concerned, was in decline. Much has been written about how it was the 'British Invasion' of the States in the early-to-mid-Sixties – in which the Stones were at the vanguard – which served to remind Americans of their deep-rooted folk legacy. Consequently, by the end of the decade, black performers like Muddy Waters and Albert King were appearing regularly on the same playbills as Jefferson Airplane and the Grateful Dead. In their home country however, the Stones were confronted by some local competition.

ROBERT JOHNSON

Robert Johnson was a bluesman who recorded a small but massively influential catalogue of recordings in the mid-1930s. Although the Stones only covered two of his songs on record – 'Love in Vain' and 'Stop Breaking Down' (they also performed his 'Walkin' Blues' at the *Rock And Roll Circus*) – Johnson was a big influence on Jagger, Jones and Richards back in the days when they were utterly immersed in the blues. So devoted is Richards to Johnson

that he owns a copy of his death certificate.

Johnson (of whom only two verified photographs exist) is a figure surrounded by myths, the most famous of which is that he did a deal with the Devil: his soul for technique. This rumour sprang from his sudden graduation from a mediocre guitarist to a man whose recordings sounded like there was another picker accompanying him. Songs like 'Hellhound On My Trail', 'Me And The Devil Blues' and 'Crossroads Blues' strengthened this myth. They and other recordings were covered by many giant Sixties and Seventies artists including Eric Clapton, Cream, Bob Dylan, Fleetwood Mac and Led Zeppelin.

BO DIDDLEY

As with Robert Johnson, Bo Diddley had an influence on the Stones' sound not immediately discernible by looking at the number of songs of his that appear on their records (three: 'Mona' and live versions of 'I'm All Right' – credited to Nanker, Phelge – and 'Crackin' Up'; additionally their version of 'Not Fade Away' brought to the fore the trademark Diddley rhythm). The pre-fame days saw their sets peppered liberally with the songs of the man born Elias McDaniel. Whereas Johnson probably had a more psychological impact on the group – affirming their belief in the power of the blues and their decision to pursue it – Diddley's influence was more direct, their nightly renditions of his material impacting on their own burgeoning ideas about how they might construct original songs, as well as arrange those of others.

Diddley actually had few chart hits himself but, in the early Sixties, the UK R&B scene was awash with his gritty, pounding R&B compositions: 'Bo Diddley', 'Diddley Daddy,' 'Mona,' 'Road Runner' and 'Who Do You Love?' were all much covered. He was also responsible for the most famous versions of two Willie Dixon songs, 'Pretty Thing' and 'You Can't Judge A Book by Its Cover'.

MUDDY WATERS

Muddy Waters was the sort of Elvis of Chicago blues: not known for writing his own material but an indisputably important and iconic figure in its history and with a host of well-loved and well-known (to its aficionados) recordings to his name. As mentioned previously, one way or another, he also gave The Rolling Stones their name.

Waters was the foremost practitioner of the Chicago electric blues sound (a style he himself called 'deep blues'), a designation applied to the new form of blues created by blacks moving from the rural areas to the nearest big city in which work was plentiful that was accessible on their local railway line in the Thirties and Forties, in which process they upgraded their previously rustic sound.

Among songs with which Waters (born McKinley Morganfield) is the main artist associated are 'Hoochie Coochie Man', 'I Just Want To Make Love To You', 'I've Got My Mojo Working', 'Mannish Boy' and 'You Shook Me'. Though he wrote infrequently, two of his songs, 'Baby Please Don't Go' and 'I Can't Be Satisfied', were covered by Them and the Stones respectively, while 'Rollin' And Tumblin'' has become a blues evergreen.

JIMMY REED

Another artist whose songs studded the Stones' sets at Ealing and the Crawdaddy. From Reed the Stones – one can postulate – learnt both that raw primitivism is nothing to be ashamed of, nor great hooks and tunes. Reed had a knack for R&B numbers that almost sounded like pop songs, so instantly hummable were they. Among them were 'Ain't That Loving You Baby', 'Baby, What You Want Me To Do' (his most well-known song), 'Big Boss Man' (not written by him but made famous by him), 'Bright Lights, Big City', 'Honest I Do' (recorded by the Stones) and 'Shame, Shame, Shame' (ripped off by the Stones for 'Little by Little'). Hand in hand with this melodic accessibility went a kind of punk approach: the most that could be said about Reed's singing, guitar work and harmonica playing was that he tried hard. Very unusually, Reed secured crossover hits, hitting the *Billboard* Top 100 a dozen times with the type of R&B then highly rare on the national charts.

When the Stones wanted to calm down the

agitated crowd at the Altamont festival, they played Reed's 'The Sun Is Shining'.

Reed's life was something of a tragedy, him drowning himself in alcohol for much of it, something which caused his epilepsy to be undiagnosed for several years, and his fits to be put down to the effects of drink. He died at the age of 50 in 1976.

WILLIE DIXON

Though he was also a musician – on stand-up bass – the name Willie Dixon was never found on many record covers but appeared with ridiculous frequency in the parentheses beneath song titles on record labels. As Richards once remarked, "I was looking at Muddy Waters records, and who wrote it? 'Dixon, Dixon, Dixon'. And the bass player is writing these songs? And then I'm looking' at Howlin' Wolf: 'Dixon, Dixon, Dixon'. I said, 'Oh, yeah, this guy is more than just a great bass player!'" A veritable one-man blues and R&B Brill Building (although his songs were always too leery of the formulaic to ever be comfortably accommodated by any genre description), Dixon's – often innuendo- laden – compositions included 'Back Door Man', 'Evil', 'Hoochie Coochie Man', 'Spoonful' and 'Wang Dang Doodle', as well as a couple of songs very familiar to Stones fans, 'I Just Want To Make Love To You' and 'Little Red Rooster'. He also wrote three songs very familiar to Led Zeppelin fans: 'Bring It On Home', 'You Need Love' (renamed 'Whole Lotta Love' by Zeppelin)

and 'You Shook Me'. Unfortunately, the names in the parentheses on Led Zeppelin records were usually – and often mysteriously – those of Jimmy Page and Robert Plant; Dixon had to take legal action for his rightful share and credit for the first two mentioned.

SLIM HARPO

One could name any number of R&B merchants as an influence on the Stones: in the early days, they covered songs by more people than anyone will ever remember. Representing those myriad artists here is Slim Harpo. Born James Moore, his music was laid-back and populist. The Stones covered a couple of his songs on record a decade apart, 'I'm a King Bee' and 'Shake Your Hips'. Additionally, his creation 'Got Love If You Want It' inspired the punning title of their live EP and their first live album (see page 162).

HOWLIN' WOLF

In 1965, The Rolling Stones were asked by US TV pop programme *Shindig* to make an appearance. Asked if they wanted a guest, they requested Howlin' Wolf. This is a measure of Wolf's influence on the group, one that, as with Bo Diddley and Jimmy Reed can't be measured simply by the number of his songs they recorded.

The Music

Wolf – born Chester Burnett – was a discovery of Sam Phillips, a full decade before the Sun label man alighted on Elvis. Phillips had heard Wolf on the radio, where he had his own show. After a contractual tussle, Wolf ended up on the Chess label and relocated to Chicago, where he became second only in importance to Muddy Waters in the Chicago electric blues scene/ genre. At Chess, Wolf was teamed with songwriter and bassist Willie Dixon. This was something with which he wasn't completely happy – "I can do my own songs better but they won't let me", he was heard to complain – but it can't be denied that most of his most famous and celebrated recordings were Dixon numbers, including 'Evil', 'Back Door Man', 'Spoonful' and 'The Red Rooster'. The latter, of course, was recorded by the Stones as 'Little Red Rooster' and became arguably the only blues number ever to top the UK charts (depending on which chart you consult.) The Stones also recorded another Wolf-recorded Dixon song, 'Little Baby', on *Stripped*. As if to prove his point that he was capable of writing his own material, a couple of Wolf's compositions – 'Smokestack Lightning' and 'Killing Floor' – themselves became standards.

Wolf's recordings were characterized by an almost supernatural menace. The Stones seem to have taken their cue from this in Sixties tracks like 'Stray Cat Blues', 'Sympathy For The Devil', 'Gimme Shelter' and 'Midnight Rambler'. Whatever the extent of the debt they owed him, they attempted to pay it back via the *London Howlin' Wolf Sessions*, a 1971 release by Rolling Stones Records on which Wolf was backed by a host of top rock stars, including the Stones' rhythm section and Eric Clapton.

CHUCK BERRY

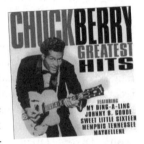

Many blues aficionados of the type the Stones ran into back in the days of the Ealing Club despised rock 'n' roll idols like Berry. To them, rock was the sell-out variant of R&B/blues, a shamelessly commercial cartoon. Yet, while Keith Richards yields to no man in his admiration for the likes of Robert Johnson and Muddy Waters, he still unapologetically retains an almost teenage-like devotion to Chuck Berry.

Not that Berry's music was actually easily categorizable as rock 'n roll. Although he – always cannily commercial – designed material like 'Roll Over Beethoven' and 'Rock & Roll Music' to provide adolescents with defiant anthems with which to bolster their solidarity about parental disapproval of their favourite music, his songs sounded as much R&B as rock.

They also sounded slightly different to everything else, what with his strangely elongated guitar licks and lyrics creating highly descriptive tableaux of middle American life. His list of hits and famous songs is ridiculously long but as well as the aforementioned they include 'Back In The USA', 'Carol', 'Johnny B. Goode', 'School Day', 'Sweet Little Sixteen', 'Memphis, Tennessee' and 'No Particular Place To Go', all sung with his incongruously clear diction.

As well as the fact that they covered more than half a dozen of Berry's songs on record, along with some songs made famous by Berry like 'Route 66', evidence of Berry's influence on the Stones can be heard in the guitar work of original Stones numbers as varied as 'Star Star' and 'Gimme Shelter'. "I lifted every lick he ever played," Richards once proudly said of Berry.

THE BEATLES

Stones aide Tony Sanchez once recalled how, when the Stones threw a party to launch *Beggar's Banquet*, Paul McCartney turned up with an acetate of the next Beatles single, 'Hey Jude' b/w 'Revolution', and put it on the turntable. Jagger could be observed scowling at the way The Beatles had upstaged the Stones yet again.

The story seems to be apocryphal – 'Hey Jude' actually appeared four months before *Beggar's Banquet* – but it does sum up the way that the Stones, though acknowledged as rock giants themselves from around 'Satisfaction'

onwards, spent the Sixties in The Beatles' giant shadow. Like everyone, they were influenced by the Fab Four by default: The Beatles' reinvention of what was possible for a British band in terms of self-composition, group format, image and song-structure filtered down to the consciousness of everyone in the same profession. However, some considered the Stones to exhibit a monkey-see, monkey-do approach, among them John Lennon, who said in 1970, "I would like to just list what we did and what the Stones did two months after, on every fucking album and every fucking thing we did." He had a point. The Beatles released the chamber music ballad 'Yesterday', the Stones followed suit with 'As Tears Go By'. The Beatles used sitar on 'Norwegian Wood', and subsequently so did the Stones on 'Paint It Black'. *Sgt. Pepper's Lonely Hearts Club Band* had carnivalesque tones and a dazzling cover. Likewise *Their Satanic Majesties Request*. The white cover of *Beggar's Banquet* followed hot on the heels of the similarly blank sleeve of The Beatles' eponymous double '*White*' album.

In retrospect, at the end of the Sixties the impression of the Stones as perennial followers, not leaders may have just been about to change, and it could be the case that the Stones overtaking The Beatles as the world's most important rock artists was only prevented by the fact of The Beatles' split. Support for this is provided by comparing the group's respective album releases in 1969, *Abbey Road* and *Let It Bleed*: for the first time, the Stones had put out a better album than The Beatles.

Part Three: Stonesology

"*These performers are a menace to law and order, and as a result of their formula of laryngitis, cranial fur and sex the police are diverted ... to quell the mob violence that they generate.*"

Daily Mirror, August 1964.

The Stones in Person

MICK JAGGER

Born Dartford, Kent 26 July 1943

Michael Philip Jagger has rather fallen from grace in recent years. Though he was always hated by 'decent' society, he was also once widely admired, his rebellious image lending him an air of integrity and alternativeness. Now he is often perceived not only as more conformist than rebellious but faintly ridiculous due to his ageing Lothario lifestyle, and even despicable for the extramarital affairs that destroyed his relationship with Jerry Hall.

Jagger had an upbringing that is pejoratively referred to as bourgeois. Mother Eva's self-consciousness about her Australian roots seemed to engender an ultra-conformism. His father, meanwhile, was a PE teacher, and instilled a certain discipline in him in this respect which has stood him in good stead in his later years – his rigidly adhered-to workout programme means he is incredibly fit for a man of his years – but which amazed young friends like Dick Taylor, who recalled to Anthony Scaduto how Jagger's father intercepted the two on the way out one day and insisted his son do his barbell exercises before they left. Mick complied uncomplainingly.

Though Jagger's upbringing – which he shared with his brother Chris, younger by four years – may have been strait-laced and stuffy, it would seem to have been reasonably loving. People frequently remarked on how well he got on with his parents as an adult. Yet Jagger certainly seemed to hold grievances about the strictures of his childhood. Paul McCartney was once taken aback – when both he and Jagger were beginning their careers – at a diatribe Jagger launched against "old people", in which he seemed to include his own parents, something to which McCartney – close to his own dad – could not relate. In the Edith Grove days, Jagger also took what seems a pointed decision to abandon his Received Pronunciation (or BBC voice) for the Mockney accent he retains to this day. There also seems to be a cold – or perhaps uncertain – core to Jagger that makes one wonder what flaw in his upbringing might have led to it. Keith Altham has commented on the fact that Jagger doesn't seem to have any genuine friends, something endorsed by comments by Richards. An apparent terror of showing his real self is a theme running through Jagger's behaviour, one manifestation of which is a bizarre tendency to imitate the accent of whoever he is speaking to.

Jagger has always been the modernizer in the Stones, insisting on them adopting new musical trends and utilising voguish producers to remain relevant to the music consumer. Richards, of course, thinks the band's strengths lie in their blues and R&B roots. Each thinks they are right and has something of a contempt for the other's standpoint. Neither will ever understand (as is the nature of these things) that it is precisely this push-and-pull, or yin and yang, which creates the dynamic that has led to their survival. Without Richards' steadying hand, Jagger would possibly have abandoned anything about the Stones' music which gives them an imprimatur – and therefore a point – while without Jagger to shake him out of his Chuck Berry ghetto, Richards would never have countenanced something like 'Miss You' or the fast tracks on *Some Girls*, which made the group of interest to a new generation.

As a plainly vain man – he insisted on having hair to his shoulders long past the point where it was seemly – it must grieve Jagger that his face is now in a state that could be described as raddled. Leaving aside the fact that he looks very good for a man approaching his mid-sixties, the contrast between him now and his remarkable beauty when in his twenties and thirties must be a heartbreaking prospect when he peers in a mirror. Not that he seems any less popular with women. However, his propensity to bed females three times younger than he seems another manifestation of the terror of ageing that Richards lamented during 'World War III'. It certainly seemed to be what ultimately destroyed his relationship with Jerry Hall, something that he appears to regret bitterly if we can interpret the lyric of 'Biggest Mistake' on *A Bigger Bang* as autobiographical.

Yet Jagger is patently not a bad person. While maybe not having many intimates, he is a reasonably friendly individual. He is also a warm and loving parent to all of his children – no matter what the circumstances of their conception or his relationship with their mother.

Even his alleged meanness seems exaggerated. An absolute Scrooge does not donate £100,000 to his old grammar school for a music centre, as he did in 2002, nor help buy singer Don Covay a bus with a chair lift after he had suffered a stroke, as he and the other Stones did in the mid-1990s.

Jagger seems to have had plenty of good times in his life but never found true happiness. Both Richards and Watts have professed confusion – or amazement – that Jagger does not seem a happy man, despite the talents, riches and loved ones he possesses.

KEITH RICHARDS

Born Dartford, Kent 18 December 1943

The difference between Richards – ex-of Dartford Technical College – and Mick Jagger – alumni of Dartford Grammar School – is superficially an obvious one. Richards has no interest in the acting, film producing, cricket websites or any other professional activity in which his fellow Glimmer Twin has engaged. Richards is a music man to the core of his being, famously able to sit working on guitar progressions for hours on end while all others around him peel away or sit with eyes glazed through boredom. Yet, though he might have failed his 11-Plus examination and thereby failed to get into grammar school, and though he may be a man of simple tastes, Richards is no idiot, as can be gleaned from this observation from him about Jagger's apparent friendlessness: "I understand the desperation of somebody like that, the insecurity that says, 'Until I am sure of myself I can't let anybody get too close, or I'll get really confused'."

Richards has latterly – by which is meant since the mid-Seventies – come to be seen as the Stone who retained his integrity. As Jagger socialized with MPs, Lords and Princesses, Richards spurned their elevated types for Rastafarians in Jamaica. While Jagger was perceived to be selling out his non-conformist principles, Richards was picking up nicknames like the 'Human Riff' and 'Mr Rock and Roll' that alluded to his supposedly perennial status of rebel and outlaw. His warmth, informality, self-awareness and friendliness are also spoken of by those who have got to know him.

That party line should not be bought without some profound reservations. Richards – and Anita Pallenberg – were deeply irresponsible in becoming junkies while bringing up young children. Their habits may well have been a factor in the death of their son Tara. Though Richards' love for his son Marlon is disputed by nobody, their daughter Angela (originally Dandelion, born 1972) was neglected by he and Pallenberg, leading Mick and Bianca Jagger to try to pick up the parental slack. Meanwhile, Tony Sanchez alleged a highly disturbing incident in Richards' life. In *Up And Down With The Rolling Stones* – the details of which book Richards went on record as stating were basically true – he related an incident from the Seventies in which Rolling Stones Records president and fellow junkie Marshall Chess rang Richards begging for help: having split a newly-bought batch of heroin with Richards, he had become paralyzed down one side after taking some. Richards hung up

on him twice and it was only because Sanchez answered the phone the third time that Chess's life was saved: Sanchez rushed around to help him. Richards, it subsequently emerged, refused to believe that the heroin had been adulterated, the denial of a man who thought getting a fix less relevant than dying. "That wasn't the action of any kind of friend at all" is Sanchez's version of what Chess said of the incident.

The Mr. Rock and Roll tag at least is justified. Richards' singular style created many of the visual clichés of rock. That self-invented shoulder-length mane of tangled hair he sported in the Seventies was the ultimate rock hairstyle and was imitated endlessly, as was that habit of having a cigarette jutting from his mouth at a diagonal angle while peeling off a lick. He is even responsible for Pete Townshend's supposedly trademark windmilling guitar playing style, The Who man having seen Richards do it at an early Stones gig at which his band played support.

Richards famously has an almost eerily unhuman constitution, able to stay up for days on end, before crashing into a sleep of several days duration. However, he has now reached the stage where he seems to live up to a caricature of himself, to such an extent that he even remarks on his image in interviews. It's also faintly embarrassing for any Briton to hear him call all and sundry "baby", although admittedly he has been an American resident since the late Seventies.

He has accepted ageing relatively well, refraining from dyeing his hair or making a conquest

Stonesology

of every passing female like his Glimmer Twin. Similar lack of ego seems to have attended his loyalty to the concept of the Stones: being celebrated as 'merely' a part of a unit rather than as an individual artist never caused him the same anguish that (initially) motivated Jagger's solo career. Though his marriage to Patti Hansen has apparently encountered some difficulties, it remains intact and his love for his two daughters with her is undeniable. In a sweet comment to a journalist when his daughters by Hansen were toddlers, he said that it broke his heart to have young children wandering around saying "I love you daddy". He has also belatedly established a good relationship with Angela.

BRIAN JONES

Born Cheltenham, Gloucestershire 28 February 1942: died 3 July 1969

When Jagger and Richards approached the so-called Elmo Lewis on that fateful day at the Ealing Club in April 1962, they were confronted by a highly unusual young man. Though only 5' 7", Lewis Brian Hopkin Jones had the barrel chest and broad shoulders of a man with a much bigger physique. He was also extraordinarily handsome, with finely chiselled features and a mop of hair more golden than blonde. In addition, he possessed clipped tones that were thoroughly incongruous in the sweaty and semi-bohemian environs of the Ealing Club on an R&B night. Though Jagger was indubitably middle class, Jones was actually posh. Not that this inhibited Jones'

lifestyle. A hedonist who had rejected the dentistry ambitions held for him by his parents, he had already sired two illegitimate children, an utterly scandalous state of affairs in an era when unmarried mothers were still frequently sent to homes to be 'reformed'.

On the surface, the young Jones was hardly pop stardom material. He had firstly the handicap of his background. The blues scene in his home of Cheltenham – a West Country town whose name rarely appears in print without the adjective 'genteel' attached to it – was naturally extremely small. But then, such environs – blissful for the middle-aged and old but tedious for the young – are possibly what originally made him yearn for the unconventional, which category artistic expression is for some reason always shoehorned into. As presumably did his family background. Jones was, to use an expression that most certainly would not have been heard in his household, a 'fuck up', amazingly insecure for someone of his material comforts, looks and capacity for personal charm. Stones aide Tom Keylock told writer Terry Rawlings, "Brian's father was one of the strangest blokes I've ever met... I remember once when the Stones played in Cheltenham, his parents came backstage and Brian turned to me and said, 'Don't let them in, I don't want to see them... I'll fucking freak out if you let them in.'"

Ian Stewart told Stanley Booth, "He had a very good education ... but ... he decided he was going to be a full-time professional rebel, and it didn't really suit him. So that when he wanted to be obnoxious, he had to really make an effort, and having made the effort, he would be really obnoxious." But there seems to have been something more to his almost psychotic shortcomings than merely kicking against background strictures. "There was something very, very disturbed about him," Jagger later said. "He was very unhappy with life, very frustrated. He was very talented, but he was a very paranoid personality and not at all suited to be in show business." This manifested itself in, amongst other things, violence toward his female partners and an anxiety to be the kingpin of the band.

Jones' increasing resentment at having to play on Jagger/Richards compositions was an insane and untenable position for a band to be in. Yet it's not quite as simple as that for, in between the sulks, the disappearances and the depressions, Jones graced the songs of Jagger and Richards with some superb instrumental decoration. In so doing, he proved – apparently without realizing it – that he had absolutely no reason to be insecure about his abilities. Perhaps he would never have developed the capacity to write songs, but he was one of the foremost innovators and experimenters in Sixties rock and pop, and his ability to master any instrument he chose to was the mark of a genius.

Bill Wyman thinks Jones was an undiagnosed epileptic. It's tempting to also suggest he was an undiagnosed schizophrenic. What else are we to make of the fact that Anita Pallenberg has referred to him as both "Talented, funny" and as "quite a bully"? Ian Stewart, in the same breath as his comments above, also said,

"Brian was really quite a sweet person."

Richards has recounted that he said to Jones, "You'll never make thirty, man" and that Jones replied "I know." "There are some people who you know aren't going to get old," Richards explained. Yet though when found in his swimming pool, Jones' body contained traces of drugs, everybody around him swears he had vehemently renounced them. Suspicious contradictions in eyewitness evidence surrounding the night of his demise abound.

By 1969, Jones seem to have become possessed of a colossal fatigue, exhausted not just by the harassment of the police and his personal and professional disappointments but – one likes to think – his own hitherto hysterical, clinging personality. Watts has said, "He got much nicer just before he died."

The irony is he died at the very point in his life at which he least deserved to.

BILL WYMAN

Born William George Perks, Penge, Kent 23 October 1936

"Some lead, some follow," is how Bill Wyman once summed up his dutiful, quiet work in his 30-year tenure with The Rolling Stones.

Wyman never did fit in easily with the Stones. Not only was he modest, uncharismatic and much older, but he did not take drugs. Jagger and Richards – and sometimes Jones – gently mocked him. "I went through a period that lasted several years where I was the scapegoat for funny remarks and sarcastic comments," he later recalled. However, there was one huge wrinkle in his façade of conventionality: far from square in sexual matters, he racked up more conquests than even Jagger. This led to him forming an unlikely friendship with Brian Jones, the only other Stone in the early days who was into groupies. Wyman's predilection for the ladies was in no way inhibited by the fact that he had been married to Diane since 1959, a marriage that was kept secret at the time as it wasn't considered good for the image of pop stars to be betrothed. Wyman came from probably the poorest background of any Stone, one of five children of a bricklayer. He changed his name by Deed Poll in 1964, although he had been calling himself Wyman, after a friend in his National Service days in the RAF, for some time.

He was the first Stone to release solo records and the first Stone to secure a solo hit single. He started the Sticky Fingers restaurant in 1989 – a place to nosh whose walls are covered in rock memorabilia – and at one point was earning more money from it than from the Stones.

The assumption for many years was that he was either a cipher or boring, he being neither handsome nor extroverted and fitting in with the tradition of the 'Quiet One' bass guitarist. All of that was rent asunder in 1986 when the press broke the story that he had had an affair with a thirteen-year-old girl named Mandy Smith. Many naturally thought badly of him for this episode (although in mild mitigation the fact that the two later married, albeit briefly, suggested this was more a rush of blood to the head caused by love than predatory behav-

iour). Wyman's most significant relationship before his Nineties marriage however was that with Swede Astrid Lundstrom, with whom he was involved for 17 years starting in late 1966 and with whom he remains on friendly terms. Richards, after ridiculing him for so long, spoke fondly of Wyman in *According To The Rolling Stones*, saying, "I love Bill dearly. He's a very funny guy with a very dry wit."

Wyman certainly showed stoicism in the face of his bad treatment by the Stones. He once turned up at an *Exile* session to find that Richards had wiped his bass part on two songs and overdubbed his own playing. When he complained that it sounded terrible, Richards and Jimmy Miller began laughing at him. For no good reason, Ron Wood played bass on four songs on *Dirty Work*. This sort of behaviour would make someone feel redundant in the best of circumstances but the fact that Wyman's talents on bass far exceeded Richards' and Wood's can only have added to this humiliation. Then there was the fact that his musical contributions to Stones songs never resulted in a writing credit and, aside from 'In Another Land', his compositions were never allowed space on Stones albums, even when the Glimmer Twins were hardly coming up with the goods themselves. ('Je Suis Un Rock Star' was better than almost anything on the chronologically previous Stones album *Emotional Rescue*.)

Since quitting the Stones in 1993, Wyman has played with oldies band the Rhythm Kings, and the surprisingly vigorous touring schedule he undertakes with them clearly indicates it is a labour of love: he doesn't need the money. He has also become an author, albeit one who usually works with co-authors. *Stone Alone* was followed by *Blues Odyssey* (also a two-part TV broadcast) and, *Rolling With The Stones*, *Treasure Island* (about discoveries of ancient treasures in the British isles), *Wyman Shoots Chagall* (his photographs of the painter) and *The Stones: A History In Cartoons*. He has also started a new family, in 1993 finally putting away the book in which he detailed the number of the women he bedded in exchange for a monogamous existence and the joy of raising three children with ex-flame Suzanne Accosta.

Asked in 2002 whether he regretted his decision to depart the Stones' ranks, he said, "Not for one minute. I never had a second thought about leaving the band. I get this question asked me daily – ten times a day probably if I'm doing interviews or meeting people backstage at a Rhythm Kings gig or something. I have no interest whatsoever. I'm great friends with the band socially. My children mix with Mick's kids. Jerry's a great friend of Suzanne my wife. That's the way it is: it's social now, it's family."

CHARLIE WATTS

Born Neasden, Middlesex 2 June 1941

"Charlie's good tonight, inee?" Mick Jagger remarked upon a drum fusillade at Madison Square Gardens in 1969. The response from the audience was an affirmative cheer.

Though as ostensibly 'boring' as Wyman, Watts has always enjoyed a popularity amongst Stones fans that his fellow poker-faced quiet one in the band's rhythm section never quite managed. It's difficult to see why. Though Watts has been involved in several jazz-oriented albums, Wyman has achieved far more as a solo artist. Wyman has also always been a considerably more interesting interviewee, Watts' off-hand manner and often one-word answers to questions making one wonder why he consented to speak to the media in the first place. Yet fans of The Rolling Stones have always found something lovable about this man whose face varies between comic and sinister (witness his skinhead *Black And Blue*-era look). Perhaps it's because of his complete disinterest in claiming the place in the rock pantheon that he unquestionably deserves: told that he is considered one of the all-time rock drummers, his response is a shrug, as though it is of no consequence to him. There seems no reason to believe that this is an act.

Charlie Watts' first musical love was, and remains, jazz. From the age of thirteen his ambition was to play with Charlie Parker. In 1964, he had published an illustrated children's book about Parker entitled *Ode To A High-Flying Bird*. His live and studio work in various jazz ensembles is, like Wyman's Rhythm Kings work, motivated by nothing other than enjoyment. Despite more than four decades as a rock drummer – or, at least, a drummer in a rock band – he still retains a jazzer's mentality, thinking what surrounds rock (the hype and the fan hysteria, not the music itself) "silly".

Watts, one of two children of a truck driver,

was one of those Britons who spent part of his post-war childhood in a 'pre-fab': emergency prefabricated housing that looked almost like cardboard boxes but many of which are still standing. Like Richards, he went to art school. However, his tenure at Harrow Art School is not mentioned in this book's Art School Rockers panel because Watts wasn't really of that ilk: he attended art school not to scrounge off the state while perfecting his musical talents but because he was aiming for a career in that area. This he achieved, securing a job as a designer with an advertising agency. He gave the job up for the Stones when their success was still far from assured.

Despite being widely respected for his musical skills, Watts has never displayed the virtuosity of drumming contemporaries like Keith Moon, Mitch Mitchell and Ginger Baker, opting instead for an unflashy, steady beat. As he himself said, "I'm not a paradiddle man." However, he also boasts the dexterity to add precisely the right metre, tempo or flavour required of a song: witness his exotic, Eastern patterns on 'Paint It Black', his booming soul playing on 'Satisfaction', his four-on-the-floor beat on 'Miss You' and his brutal pounding on 'When The Whip Comes Down'. His finest hour as a drummer was the *Some Girls* album, on which his unusually frenetic work only underlined the impression of a band with revitalized energies.

Watts famously hates touring but accepts it as a corollary of being a musician, which he loves. Unlike guitarists and songwriters, drummers have to come to terms as they age with a decline in ability that is beyond their control: the arms simply do not move as fast nor as steadily as they did previously. Should Watts ever be reduced to someone who can't play more than a couple of fast tracks live without needing a ballad break, it's doubtful that he'll feel much anguish about it. He once said of the Stones, "I love this band, but it doesn't mean everything to me. I don't really care if it stops."

This impression of Watts being the sanest Stone took a severe dent when he embarked on a two-year period of self-destruction in the early- to mid-Eighties in which he indulged in alcohol, amphetamines and heroin. It was behaviour so uncharacteristic that many people simply found it unbelievable. However, what was characteristic was the way he cleaned up: the impetus wasn't a drug trafficking charge but a simple decision that enough was enough and that it was time to resolve his mid-life crisis. He came off drugs with no professional help and the first the wider public knew of his problems was after he had cleaned up.

Though he often stands silently and gives off a lugubrious air, he is a popular man. Nobody dislikes Charlie Watts. Remarkably, he is genuinely good friends with both Jagger and Richards, two people who often have so little to say to each other these days. His essential decency and good nature are revealed by these touching comments from his wife, Shirley, from 1997: "He has an incredible depth of sweetness in his nature... Actually the most irritating habit he has is chewing his nails. He never, ever criticizes me so he's never told me what I do to irritate him."

MICK TAYLOR

Born Hatfield, Hertfordshire 17 January 1947

In many ways, it sometimes seems that Mick Taylor never was a Rolling Stone. Not that he wasn't massively influential or displayed vast gifts in his five-year membership. It is just that the sands of time, the colossal charisma of Ron Wood and Taylor's own subsequent lack of success in music has served to make his face and name fade. Then there is the Stalinist approach to the band's official biography *According To The Rolling Stones*, to which he (like Wyman) does not seem to have been invited to contribute, and the way that Keith Richards never seems to miss an opportunity to imply that there is somehow something wrong with being a lead or virtuoso guitarist and that interacting with fellow-rhythmist Ronnie is much more fulfilling. All of these things have served to make it seem like Taylor's tenure is a dream that never really happened.

The evidence that it did happen is there to hear in some of the most famous and remarkable rock records of all time: 'Honky Tonk Women' – his contribution to which by common consent lifted the song to new heights – *Sticky Fingers*, *Exile On Main St.* and 'Angie' among them. As mentioned previously, Taylor's very presence in the ranks caused the invention of the decadent riff-propelled Stones sound

that the public now indelibly associates with the band.

Taylor was inspired to play guitar by an uncle and although few of his family played musical instruments he recalls a childhood immersed in music. He formed his first band when he was either thirteen or fourteen. Though his parents had taken him to see Bill Haley and his Comets when young, it was R&B and blues to which he gravitated rather than rock 'n' roll. Major influences were Buddy Guy, Junior Wells, Muddy Waters, Jimmy Rogers and B.B. King. Taylor's break in the music business was not quite a let's-do-the-show-right-here fairytale but pretty close. When he was fifteen, John Mayall's Bluesbreakers had played a gig in Welwyn Garden City, near Taylor's home town of Hatfield. "Eric Clapton didn't show up for the gig and I asked if I could sit in with them and he said yes," Taylor later recounted. "He must have been quite impressed because he took my number and got in touch with me a couple of years later when Peter Green left." That Taylor's quote mentions two of the finest guitarists in Britain (if not the world) at the time indicates the level on which this precociously gifted young man was now operating. When Taylor contributed his mellifluous lines to the Bluesbreakers' 1967 album *Crusade* he was just 18.

Taylor wasn't too overawed when asked to join the Stones. Not only had he shared the bill with luminaries like Jimi Hendrix and Albert King when with the Bluesbreakers, but he saw the Stones as if not peers then people from the same British blues background as him. Nor – as his brilliant playing on their records attests – was he overwhelmed by their abilities. What does seem to have overwhelmed him is the Stones' lifestyle, particularly the drugs. By the time he left the group he was a heroin user. Though he has been too diplomatic to mention it, something that also probably affected him is the moral shortcomings of Jagger and Richards: though he hung around with Keith (and strangely, was quite friendly with Bianca Jagger), Taylor's self-effacing and shy nature meant that he had more in common with Watts and Wyman. His lack of credit for songwriting has been covered elsewhere but in an interview in 2000 he spoke darkly of lack of satisfaction over his performance royalties from Stones records. Asked if he still got compensated for the Stones records on which he played, he replied, "No, not as much as I should. Unfortunately, in this world things are not fair."

It was Andy Johns who suggested in 1974 that Taylor join Jack Bruce's new band. Taylor took up his suggestion but this exciting matching yielded gigs but no records. Taylor was given a big budget to record a solo album in the late Seventies. It was good stuff but sold badly. Nonetheless, his skills are widely enough known of for him to have been invited to play on records by people like Mike Oldfield, Little Feat, Bob Dylan (with whom he also toured) and Joan Jett.

"I felt I was their equal as a musician...in fact I ended up feeling superior", Taylor once said of the Stones. He has also admitted that when he left he thought the band was past its peak and was headed inevitably for some sort of demise. It's a cruel twist of fate then that the Stones are still thriving – commercially anyway – three decades after his departure while he plays solo gigs at small clubs in between his session work. For those who consider his contributions to the Stones underrated, though, it provides a glimmer of pleasure that this doesn't seem to upset him too much. "I'm actually enjoying playing more than I ever have," he said in 1989.

RON WOOD

Born Hillingdon, Middlesex 1 June 1947

In a sense, 'Woody', as many friends call him (and apparently he prefers 'Ron' to 'Ronnie') has had a more interesting professional background than any of The Rolling Stones. Whereas Jagger, Richards, Watts and Wyman were all in the same band from their teens or twenties, Wood was in several different groups before his stint in the Stones began, all of which were high quality and most of which made brilliant records. His pre-Stones CV comprises UK R&B group The Birds, the Jeff Beck Group (who in many people's opinion invented heavy metal), freakbeaters The Creation and The Faces. He was also principal collaborator with Rod Stewart in the solo career the latter ran in parallel with The Faces. The actually quite folky albums that Stewart made for Mercury between 1969 and 1974

– especially *Gasoline Alley* and *Every Picture Tells A Story* – contain some of Wood's most interesting and impressive recorded guitar work, a lot of it acoustic.

Wood, though, had always wanted to be a Stone. Meeting the band at the 1969 Hyde Park gig and asked by them when they were going to see him again, he claims he thought, "Sooner than you think", so sure was he that his destiny lay within the group. Little did he know that the Stones had tried to poach him mere weeks before. The late Ronnie Lane of The Faces related how he had taken the call from the Stones during the early rehearsals of The Faces, and told the caller that Wood was happy where he was. Wood only learnt of this frustrated overture in the mid-Seventies.

Wood grew up in a council house in the bosom of a loving family. His future best mate, Rod Stewart, once observed of him that Wood spoke of his father as if he were a 'hero'. Wood came from a musical family and so never had the experience of his parents pestering him to aim for a 'real' job. His older brother Art was the leader of Sixties R&B group The Artwoods. Wood, of course, was another art school rocker but actually had a genuine talent in that direction, as proven by the career he still maintains as a sideline, creating for commercial sale pictures of popular culture icons.

It is commonly accepted (i.e. this is the party line) that Wood is utterly immature but utterly lovable. Though his diplomatic skills gave him a role of mediator during 'World War III' (and possibly saved the band thereby), one can't help but get the impression that one of the reasons that Jagger and Richards hold him in such high regard is due to how supine he has been about his songwriting credits, which have – suspiciously – been as meagre with the Stones as they were common with The Faces/Stewart. This situation and his long-term salary status is something Wood may not have challenged because he wasn't in a position to. He apparently achieved the quite remarkable feat of shocking and dismaying even The Rolling Stones with his tendency for excess. Though he occasionally relapses, his dependencies are now behind him.

There are indications that the other party line about him being 'luvverley' is not completely true. Though gregarious and chirpy, his comments in *According To The Rolling Stones* display a streak of callousness. At one point he refers to the fact that Mick Taylor had sent the band a note backstage in 2003 saying, "I've got no confidence, I'm really depressed and short of cash" and seems to find it amusing more than anything. He also suggests that Bill Wyman's songs never made it onto Stones records because they were "useless". One would think that Wood would understand that the reason for both of those scenarios was the same as for his own infrequent credits.

Wood has, interestingly, in some ways filled the role in the Stones occupied by Brian Jones in the mid-Sixties. He displays Jones' ability to master just about any instrument if he turns his mind to it – although will probably never be in the latter's league as a multi-instrumentalist because of an attention span that Watts likens to that of "a gnat".

One can't help but feel that the decision to enlist Wood in the Stones – a decision they have effectively admitted was as much for personal as musical reasons - has not been ultimately good for either them or him. Richards frequently says things like, "After playing with Mick Taylor for four [sic] years, I had almost gotten used to the Stones' sound being myself and Mick Taylor's style. Woody and I can start playing together until we don't know who played the last lick. It's as close as that. We both become one instrument." He doesn't seem to understand that apart from one great honeymoon album – *Some Girls* – his and Wood's intermeshing style has increasingly led to sonic porridge where it hasn't just resulted in tinniness. Wood's and Richards' guitar interplay is simply no match for the fat, rasping power of the band's sound when Richards was working alongside Taylor. Additionally, Wood's songwriting talents have stagnated. In typically blunt style, Glyn Johns has said Wood's employment was "absurd" and that "the man was an extraordinary musician and he's being completely wasted". Observing that Wood was less a band member, more a court jester, he opined "I think that's unnecessary and it's degrading".

Almost Stones

POSSIBLE REPLACEMENTS FOR BRIAN

Though the dismissal of Brian Jones from The Rolling Stones in 1969 did not involve the intensive, formal auditioning that attended the quest to replace his replacement Mick Taylor, there are several people who either did, are rumoured to or might have crossed the minds of the band as a new Rolling Stone at the time...

Jimmy Page Bill Wyman has revealed that in 1965 the band were considering asking the now erratic Jones to leave, and had in mind the then prolific session-guitarist Page (who would have been a familiar face from Andrew Oldham's Immediate label sessions) to replace him.

Al Kooper Though his contributions to 'You Can't Always Get What You Want', were on keyboards and horn, Kooper did some guitar overdubs on an ultimately unreleased version of 'Memo From Turner' at around the same time. His multi-instrumental skills would have been the closest the Stones could have got to finding someone to replicate Jones' role as a human mellotron.

Eric Clapton Always a good mate of the Stones and kindred spirit (like Keith, he was an art school boy and steeped in the blues), Clapton was apparently discussed by the band as a candidate to replace Jones (though the Stones themselves seem vague on this). Certainly a Stones boasting the virtuoso guitar talent of the original Yardbirds, Cream, Blind Faith (with whom he was playing at the time of Jones' dismissal) and Derek and the Dominos is an intriguing alternative-universe idea. In retrospect, however, Clapton's career has proved him to be more comfortable as a (hugely successful) loner.

Dave Mason The Traffic guitarist played (uncredited) on at least a couple of tracks on *Beggar's Banquet*. (He plays the Indian instrument the shenai on 'Street Fighting Man' and mandolin on 'Factory Girl'.) A hidden man in rock but respected by his peers, he played with, amongst others, Jimi Hendrix, Wings, George Harrison and Fleetwood Mac.

Ry Cooder We shall presumably never know the truth about Cooder's allegations of exploitation by the Stones at the *Let It Bleed* sessions, nor whether, had they not had that row, the group would have asked him to join permanently. We do know that his contributions to 'Love In Vain' and 'Sister Morphine' indicated a man who had the ability to garnish Stones basic tracks for the better.

POSSIBLE REPLACEMENTS FOR TAYLOR

It's often said that the category of 'Greatest prime minister Britain never had' is one bulging at the seams. Much the same can be said

of guitarists who were supposed to have been in the frame to replace Mick Taylor in The Rolling Stones in 1975. "Even Segovia tried out," Keith Richards once laughingly said of the number of people auditioned by the band in the wake of Taylor's resignation. Actually Segovia is possibly the only famous guitarist whose name was not mentioned in connection with the job. Some were auditioned formally, some not, but all of the names below seem to have been seriously considered by the group as a Stone.

Jeff Beck The quicksilver talent of Jeff Beck is doubted by no-one. Jimi Hendrix considered him to be a superior guitarist to Eric Clapton, for instance. Unfortunately, Beck is also a notoriously idiosyncratic and temperamental individual, something illustrated by the fact that he stormed out of the chance of a lifetime that the Stones auditions represented because – according to Ron Wood – he couldn't handle a mere three chords all the time. None of his contributions appeared on the *Black And Blue* album: the band wiped his guitar work in retaliation for his sarcastic comments. A track he had worked on turned up, *sans* the Beck-isms, as 'Slave' on *Tattoo You*.

Eric Clapton (again) Clapton had had his ups and downs since a vacancy in the Stones had previously occurred. Supergroup Blind Faith had turned out to be less than super, breaking up after recording one lacklustre album.

After recording a so-so eponymous debut solo album, Clapton proceeded to put together a supposedly anonymous group containing relative nobodies and with even his own famous name disguised or downplayed – Derek and the Dominos – who turned out to be far more super than the star-studded Blind Faith. Their single 'Layla' is now recognized as a rock classic. Problems in his love life led to serious drug addiction but, by 1974, he had recorded the brilliant *461 Ocean Boulevard* solo album, which yielded the hit, 'I Shot The Sheriff', a Bob Marley cover that showed that he shared Richards' love of reggae. Ostensibly, then, the perfect candidate. However, he never approached the band and Richards has recently said, "He expected us to call, although I only just found out. 'Why didn't you call me?' 'Because you're too damn good – and your own man'. If there's anybody lazier than me, it's Eric."

Peter Frampton One of two ex-members of Humble Pie to audition for the Stones in this period. A moderately successful solo artist in '75, his name was suggested by both Ian Stewart and Bill Wyman. However, his fluid but not showy style was rejected by the Stones who mattered – or perhaps his nice-verging-on-fey personality struck Mick and Keith as being too similar to Mick Taylor. Either way, the rejection was almost certainly a good thing for Frampton. The following year, his double in-concert album *Frampton Comes Alive* started its journey to being the biggest-selling

live album of all time up to that point, and he became a superstar.

Rory Gallagher A star in his own right with chart albums to his name and a reputation as both a good blues-rock songwriter and a coruscating guitarist. Glyn Johns recommended the Irishman to the Stones. He was actually the first to try-out, jamming for two nights in Rotterdam in January '75.

Nils Lofgren The Washington D.C. native Lofgren had made his reputation with a quartet of albums with his superb group Grin. By 1975, Grin were history, and Lofgren was embarking on a career as a solo artist. Lofgren spoke to Richards after Taylor's departure but says that they really needed a "mate" rather than someone with his mellifluous guitar skills. What a strange situation it would have created had the diminutive Lofgren been recruited for the Stones, one that George in Seinfeld might have described as "when worlds collide", for Lofgren was one of the Stones' metaphorical progeny. Steeped in the lore of rock that the Stones had done much to create, he was not only a Keith Richards look-alike but, in 1975, issued a song detailing his concern about Richards' drug habits called 'Keith Don't Go (Ode To The Glimmer Twin)'.

Harvey Mandel The Detroit-born Mandel was tried at the request of Jagger, who wasn't completely convinced by Wayne Perkins (see below). Mandel had released some solo albums but was best known for having been lead guitarist of Canned Heat. He had also been a member of one of John Mayall's many bands.

Steve Marriott Though more acclaimed for his gravelley, soulful vocal style, the cockney Marriott had been guitarist in two highly successful groups, the soul-pop-turned-psychedelic Small Faces and the boogie men Humble Pie. Neither of those groups had had someone of the financial nous of Prince Rupert Loewenstein advising them and, consequently, Marriott was broke by the time of the Pie's disintegration in the mid-Seventies. Unlike most of the axe-slingers who tried out for the role left vacant by Taylor, he was not a virtuoso but did have a playing style with plenty of raw power. His ex-colleague in the Small Faces, Ian McLagan, swears to this day that Richards wanted Marriott to get the job but that Jagger nixed it: he wasn't prepared to have anyone in the group who was a better singer then he.

Jimmy Page (again) Since he had first been considered for a guitarist's role in The Rolling Stones, Jimmy Page had done rather well for himself. In 1968, weary of unfulfilling session work, he had set up a band called Led Zeppelin. Their 'cosmic blues' often raised eyebrows – the way that often well-known blues songs and riffs were attributed to band members led to several legal settlements and changes of credits – but massively successful. Zeppelin were, in fact, for much of the Seventies, bigger money-spinners than The

Rolling Stones could dream of being, although nothing like as famous to the general public, mainly due to their eschewing of the single format. That being the case, it seems unlikely that the Stones would have thought Page would leave Zeppelin, or that Page would be interested in an overture from the Stones, but Watts has subsequently confirmed that "Jimmy came and played with us at that time."

Wayne Perkins Possibly recommended by Bill Wyman, on whose *Monkey Grip* solo album he had played, the native Texan Perkins apparently was under the impression that he had the gig as the new Rolling Stones guitarist when, after playing with the band in London and actually living with Richards for a month, he was asked to attend the March '75 Munich sessions. Perkins was a well-known session player, having appeared on product by artists as diverse as The Everly Brothers, Joni Mitchell and The Wailers. It's rumoured that Richards decided against him because his style was in the virtuoso mould of Taylor. Following the shattering of his dreams of being a Stone, a further cruel blow was in store for Perkins: a track he had played on, 'Fool To Cry', shortly became inescapable as it became a hit around the world.

And there were more. The names of Robert A. Johnson, Shuggie Otis, Chris Spedding and Mick Ronson have also been mentioned in relation to the role. The most bizarre alleged candidates, though, must be Ry Cooder (who had described them in print as "reptilian") and Geoff Bradford, who had been a member of Little Boy Blue and the Blue Boys and whose elevation to this role would have been the Cinderella-getting-to-the-ball story of all-time. (Bradford denies all knowledge of it; although in any case it's far more likely that he would have been under consideration in 1969.)

WANNABE STONES

It's a little remembered fact that for many years, The Beatles were not held in as high regard by musicians as they are today. Though the Fab Four were naturally always popular with the wider public, it was only with the CD reissue of their catalogue in 1994 and the concurrent championing of them by the Brit Pop groups, especially Oasis, that they acquired a cool once more. Prior to that, the set-up and music of The Rolling Stones was considered to be the template/archetype for a rock band, and their anti-authoritarianism a requisite rock 'Attitude'. (Nowadays, the latter has become a *reductio ad absurdam* which Pete Townshend has described as the "kind of silly teenage thing that 'If you get in my way, I'll squirt at you' thing." For proof of this, witness Oasis, whose bad-boy behaviour is not a reaction to a society teeming with injustices – most of which were swept away by the Stones' generation – but simply because they imagine they think

it looks cool.) Accordingly, talk of the new hope of popular music would usually centre around a band who looked and sounded like the new Rolling Stones. There have been many in this category but the most notable are listed below.

THE PRETTY THINGS

Formed by Jagger's and Richards' ex-colleague Dick Taylor, for a brief period this band was actually in danger of eclipsing the Stones in terms of notoriety. They had probably the longest hair of any group in around 1964/65 and Taylor's beard only added to their bohemian appearance. Named after a Bo Diddley song, they played the same kind of authentic and gritty R&B as the Stones, though Phil May's reedy vocals denied them power, as did their initial inability to translate their capacity for good singles ('Rosalyn', 'Don't Bring Me Down', 'Midnight To Six Man') into solid albums. Having already made line-up changes along the way that emphasized that May and Taylor were the nucleus, when their contract with the UK Fontana label expired, The Pretty Things morphed into a completely new-sounding proposition, embracing psychedelia wholeheartedly and recording *S.F. Sorrow*. The latter – released in December 1968 – was arguably the first album to feature a storyline across its entire length (it was released before The Who's own rock opera *Tommy*) as well as being a fine piece of work itself. Taylor departed at this point, and May recorded another good album,

Parachute which, though now forgotten, was voted Album Of The Year for 1970 by the staff of *Rolling Stone* magazine. They were subsequently signed to Led Zeppelin's Swan Song label but still didn't quite manage to hit the big time. The band have since continued to record on and off, with ever-changing line-ups.

THE FACES

In Summer 1972, The Rolling Stones and The Faces were touring America at the same time. Although they were both five-piece R&B-inflected rock 'n' roll bands fronted by an extrovert singer, it was The Faces (on the face of it) who were the mere pretenders. Yet renowned rock critic Dave Marsh spoke for many when he observed, "I'd take one Rod Stewart for five Mick Jaggers any day." While the Stones were increasingly taking on an image of hauteur, the rip-roaring unpretentious party atmosphere at Faces gigs, and their friendly and often inebriated personalities, gave them the aura of rock's Everymen.

The band comprised three remnants of the Small Faces following guitarist/vocalist Steve Marriott's abandonment of those classy pop-psych merchants, plus Ron Wood and his exquisitely gravel-throated singing mate Stewart. Their product was patchy – of their *oeuvre* only the 1972 album *A Nod's As Good As A Wink* achieved a real consistency – but it didn't seem to matter much because their records seemed to meld into the excellent solo albums of Stewart, which frequently used their personnel, either extant or in various configurations.

Ironically, Stewart would come to epitomize rock ego even more than Jagger had. Also ironically, Wood allegedly helped destroy The Faces by moonlighting for the Stones prior to joining them.

THE NEW YORK DOLLS

The parallels between these early Seventies New York rockers and the Stones were ones of almost parodic levels. Singer David Johansen uncannily resembled Jagger in his rubber-lipped-but-handsome features and pouting onstage demeanour, while guitarist Johnny Thunders resembled Richards via his crow's-nest coiffure and his junkie lifestyle. The aforesaid pair also operated a songwriting axis that mirrored that of the Glimmer Twins. Their songs were superficially just enjoyable pastiches of bad-boy sloganeering, but actually evinced a sort of coarse thoughtfulness in their dissection of the *demi-monde*. The Dolls made two albums – an eponymous one in 1973 and *Too Much Too Soon* the following year – but neither captured their trash-cartoon version of rock effectively due to maladroit production. Nonetheless, they became a big influence on UK punks.

MOTT THE HOOPLE

Asked by the NME in the early Seventies who were the new Rolling Stones, Mick Jagger responded that it might well be Mott The Hoople. A band that varied between quintet and quartet status, they hailed from rural

Wannabe Stones

Herefordshire, England, with the exception of frontman Ian Hunter, who came from Shrewsbury in rural Shropshire. Their strange name was derived from the title of a novel, and was suggested by their manager and producer Guy Stevens. Though building up a fanatical live following, the band didn't really shine on record until David Bowie took them under his production wing and gifted them the 1972 hit 'All The Young Dudes'. They subsequently took their cue from the way that song mythologized rock music, their brilliant 1973 album *Mott* being virtually a concept album about being a struggling band. Things started to go downhill when lead guitarist Mick Ralphs left to form Bad Company and their only other album, *The Hoople*, was patchy. Deciding to split, they executed the perfect finale with a fabulous single called 'Saturday Gigs' that waxed nostalgic about their career and movingly bade farewell to their fans.

AEROSMITH

Like many bands whose membership grew up listening to the Stones, Aerosmith often seemed more like a 'square' movie mogul's idea of a rock band than the real thing, so studiedly Stones-esque were their visual style and musical mannerisms. The fact that frontman Steven Tyler was a dead ringer for Jagger only added to the impression, as did their later descent into the sort of drug-drenched excess that came so naturally to Keith Richards but,

in the hands of bands like Aerosmith, seemed rather like blind adherence to what was now a rock 'n' roll tradition. Regardless of the musical, sartorial and attitudinal clichés, though they did, occasionally, make some fine music, especially *Toys In The Attic* (1975) and *Rocks* (1976).

THE CLASH

They may have sang "No Elvis, Beatles or The Rolling Stones" in their B-side '1977', but The Clash were no more immune than any other young men of their generation to the allure of the music and myth of rock's ultimate Gods. Rhythm guitarist/vocalist Joe Strummer idolized the band during the Sixties when in boarding school, and lead guitarist/vocalist Mick Jones cultivated a look in around 1978 that made him the spitting image of Keith Richards circa 1972. Of their six albums, their third, *London Calling* (1979), was the one on which they most resembled the Stones. A double set, it could plausibly be posited as their equivalent of *Exile On Main St.* – only they were what The Rolling Stones would have been if the Stones had come after punk rather than helping to cause it. Though their music and image was rebellious and turbocharged, it had a mateyness and a tender heartedness – their lyrics acknowledging the harsh realities of the lives of their fans – that was antithetical to kings of *hauteur* and decadence like the Stones.

THE ROUGH GUIDE TO THE ROLLING STONES

THE BLACK CROWES

Even the name of this group somehow seemed a tip of the hat to the Stones or, more specifically, to a 1976 review of one of their gigs in which Charles Shaar Murray likened Richards and Wood visually to a pair of diseased crows. In fact, the name originated with a children's book titled *Mr. Crowe's Garden*, but so closely did they model their decadent, rooster-haired, bell-bottoms-dragging-in-their-own-urine sound and look on the Stones (albeit with a pinch of The Faces) that the jump to that conclusion was forgivable. Almost as if acknowledging how steeped they were in classic rock, Jimmy Page hired them to back him on *Live At The Greek*, a 2000 in-concert performance of mostly Led Zeppelin songs. Also inevitably, the Crowes played support to the Stones, opening for them on their 1995 European tour.

THE SEX PISTOLS

The London quartet who exploded upon the nation's consciousness with a four letter outburst on live TV in late 1976 were probably the last band to truly shock 'decent' society. They were shocking because their public attitude did not conform to the conventions of celebrity behaviour to which even the Stones had had to adhere in order to maintain a commercial viability. Though they used obscenities in their everyday vocabulary as much as the Pistols, the Stones would never have sworn on television or radio for fear of being boycotted. To some extent, that is what happened

to the Pistols – but that gave them an outlaw cachet that only increased their legend and their record sales. Had the Stones indulged in such behaviour in the Sixties, even people of their own generation would probably have been genuinely disgusted by it, and would have stopped buying their product. But then the Pistols' generation were one whose more liberal values the Stones had helped to create.

Nonetheless, there was no way the Pistols' posturing and their brilliant but often disturbing music would have allowed them to cross over into the mass market and, after a succession of hits and one album, they imploded. Occasional reunions of the original line-up still happen, somewhat undermining one of their avowed *raisons d'être*: the fact that they were under thirty.

STONES WOMEN

The partners of the individual Rolling Stones have themselves often been larger-than-life personalities. They have also, of course, frequently acted as muses for classic Stones songs. Here we profile the most significant of them.

CHRISSIE SHRIMPTON (MICK)

When then-NME journalist, later Stones PR man, Keith Altham went to the Station Hotel, Richmond to see the Stones for the first time, he was confronted outside by the sight of what he thought was two girls having a fight. The pair turned out to be Mick Jagger and Chrissie Shrimpton. Such tempestuousness was a characteristic of their three-year relationship. Shrimpton – sister of famous Sixties model Jean 'The Shrimp' Shrimpton – was considered by Jagger to be wretched and neurotic, something that came out in his many songs about her, including 'Stupid Girl' and '19th Nervous Breakdown'. Their tormented partnership staggered on until December 1966, the termination of which by Jagger resulted in Shrimpton taking an overdose – which either proves Jagger was a cad or that she was the neurotic Jagger always believed. Following her recovery, Shrimpton sent Jagger her medical bills. Jagger refused to pay them and sent them back. Later, Shrimpton unsuccessfully tried to sell Jagger's love letters to a tabloid newspaper.

MARIANNE FAITHFULL (MICK)

If ever a couple were considered to epitomize the values of the Sixties, Mick Jagger and Marianne Faithfull were it. Their unmarried state upon the announcement of Faithfull's pregnancy in 1968 was genuinely considered a slap in the face by those who considered themselves to abide by certain values (not all of which people were in the ruling class or older generation by a long shot). Jagger at that point – with his hair growing longer and longer – seemed like a very well-turned out savage who was gradually contaminating his previously clean-cut lady with his unspeakably loose morals. Certainly the change in Faithfull from the virginal figure she appeared to be on the release of her first single 'As Tears Go By' in 1964, to the well-spoken whore image she obtained via both the 1968 unmarried pregnancy and her role in the soft-porn biker movie *Girl On A Motorcycle* the same year was spectacular. The belief that such 'degeneracy' had dire consequences was confirmed in many people's eyes by Faithfull's miscarriage and her suicide attempt in Australia in 1969.

However, Faithfull's true descent began in the early Seventies. Having walked out on Jagger – and stymied his attempts at any reconciliation by letting herself go fat – she became a street junkie, famously living on a wall in St. Anne's Court in Soho, London for several years and losing custody of her son Nicholas to her ex-husband John Dunbar due to her drug abuse. She reports that she was well-looked after by the Soho tramps, and that she was able to go back to her mother's house once a week for a bath. From this unimaginable low depth – the pain of which must have been made all the more exquisite because of the heights she'd fallen from – Faithfull effected a spectacular comeback in the late Seventies with the albums *Faithless* and *Broken English*, in which she reinvented herself as a smokey-voiced survivor-figure.

Faithfull inspired the Stones songs 'Let It Bleed' ("parking lot" was her and Jagger's pet name for her genitals) and 'You Can't Always Get What You Want' and – jointly with Pallenberg – 'Wild Horses'. Her reading habits brought about the composition of 'Sympathy For The Devil'. Her most significant contribution to the Stones' canon, though, was 'Sister

Anita Pallenberg (BRIAN, MICK AND KEITH)

As the lover of the principal three original band members and a muse to some classic Richards songs, as well as, you might say, his partner-in-crime during the heroin years, Anita Pallenberg is the woman who looms largest in the story of The Rolling Stones.

Born in Rome in 1944, Pallenberg was a model and actress when she met Brian Jones in 1965 after blagging her way backstage via Danish tour photographer Bent Rej, at a Stones gig in Munich. She did not live up to the clichéd image of a model, being highly intelligent and fluent in several languages. Pallenberg was very attractive as a young woman, although for some her beauty was curdled by a certain degree of malice. She is said to have dabbled in black magic, to have taken whips into Brian Jones' bedroom, and was by her own admission behind the ill-judged decision of Jones to pose for a photograph wearing a Nazi uniform while using his jackboot to crush a baby doll. Keith Altham has said of her personality, "I was kind of attractively repelled by her. She had those kind of venomous good looks." She and Jones were for a while the epitome of a glamorous couple, both blonde and beautiful – identical looking in a certain light – and both cultural icons.

However, both Jones and Pallenberg had considerable egos. and spiteful temperaments. Mutual violence marked their affair. It was a beating Jones inflicted on her that drove Pallenberg into the arms of Richards. Though Pallenberg would appear to have found true love with Keith, abandoning her film and modelling careers for the role of common-law-wife and mother, this domestic bliss didn't prevent her having the fling with Jagger on the set of *Performance* that briefly threatened to destroy the Stones. Among classic, and not so classic, Stones love songs that she at least partly inspired are 'You Got The Silver', 'Wild Horses', 'Coming Down Again' and 'All About You'. Additionally, and though it's not specifically a love song, 'Gimme Shelter' would possibly never have been written had Richards not met her.

Despite her beauty and wealthy lifestyle, Pallenberg has endured more than her fair share of trauma. There was the death of her and Richards' son Tara in 1976. And there was trauma of another sort – in which Pallenberg was cast as the villain – in 1979, when a youth named Scott Cantrell shot himself dead in her and Richards' home when Richards was away. Pallenberg was cleared of any legal blame but the parents of the boy were scathing about why a 17-year-old would be in her bedroom in the first place.

Sanchez claims that Pallenberg once said to him of Jagger, Jones and Richards, "I'm certain that any one of them would break up the band for me". The power she held to bewitch three men at once has faded with her looks. With Richards now firmly attached to Patti Hansen – one of his few partners following the break-up of their marriage of whom Pallenberg approved – and with son Marlon and daughter Angela grown and both married, Pallenberg now lives quietly in London, working as a drug counsellor.

In a relatively recent interview, she said that one benefit of not being attached to Richards anymore is that she no longer felt obliged to be loyal to The Rolling Stones.

Morphine'. She provided a harrowing lyric to a melody Jagger had devised and the Stones worked it up into a haunting piece of work on Sticky Fingers.

BIANCA JAGGER (MICK)

The woman who was to become Mick Jagger's first (and, by his reckoning, only) wife was born Bianca Perez Moreno de Macias on 2 May, 1945 in Nicaragua, Central America. Though her father was a successful businessman, she fell on hard times when her parents' marriage ended when she was ten. She studied political science in Paris after winning a university scholarship. Jagger met Bianca in Paris in 1970. Many remarked at the time on how similar the two were facially. They married in chaos in May 1971. Jagger hadn't realized that the law in France stated that anybody could attend a wedding in a public building. It wasn't just the *melée* at what should have been a happy and intimate affair that caused Bianca to state that it was the worst day of her life: Jagger asked her to sign a pre-nup on the morning of the wedding. On her wedding day, Bianca was already pregnant and gave birth to a daughter, Jade, in October 1971.

It was Bianca who was behind the Stones' decision to stage a rare benefit gig to help victims of the 1972 earthquake in her home country. Bianca's plan to build a clinic with the $280,000 raised was stymied by the corrupt Somoza regime in power at the time and it was instead donated to a founda-tion to build homes for the earthquake victims. Following the displeasure she incurred by resisting the Somoza regime, Bianca felt afraid to go back to Nicaragua until the regime fell in 1979. Despite this, during her marriage to Jagger, Bianca was known not so much for her political beliefs but as a socialite and partygoer, one of the regular faces at New York's Studio 54. She was also considered to be a rather imperious and haughty figure, especially in the informality-loving rock circles in which her husband moved. The Stones crew hated her, nicknaming her "Bianca the Wanker". She in turn hated the Stones' machinery, contemptuous of an attitude toward women that grated on her feminist principles. The image of Bianca as a freeloader amongst her detractors was only strengthened by the record-breaking divorce settlement she obtained against Jagger, as did the fact that she decided to retain the Jagger name, which she used as she embarked on an ultimately failed career as an actress.

However, she then proceeded to effect a remarkable image transformation, getting involved in politics in Nicaragua (whose revolutionary Sandinista government she initially supported), El Salvador (whose death squads she campaigned against) and Bosnia. Her previous image as a jet-setter now seems a distant memory. As she herself said, "Early on, when I began my humanitarian work, I understood that in order to gain credibility I needed patience, commitment and unwavering perseverance. And I needed to ignore the sceptics.

I thought there would come a time when they couldn't deny my accomplishments."

Jagger doesn't talk much about his female muses, so one can only guess at which songs Bianca inspired apart from the obvious 'Respectable', but it seems safe to assume that several of the love songs on *Sticky Fingers*, *Exile On Main St.* and *Goat's Head Soup* were about her. It also seems sadly plausible that some of the songs about disillusion with a love affair on *It's Only Rock 'N' Roll* were ones that traced the trajectory of the pair's disintegrating relationship ('If You Can't Rock Me', 'If You Really Want To Be My Friend', 'Short And Curlies'.)

JERRY HALL (MICK)

Though Jerry Hall and Jagger are now technically separated, it's safe to say that Hall is the love of his life, both because of the length of their partnership and the permanent bond that their closeness and their four children seems to have created: they and their brood still live under the same roof, albeit in separate parts of the house. Jagger met the – to use tabloid parlance –'leggy Texan model' in 1976 at a Stones Earl's Court gig. At the time, she was the girlfriend of Roxy Music's Brian Ferry. She appeared on the cover of that band's *Sirens* album. Hall, born in 1956, was one of five children – all girls – from a family of a type that Americans call 'white trash'. Her father was an abusive alcoholic. Her mother had a certain down-home wisdom – although Hall trumped

her with her own insight. Hall has recounted an exchange between them in a quote that has been endlessly repeated: "My mother said it was simple to keep a man: 'You must be a maid in the living room, a cook in the kitchen and a whore in the bedroom'. I said I'd hire the other two and take care of the bedroom bit."

Hall left home at sixteen to go to Paris to try to become a model. Surprisingly, considering her height and her unconventional, equine face, she succeeded, becoming one of the highest-paid models in the world. She left Ferry for Jagger in 1979, though their Hindu beach wedding in Bali didn't occur until 1990. It was annulled in 1999.

Though she had a couple of small acting roles (including *Batman*) her film career failed to take off. However, in recent years, she has successfully appeared on stage, including the part of the older woman in a London West End production of *The Graduate*.

Amongst others, Hall inspired the Stones song 'Miss You' and – it is suspected – the bitterly regretful 'Biggest Mistake'.

PATTI HANSEN (KEITH)

The pairing of rock 'n' roll outlaw Keith Richards with Patti Hansen, a remarkably beautiful and wholesome all-American girl, always seemed unlikely. However, though the pair are reported to have had their troubles – Hansen comes from a Christian family and re-discovered God during one of Richards' lengthy absences, leading to conflicts upon

Stonesology

his return from the road – it has now endured for a quarter of a century. They met in 1979 at Keith's birthday party. Hansen at the time was a 22-year-old model. They married in 1983 on Richards' 40th birthday. Hansen gave up her career to have a family and the pair have two daughters, Theodora (born 1985) and Alexandra (born 1986), whom Richards calls his "best friends". Like Jagger's daughter Lizzie, Theodora has followed her mother into modelling and she and Lizzie appeared together on the cover of *Nylon* magazine in August 2004 under the heading "Jagger & Richards – Sex, Jeans & Rock 'N' Roll (The Next Generation)".

Perhaps it's because Hansen met Richards when the latter was past his peak as a songwriter that the guitarist doesn't seem to have written much in the way of great musical tributes to her. Flattering though it must be to be anybody's muse, one imagines that the joy Hansen experienced for inspiring material like 'Little T&A' ("She's … My tits and ass with soul") was somewhat limited.

SHIRLEY WATTS (CHARLIE)

The wife of Charlie Watts enjoys a unique status: she is the only Stones partner to have been with her man since the 1960s. While other marriages and partnerships have fallen by the wayside, she and Charlie have persevered in a union that seems genuinely happy. This is not to say that they have experienced uninterrupted bliss. Watts' drug- and drink-sodden

mid-life crisis in the mid-Eighties was roughly simultaneous with Shirley's own battle with alcoholism.

Her husband's job has enabled Shirley to indulge her passion for horses, with the two running a successful stud farm. They also have a mutual passion for art, while Shirley is a talented amateur sculptor. They have one daughter, Seraphina, born in 1968.

Shirley Watts is most famous to Stones fans for two memorable quotes. One is when she said in 1966, "Charlie's not really a Stone, is he? Mick, Keith and Brian, they're the big bad Rolling Stones". The other is from 1989, when she said, "I've always hated the way rock music and its world treat women and particularly The Rolling Stones' attitude. There is no respect."

MANDY SMITH (BILL)

By his own account, Wyman has notched up more conquests than probably the rest of the Stones put together. With such a record something had to give. In February 1984, Bill Wyman was attending a Rock Awards ceremony when he spotted an elfin blonde beauty. He was instantly smitten. So much so that when the girl – named Mandy Smith – turned out to be just thirteen, it didn't stop him embarking on a love affair with her. When the story reached the media after the pair's affair had ended there were calls for Wyman to be prosecuted. When he wasn't, people assumed that was the end of the matter, but there was a bizarre postscript: Wyman and Smith were reconciled and got married in 1989. The marriage was extremely brief but, in an even more bizarre postscript, Wyman's son Stephen announced his engagement to Mandy Smith's mother, although the marriage ultimately didn't happen.

STONES AIDES

Many of the people who have formed part of the Stones' entourage over the years are just as larger-than-life as the band members themselves. Here are profiles of some of the people who have shaped the band's careers and/or images and/or lives.

ANDREW LOOG OLDHAM

Though Andrew Loog Oldham admits he was only hours behind the rest of the music industry in discovering the Stones, the idea that the band would have been the band they were without him at the helm seems unlikely. With Oldham's nose for headlines – acquired in his previous job as plugger – they became something more than a mere group but the Way Of Life Oldham bombastically boasted they were to fill up space on the back of their first LP.

Oldham was born in 1944. He had the privilege of a public school education courtesy of the genuinely caring married lover of his single mother. He was clearly bristling with energy and ambition as a young man. By the time he made his fateful visit to the Station Hotel, Richmond at the age of 19, he'd already worked for fashion-designer Mary Quant, and

had carved out a niche for himself in music PR. (His pop career though was a myth.) He wasn't interested in and didn't understand the blues or R&B, but did understand star quality.

Keith Altham has said Oldham, like many managers in those days, had little business nous but had flair, imagination and creativity in abundance. This was manifested in his rapid realization that trying to make the Stones the 'London Beatles' was the wrong strategy and that he should do almost the exact opposite by marketing them as the antithesis of The Beatles. "I think that was the thing that helped take them up," said Altham. "In those days you became a Beatles fan or a Stones fan and The Beatles were kind of all-round family entertainment. To a lot of people in the business [the Stones] weren't going to have a very long career because they were not going to be accepted by the Establishment."

Unthinkably, this anti-Establishment aura actually contributed to a long career. Though Oldham wasn't the all-seeing manipulator he might have imagined himself to be – it was the band who insisted on dressing causal when his sartorial vision didn't extend beyond matching hound's-tooth suits – he had the perspicacity to change course when he saw which way the wind was blowing, hence the "Would You Let Your Daughter Go With A Rolling Stone?" headline and an incident in the early days in which he arranged for the press to be present as the Stones were turned away from the Savoy restaurant for not wearing ties (as he knew they would be).

Pictures of Oldham from the Sixties show a man who is as cool (stylish clothes and wrap-around shades before the latter became a cliché) and good-looking as any Rolling Stone. Though he had swiftly abandoned his first ambition to be a recording artist when he realized he didn't have the talent, for a while Oldham imagined that he could turn himself into an English Phil Spector. He had met the legendary American studio mastermind before the Stones and – as he did with so many older or more power-ful male role models in his life, presumably to replace the father he never knew – become besotted with him. However, the various pro-ductions he oversaw as his wealth increased – some of them under the mildly sniggersome name The Andrew Loog Oldham Orchestra – were Spector-Lite. He kept his grandiosity to himself when overseeing the Stones' records (though Richards blames him for the shoddi-ness of the released version of 'Have You Seen Your Mother'). "He wasn't like an overbearing producer," engineer Dave Hassinger recalls of Oldham. "He didn't tell them how to play but he ran things from the control room. I think Andrew was an excellent producer because he could sense when not to get involved. I think he understood the Stones probably better than anybody. Too many producers try to leave their imprint on what they do. Andrew wasn't that way. Andrew was very smart. Very bright guy. Andrew didn't ever leave when they were recording. He was there. He was the, you might say, manager – managing everything else other

than the Stones. Making sure everything was ready, that kind of thing. He just didn't butt in. Andrew knew just how to not only get along but keep things moving. It's almost like Andrew had no ego. He was perfect for that. I look at Andrew as the perfect person to have in that position at that stage of their careers."

In 1965, Oldham set up the independent record label Immediate with Tony Calder. The Small Faces, The Move, Fleetwood Mac, PP Arnold, The Nice, Amen Corner and Chris Farlowe all made good-to-great records for it but more importantly Immediate broke the hegemony of the crusty, only-listen-to-classi-cal-myself types then running the UK music industry. Nonetheless, when it went under in 1970, it left bitter feelings amongst some of its artists. Oldham countered with the asser-tion that the reason the Immediate artists didn't see any money from their chart plac-ings is that the label had to obtain them by hype. There is also the fact that his procuring of Allen Klein as Stones co-manager resulted in a financial position which led them to have to leave the country, although he points out he can hardly be blamed for deals made between the band and Klein after he himself had left the picture.

Oldham maintained a desultory career as a producer and manager after the Immediate dissolution but a move to Colombia – where he married a famous native soap star – took him off the radar of his previous profession, one that he only really emerged back onto with the publication of the first two volumes of his autobiography. In the mid-1990s, he collaborated with Tony Calder and Colin Irwin on a book about ABBA, which posited them as the greatest pop group of all time. Something which in a way summed up Oldham's take on popular music is the fact that the index listed more references to "Agnetha's bottom" than to some of their hits.

IAN STEWART

Though Ian 'Stu' Stewart was eased out of The Rolling Stones partly for looking insufficiently like pop star material, in a way his personality was the epitome of the sprit of the Stones. He was so much his own man that he refused to play minor chords, lifting his hands when one occurred in a Stones song. In addition, he was also the only member of the Stones inner circle with the courage to decline to be sycophantic toward them as they became incrementally more celebrated (a memorable insult was, "Come on my little shower of shits, my three chord wonders, you're on"). As well as being the Stones' head roadie and occasional pianist (when the keys were to his satisfaction), Stewart helped run the much in-demand Rolling Stones Mobile Studio. He also did occasional session work, including for Led Zeppelin, who titled the Physical Graffiti track 'Boogie With Stu' in acknowledgment of his contribution to it and gave him a lucrative co-writer's credit. He died of a heart attack in December 1985. "Who's gonna tell us off now

when we misbehave?" Richards remarked of the unaffected, harrumphing figure now forever absent from the Stones' lives.

NICKY HOPKINS

If rock session musicians had such things as CV's, that of Nicky Hopkins would have been the most mind-bogglingly star-studded of them all. Sometimes it seems that there is barely a classic recording of the late Sixties and Seventies that is not graced by his ornate keyboard work. That's him on The Beatles' 'Revolution', The Who's *My Generation* and *Who's Next* albums, and John Lennon's 'Jealous Guy', as well as various recordings by luminaries like Jefferson Airplane and The Steve Miller Band. He's also all over 'Sixties Kinks albums and Ray Davies even wrote a song about him, 'Session Man'. Naturally, Hopkins played on the track (harpsichord). Hopkins also appeared as a *bona fide* group member on records by The Jeff Beck Group and Quicksilver Messenger Service.

It was Ian Stewart's dislike of the direction in which the Stones' music was going that brought Hopkins into the Stones' camp. He started working with the group on *Between The Buttons* at a time when Stewart was declining to play on their records. With no disrespect to Stewart, the result was a net gain for the listener, as can be discerned by bearing witness to Hopkins' menacing, snaking playing on 'We Love You', his surreally trebly contribution to 'She's A Rainbow', the sublime extended intro-

Stonesology

Glyn Johns

Glyn Johns has long been renowned as first, a world class engineer, then a top producer, his credits having graced the albums of people like The Who and The Beatles. He has also long been a mate of the Stones. Somehow, though, their relationship has always been fractious and never resulted in significant or sustained periods of collaboration.

Johns was amongst the first to spot their talent, engineering the January 1963 IBC demos. From there he worked for them sporadically, recording the UK *Got Live If You Want It!* EP and the unrelated US album of the same name, as well as occasional studio tracks like 'As Tears Go By' and 'Have You Seen Your Mother Baby...?'.

Johns engineered the whole of the *Between The Buttons* and *Satanic Majesties* albums (the latter as the senior production staff member following Oldham's departure). *Beggar's Banquet* through *Exile* saw him working under the command of Jimmy Miller, the man whom he had of course nudged the Stones into acquiring as a producer.

He received a full co-producer's credit on the live *Get Yer Ya-Ya's Out* album. He contributed mixing work to the *It's Only Rock and Roll* album, during which he had a blazing row with Mick Taylor, whom he considered to have turned from an egoless boy into a self-indulgent bore of a man. Many would suggest that it was Johns – notoriously temperamental – who was the problem, and would point to the fact that another blazing row – with Keith Richards – saw him leave the *Black And Blue* sessions early.

duction to 'Loving Cup' and the breathtaking solo in the middle of 'Angie'.

Hopkins was always a sickly figure – Truman Capote once said he "...has the mark of death on him" – and he died prematurely in September 1994 of Crohn's Disease, aged 50.

ALLEN KLEIN

Not only did Paul McCartney go to court to break up The Beatles' business partnership specifically so that he did not have to be managed by Allen Klein but the Rolling Stones also became bitterly disenchanted with the services provided by the New Yorker. They fired him in the summer of 1970 and, bitterly unhappy at the way he had handled The Stones' finances, instigated a $29m lawsuit against him. (The case was settled out of court.) Yet the fact that Keith Richards had said that on balance he is glad that the Stones were managed by Klein reflects Klein's success at the one thing he is acknowledged to be good at: obtaining money from record companies on his client's behalf.

Trained as an accountant and possessing the hide of a rhinoceros, he was able to do for pop stars what they were too intimidated or unworldly to themselves: work out whether their record companies were withholding rightful earnings from them by creative accounting. By taking on the accounts of first the Stones and The Beatles and by using his bluff New Yorker's manner (which seemed very menacing to middle-class record execs in England, to whom it was a movie gangster's mien) he successfully renegotiated what had been insulting contracts to reflect those artists' importance to Decca and EMI respectively. Unfortunately, the Stones subsequently felt utterly frustrated at their inability to get hold of the monies he obtained for them.

The Stones' break with Klein was bitter indeed but they are linked to him for all eternity through his ownership of the masters of their Sixties catalogue.

JIMMY MILLER

Jimmy Miller was the kind of larger-than-life figure who could be mistaken for a rock star himself. A towering man with a Texan drawl, he was actually gifted to the Stones by Glyn Johns when Jagger told the engineer after *Satanic Majesties* that they were thinking of getting an American producer. Johns later said, "I [thought] 'I don't think my ego could stand having some bloody yank in here telling me what sort of sound to get for The Rolling Stones'." Because Johns knew – and liked – Miller from his recent work with Traffic, he nominated him. "Jagger actually took the bit", Johns said. Whatever the machinations behind his appointment, Miller was a huge and positive influence on the Stones, his highly receptive ear and musician's sensibility adding a dimension to their music that Oldham never could. He famously played drums on 'You Can't Always Get What You Want' after Watts couldn't get right the rhythm Miller suggested to him, and Watts even said subsequently, "Jimmy actually made me stop and think again about the way I played drums in the studio and I became a much better drummer in the studio thanks to him."

In addition to the Stones, Miller produced The Spencer Davis Group (with whom he co-wrote 'I'm A Man'), Traffic, Blind Faith, Spooky Tooth, The Move, Motorhead, Johnny Thunders and Primal Scream. It has to be said that some of the acts for whom he recorded following the break with the Stones seemed to want him for his association with Jagger and co: witness the ludicrous if enjoyable Primal Scream Stones pastiche 'Rocks' that said band recorded after working with him.

Miller never seemed to quite recover form the drug problems he picked up while working for the Stones before his death from liver failure in 1994 aged 52. It seemed he made the mistake of so many who hung around with the group in thinking that his constitution could handle the same abuse that Richards' could. Richards observed of his exit from the Stones' camp, "Jimmy Miller went in a lion and came out a lamb. We wore him out completely..."

DON WAS

When Don Was was appointed co-producer of *Voodoo Lounge*, it was the beginning of a relationship which the band found so fruitful that at the time of writing there seems little prospect of it being ended by either side.

One of the main attractions of Was to the Stones is the fact that he is a musician, having made his name in the Eighties with the group

Was (Not Was). He subsequently became better known as a producer. He has certainly overseen the recordings of some real luminaries, Bonnie Raitt, Iggy Pop, Ringo Starr, the B-52s, Willie Nelson and Bob Dylan among them. He has played on various tracks on the Stones albums he has overseen since then: *Stripped*, *Bridges to Babylon* (on which he was billed as executive producer; translation: managing the chaos) *Forty Licks*, *Live Licks* and *A Bigger Bang*.

KEITH ALTHAM

Keith Altham grew up with The Rolling Stones. As a young reporter on the NME, he saw some of their first publicity shots. "The first time I ever saw a photograph of them, I thought the Four Stooges had arrived," he says. "They had those pudding basin haircuts which were kind of like an attempt to do a Beatles almost in the early days and they just looked silly to me." In time, he became a firm friend of the band, and particularly of Ian Stewart. He was in Olympic studios with the group on the night that the news came through that Brian Jones had died. When the Stones long-term PR man Les Perrin (an amusingly strait-laced spokesman for the increasingly debauched Stones) fell ill in the late Seventies, Altham seemed a natural choice to replace him.

Altham quickly became disillusioned with his role, finding that he was effectively PR not for the band but for Jagger, of whom he says, "I just found I was dealing with a different person completely. The Jagger I knew had disappeared. I hated the suffocating sodding group of people that he seemed to have got around him, particularly in America where you had to go through some sort of corporate pecking order before you could actually talk to him. That used to get right up my nose – and of course I got right up their nose[s] by going straight to him, because I couldn't hang around for three months sometimes for a decision while everybody covered themselves." His loyalty to the band – which had led him as a journalist to give a glowing review to *Satanic Majesties* (even though he didn't like it) because he wanted to show solidarity with them after all they had been through in '67 – was severely tested. However, when he left his job in 1982, it was not voluntary: Jagger sacked him at a time when he was about to appear on the front covers of three magazines through Altham's efforts.

Altham was one of the most successful music PR men of all – witness his client list and profiles in his autobiography *The PR Strikes Back*. He also merits an important footnote in rock history: it was his suggestion to Jimi Hendrix that he adopt the gimmick of setting fire to his guitar on stage.

PRINCE RUPERT LOEWENSTEIN

It's an amusing fact of the Stones' history that their financial adviser/accountant for the last three decades has been the unlikely aristocratic figure of Prince Rupert Loewenstein. "Of Bavaria" is the answer to both your immediate question ("Of what country?") and your second question ("Shouldn't he be king at his age?") In any case, even if Bavaria did exist as a monarchy, Lowenstein's claim to the throne has been disputed on the grounds that his forebears were mere counts.

Jagger met Loewenstein socially in 1968. When Jagger began asking the latter about matters financial, Loewenstein thought he might need some kind of tax shelter in which to stow his unassailable riches. In fact, his new client turned out to be teetering on bankruptcy. Loewenstein's colleagues at bankers Leopold Joseph, where he was MD, were against him taking on the Stones, as they might be bad for their image. Loewenstein won out and saved the Stones from financial ruin – and possibly saved the Stones *per se* – by telling the group to leave the country. More than three decades later, he is still with them, routinely cutting deals that see the band successively breaking all records for tour grosses.

Bobby Keys

Texan saxophonist Bobby Keys and Keith Richards were born on the same day. As well as this and their expertise on their chosen instruments, they also had another connection: their once-prodigious consumption of narcotics. Keys first played with the Stones on *Let It Bleed*'s 'Live With Me'. His sax break in 'Brown Sugar' achieved instant immortality and he is associated with some of the greatest Stones music. Some Stones insiders considered Keys to be a bad influence on Richards and it is rumoured that this is behind the fact that he wasn't to be found on the Stones' records for a period after the Toronto bust. Nonetheless, the bond remains strong between him and Keith and Keys has guested on Stones records and tours regularly since, including the 2005 Bigger Bang US tour.

STONES PLACES

The Stones have roots in, and associations with, various localities. Here is a selection of geographical locations associated with The Rolling Stones, as individuals or as an entity. Actual street addresses have not been printed in order to ensure that current residents are not plagued by over-enthusiastic people sporting lapping-tongue t-shirts.

DARTFORD

Though local industries include the manufacture of cement, chemicals and paper, Dartford, Mick Jagger's and Keith Richards' hometown, is a commuter town, one which has no real major sources of employment and therefore is a location from which people travel to the nearest major city – London – to work. Naturally such a town is rather sleepy, a quality which makes it attractive to the middle-aged and elderly and drab to the young. Its name is an abbreviation of 'Ford on the River Darent', a reference to a geographical landmark of two thousand years ago. The census of 2001 showed its population to be 85,911.

Both Jagger and Richards were born in 1943 at Dartford's Livingstone hospital, on East Hill. Jagger's family lived initially in Brent Lane. By the time his brother Christopher was born in 1947, the family had moved to Denver Road in West Dartford, a street running immediately parallel with Chastilian Road, in which was located the home of the Richards family. Running off Chastilian Road is Wentworth Drive, in which is located Wentworth Primary School, or Wentworth County Primary School as it was known when Jagger and Richards attended it from the ages of seven to eleven. "I can't remember when I didn't know (Keith)," Jagger has said. "We used to play together, and we weren't the closest friends, but we were friends."

1954 was a year of upheaval all round for the still-not-really cemented Jagger and Richards bond. As if to emphasize the class divide between the pair's families, in that year Jagger's family went onwards and upwards when they moved into Newlands, a three-bedroomed house with a garden in Wilmington – an area just to the south and not technically part of Dartford – while Richards' family moved downwards, although it wasn't meant to be like that, as they were allocated housing on Spielman Road on a council estate called Temple Hill, several miles to the north of his previous neighbourhood. "This fucking soul-destroying council estate at completely the other end of town." Richards later said of it. "… a disgusting concrete jungle of horrible new streets full of rows of semi-detached houses… Everyone looked displaced."

Even had they not been geographically separated at that point, the future Glimmer Twins were destined to be broken up in the same year by another indication of England's class divide: the 11-Plus. As happened so often to friends and acquaintances in those days, one of the pair passed the 11-Plus exam – and was rewarded with a place at a grammar school, the type of pedagogical institution for those whom it was considered had the intelligence to handle office work or more. The other's failure consigned him to a technical college, the type of institution reserved for pupils who were considered to have a future only in manual professions. Jagger's secondary school was Dartford Grammar School on West Hill, an illustrious academy founded in 1576. There, he passed seven O-levels and two A-levels. He wasn't exactly a model pupil – an air of indolence and insolence about him even then – but he would become without question the most celebrated of its alumni. In March 2000, he returned to it to open the Mick Jagger Centre – a section for the musically inclined on the school grounds. Richards, meanwhile, attended Dartford Technical College, which was quite a long journey from Spielman Road. Jagger has recalled sometimes seeing Richards passing on his bike in this period of geographical and social distance between them. Their only real contact at this time seems to have been an incident when Richards bought an ice cream off Jagger when the latter was working on an ice-cream trolley outside the town library, which is not too far from Dartford Grammar.

The other notable Dartford landmark featuring in the pair's formative years is, of course, Dartford railway station, which, on the day in 1961 that they met on a train coming out of it, had three platforms but now has four. "In a town like Dartford, if anybody's headed for London or any stop in between, then in Dartford station, you're bound to meet," Richards later shrugged. Maybe so, but there seems something slightly symbolic about the fact that the station is located at a position more or less equidistant between Spielman Road and West Hill.

CHELTENHAM

Cheltenham, a town in the west of England, is best known for three things: being a place whose waters historically had supposedly restorative powers, being the location of GCHQ (the government surveillance centre) – and being the home town of Brian Jones.

Like Dartford, it has a quietness that is highly attractive to those over thirty and anathema to those under it – only to the nth degree. Cheltenham is a town of almost parodic, comedy-sketch-show gentility. It was certainly no place for a free spirit like the young Jones.

"Brian couldn't stand Cheltenham," Alexis Korner told Stanley Booth. "He simply loathed Cheltenham... He couldn't stand the restrictions imposed by his family on his thinking and his general behaviour."

If Jones hated his home town, by the time of his death, it seems that there were no feelings of reciprocation on this score from the populace. Stones secretary Shirley Arnold, who attended his funeral, observed, "The whole of Cheltenham came out just to stand and watch."

CHELSEA

Kings Road (actually always referred to as 'The King's Road') in Chelsea, south-west London is divided into two ends. The street is bisected by Beaufort Street. Turning right into the King's Road from Beaufort Street takes one into an upmarket area with shops groaning under some of the highest rents in the land, off which are sundry plush 'squares' (actually U-shaped residential streets) stuffed full of posh houses. Turning left out of Beaufort Street, however, puts one into a decidedly less posh end, one that gets incrementally less salubrious until it reaches the notorious World's End council estate. Edith Grove, where Brian, Mick and Keith lived together in 1962/63, is actually the street immediately past the World's End Estate. The latter wasn't built until the 1970s and in '62 was a slum of terraced housing that Jagger, Jones and Richards could see from their home.

Stonesology

As mentioned previously, the conditions in which they lived were dire, although not always of their own making: Richards has recalled how each room they occupied in their house would be condemned as unfit for human habitation, necessitating a regular move to a new one.

What a difference a few years make. Having made hit records and small fortunes, the Edith Grove Stones triumvirate had graduated (following moves to different areas of London) to other areas of Chelsea that were physically only a few hundred yards away but materially a universe removed from the site of their former residence. Jones actually lived at various residences in the SW3/SW7 area over the period up to 1968, including a Chelsea Mews cottage, a flat in Belgravia and a flat in South Kensington.

A stroll down to the end of Edith Grove takes one into Cremorne Road, a curve of a street that melds into Cheyne Walk, a riverside avenue into which Jagger moved in 1969. Richards followed his example a year later. Though the bohemian/ artistic likes of George Eliot, Oscar Wilde and Ian Fleming once dwelled there, Cheyne (pronounced "Chay-nee") Walk is a hugely plush area usually inhabited by real, not pop, aristocracy. Its other end, incidentally, meets the beginning of Beaufort Street. Both Jagger's and, especially, Richards' Cheyne Walk houses were the scene of previously referred to busts by the Metropolitan Police Force. Wyman still maintains his London home a stone's throw from Cheyne Walk.

OTHER STONES LONDON LANDMARKS

The London School of Economics Located in Houghton Street in central London, it was founded in the late nineteenth century after a Fabian Society bequest. A highly prestigious institution – boasting over 7,000 pupils, it is unrivalled in social sciences and in attracting foreign students – Jagger was still attending it when the band's first single was released

Olympic Studio Located in London suburb Barnes and once the group's UK studio of choice, it still exists but is now very different to the cosy but high-tech studio in which the band made some of their greatest Sixties records.

Regent Sound Studio Located at 4 Denmark Street – whose proliferation of song publishers made it London's Tin Pan Alley – studio head Bill Farley recollects UK recording artist Max Bygraves saying to him "Farking 'ell – it's the kind of place where you wipe your feet on the way out". This didn't prevent the Stones making a classic debut album there, as well as the hit 'Not Fade Away'. Amazingly, even The Beatles recorded at this insalubrious venue, working on 'Fixing A Hole' there in February 1967. The studio is now long gone. For several years, its premises were occupied by the rock bookshop Helter Skelter, whose manager Sean Body specifically chose the site because of its rock connections.

Hyde Park The scene of the band's live inauguration of the Mick Taylor line-up in July 1969, which unexpectedly turned into a wake for Brian Jones. Attendance figures for the event at the massive park, situated adjacent to Hyde Park Corner which leads into London's West End, have always been conflicting but have varied from between 250,000 people to half a million.

The 100 Club Most of the pub and club venues at which the Stones gigged in their early years are now closed or transformed. Only Ronnie Scott's on Frith Street in Soho and The 100 Club on Oxford Street remain *in situ* as music venues, and the 100 remains a favourite location for the Stones, among others, to perform informal, limited-invitation bashes.

TOWN AND COUNTRY

All of the Stones retain residences in west or south-west London, as well as various rural piles. The Watts run a successful stud farm in the West Country. Jagger bought the palatial Stargroves near Newbury, Berkshire in 1970, and tracks from *Sticky Fingers* and *Exile* were recorded there using the Rolling Stones Mobile Recording Unit – a facility also used there by The Who, Led Zeppelin and Deep Purple. The house was acquired by Rod Stewart in 1998. Meanwhile, Wyman maintains a stately manor house in Suffolk in East Anglia.

Sussex is a county in south-east England, separated from London by the county of Surrey.

Its southern edge sits on the Channel coast. In the late Sixties, both Keith Richards and Brian Jones had homes in it. However, following the schism caused by the transfer of Anita Pallenberg's affections from Jones to Richards, they were the proverbial universe apart, despite being geographically relatively close. The county is divided neatly down the middle into West and East Sussex and it is poetically appropriate that the Stones in question lived either side of this geographical division.

When Jagger, Richards and Watts journeyed up to Jones' house, Cotchford Farm, on the grim day in the Summer of 1969 when they sacked Brian, Richards remembered thinking, 'Wow, nice joint'. That he should be so distracted by such matters when the band were just about to – in Charlie Watts' later phrase – take away from Brian "his one thing, which was being in a band" is testament to the beauty of the house that Jones had bought in November 1968. Not only was Cotchford Farm beautiful, it was steeped in literary myth, for it was here that one of the classic characters of children's literature, Winnie The Pooh, was created.

Cotchford Farm – about an hour's drive from London – started out in the sixteenth century as a farmhouse. When it was bought by the journalist and writer A.A. Milne in the mid-1920s, it became – via some landscape work – a wealthy man's pastoral retreat, although Milne's family did move in permanently in 1940. Milne created a character based partly on a teddy bear his son Christopher was given as a first birthday present and partly after a

279

Canadian black bear in London Zoo. Many of the adventures of Winnie The Pooh and his friends took place in nearby Ashdown Forest, while the bridge from which the characters played the game of Poohsticks actually existed not too far away. The house was sold by the grown Christopher – always ambivalent about his place in literary history – in the 1950s to a couple called the Taylors (who would also rent it to the actor Richard Harris). Jones bought the house from the Taylors for £35,000 – a massive sum then.

Jones famously loved Cotchford, finding it the proverbial place of tranquillity far from the madding crowd (which we should remember included corrupt police officers and rapacious journalists). He seemed to present a different face to the locals than to people in the metropolis, who often knew him as a bully and an overgrown infant: his Cotchford housekeeper's comment that "you couldn't have wished for a nicer boy" seems to reflect local opinion.

The Taylors had surprised the locals by putting a swimming pool into the grounds of Cotchford, seeming to betray their unfamiliarity with the damp English weather. It was in this pool, of course, that Jones met his fate.

Richards' Sussex domicile – which he still owns – was Redlands. Located in West Wittering, West Sussex, it is, in its own way, as breathtaking as Richards felt Cotchford Farm to be: how many houses have their own moat? And an Elizabethan thatched roof? The most famous drug bust of all time, of course, took place here (see the Toronto section below for

the second most famous). Redlands seems to be particularly susceptible to fire, two major blazes having occurred there in Richards' tenure as owner, the most serious one in July 1973, which left it virtually gutted. The water rats that once lived in the moat prompted a line in the *Let It Bleed* song 'Live With Me' ("My best friend he shoots water rats and feeds 'em to his geese").

NEW YORK

In the late Seventies and early Eighties, The Rolling Stones were effectively a New York band. Mick Jagger and Keith Richards were then permanently in residence in the Big Apple, while Ronnie Wood spent lot of time in a home there. Jagger lived in a building adjacent to the Dakota, where John Lennon lived, and outside which he was murdered. Gradually, the New York triumvirate separated, Richards moving his growing new family to Connecticut, Jagger going back to England to live in a house in Richmond, Surrey, with Jerry Hall and their children that was – surreally – next door to Who guitarist Pete Townshend's home, and Wood switching between homes in London and Ireland.

The greatest legacy to the Stones' New York days is the *Some Girls* album, which is dripping with references to the city's landmarks and issues.

"It's definitely an important part of their careers, and their lives," Bill German, a New Yorker who ran the *Beggar's Banquet* fanzine for many years, has said. Every night, they were going out and playing unannounced with any bands that they liked, and it was all unrehearsed. I don't think they could have done that in any other city."

TORONTO

Canada is often alleged to be a boring country. Not when the Stones come to town. When in 1977, the band flew in to record a live set, the upshot of their visit was one scandal that caused the Canadian dollar to tumble on the world's markets and another that left a huge question mark over the group's career and a big headache for the country's government. Richards' infamous Mounties drug bust took place at the Harbour Castle Hotel in Harbour Square, overlooking Lake Ontario (he said he was disappointed that they were not in their famous uniforms.) It was in the same hotel that Margaret Trudeau, wife of the Canadian prime minister Pierre Trudeau, met Ronnie Wood. Margaret was a woman who was perceived to be bored with the life she had found herself trapped in by marrying a man two decades older than her. As a former hippie, she seemed to feel more comfortable with the likes of the Stones than with stuffy politicians. Trudeau later said that the real story was that she had met Wood in a hotel corridor and that he had invited her to take photographs of the band's El Mocambo gig. The following day she found herself looking after Richards' son

because Richards was too out of it to do it himself. She also said she drank, played dice and smoked a little hash with the group. The way the story was presented in the press was that she was having an affair with Mick Jagger. "Unbecoming" was the word being bandied about by people who cared about such things – although this was understandable considering the political ramifications of the drug bust just days before.

After his experiences there (he was assaulted by a member of the public when attending court) one would imagine that Richards would never want to see the city again, but the band now have a long-standing tradition of practising for their North American tours in Toronto, having done this in 1989, 1994, 1997 and 2005, usually at a school or college. This choice of location is considered to be not unrelated to the fact that their concert promoter Michael Cohl lives in the city, although the lack of hassle from the press and the good exchange rate are also presumed factors.

THE STONES IN PRINT & ON SCREEN

This doesn't pretend to be a comprehensive list of Rolling Stones books, films, television shows and internet sites. There are far too many to review them all. However, below we discuss some of the more important ones.

BOOKS

ACCORDING TO THE ROLLING STONES

Mick Jagger, Keith Richards, Charlie Watts, Ronnie Wood (2003)

The Stones waited until their fortieth anniversary before putting out their own version of their story (unless one counts the Sixties puff book *Our Own Story*; *passim*). It was a sort of equivalent to The Beatles' *Anthology* book of a couple of years before: a large format, lavishly illustrated hardback. Sales of the hardback seem to have been poor, judging by the fact that when it went into paperback it was considerably scaled down to an A-format with just plate sections serving as illustration.

A certain pettiness attended the project. While one could understand to an extent Bill Wyman not being invited to participate on the grounds that his own lavish book *Rolling With The Stones* (see below) had already appeared, why no contributions from Brian Jones (the fact that Lennon was dead didn't stop The Beatles ensuring his views were represented in *Anthology* by hunting down old interviews and excerpting them) or the still very much alive Mick Taylor? Instead we have Ronnie Wood quoted throughout, as though his recollections of, say, being in the audience at Hyde Park in '69 are of comparable significance.

One could make a case for the Stones' concentrating on the latter part of their career herein as being a useful antidote to the way biographers always focus disproportionately on the early years but the fact that, by the time of Mick Taylor's departure, we are only halfway through the book feels like nothing other than misplaced priorities – underlined by the fact that much of the rest is padded out with tedious descriptions of the band's ever-more elaborate stage sets. Additionally, the fact that the 1967 drug busts and imprisonment is dispensed with in little more than a page is absurd.

There are a couple of nice surprises in the book. One is that complete freedom of speech seems to have been allowed – possibly due to Charlie Watts (someone generally acknowledged as a man of integrity) being the consulting editor. Ron Wood makes some acid comments about his protracted employee status, and the way Stones songwriting credits are sometimes mysteriously assigned, while Giorgio Gomelsky – in one of a series of outsider's guest essays distributed throughout – suggests that the Stones should do something financially for the blues music that they had done so well out of. The biggest and most pleasant of the book's surprises are the contributions of Charlie Watts, who is here really talking extensively about the Stones in public for the first time. He offers consistently intriguing comments, throwing new light onto many parts of the band's story.

IT'S ONLY ROCK 'N' ROLL

Steve Appelford (1997)

Appelford uses both secondary sources and original interview material to tell, as the subtitle puts it, 'The Stories Behind Every Song'. Where there is a story to tell, he relates it well – he has a nice turn of phrase – but, as we know, very often, especially in those high-quality but ludicrously prolific Sixties, there isn't an attendant tale and Appleford is reduced to discursiveness. Additionally, hiving off the non-album tracks – which includes some of the greatest and most important Stones songs – to an appendix is a bad move.

A JOURNEY THROUGH AMERICA WITH THE ROLLING STONES

Robert Greenfield (1974)

Originally published as STP: Stones Touring Party but actually better known by the above title, which it was re-christened upon its 1975 paperback release, this book is a document of the 1972 American tour, the quintessentially debauched Stones road trip. Greenfield captures the group as epitomizing rebellion even as they approach the age of thirty but on the cusp of becoming Establishment. Considering the access he had, it's a surprisingly unexciting read, with visits to the Playboy mansion, encounters with groupies and audience riots passing uninterestingly by like so much landscape, although Greenfield is funny when dealing with the restless crowd at a Boston venue when they realize that the gig might be cancelled after Jagger, Richards and a couple of others are arrested following an altercation with a cop.

A snapshot of a time and place that should have been better.

MICK JAGGER

Anthony Scaduto (1975)

Scaduto had written the first proper biography of Bob Dylan. The subject of Jagger for his next rock biography must have seemed natural. Such was the mystique Mick was still perceived as possessing by the public in those days that people didn't laugh when it was suggested he had the image of the Devil, hence the original subtitle of this work, Everybody's Lucifer. Having no access to the Stones themselves – Keith found it strange that the author hadn't approached him, someone who had known Jagger longer than just about anyone – Scaduto spoke to, amongst others, Dick Taylor, Alexis Korner, Andrew Loog Oldham, Chrissie Shrimpton and Marianne Faithfull. The book is often annoying. Written in a style approaching that of a novel ("Jagger remained silent… he had never felt more excited, more certain of himself"), one is often not sure whether or not what one is reading is simply speculation, Scaduto's list of sources at the back notwithstanding. Scaduto also started a long tradition amongst Stones biographers of dealing in depth with the pre-fame days but condensing the later years into a few pages. Nonetheless, an absorbing read.

OLD GODS ALMOST DEAD

Stephen Davis (2002)

Though the Robert Graves-derived title sounds vaguely contemptuous, this book by the author of the notorious Led Zeppelin biog Hammer

Of The Gods is actually petty impartial. Though he has around 550 pages to work with, covering the whole of the Stones' career makes for a rather whistlestop, breathless feel and Davis' necessarily economical style means he makes statements which come worryingly unattached to sources. Nonetheless, entertaining and authoritative-seeming.

OUR OWN STORY

The Rolling Stones ("As we told it to Pete Goodman") (1964)

A quickie paperback put together by Beat Publications, this is the kind of pop group biography that is now consigned to history. A-format, nearly 200 pages of quite dense text, illustrations restricted to two photographic plate sections and line drawings, it's precisely the sort of wordy stuff that would cause crinkled noses amongst today's computer- and TV-oriented generation of pop fans. Not that it's a particularly illuminating read. A puff piece is not going to tell the truth about a band. Ian Stewart for instance is quoted as saying "I left for one or two reasons that aren't now worth going into". However, as a snapshot of an era it evokes mild interest, not least in the way it reveals that one correspondent who objected to the band's *Juke Box Jury* appearance was reduced to rage because "the Stones not only smoked through the programme but only one of them had the manners to stand when a young lady was shaking hands with them."

THE ROLLING STONES – THE FIRST TWENTY YEARS

David Dalton (1981)

At the time of its release, the title of this 12-inch square paperback seemed pretentious and almost stupid. The band hadn't quite been going two decades by then and in any case the fact of them making it to twenty years wasn't necessarily a good thing to many former fans, let alone something to so exult in.

The format is unusual. Dalton alternates a straight biography with contemporaneous news clippings. There is also a mock tabloid section printed on pulp paper (the rest of the book is glossy) featuring some of the more sensational and inaccurate Stones stories from down the years. A pull-out blueprint of one of Keith's guitars is also included, plus a session-ography. It's a sort of large format, illustrated version of Dalton's earlier *The Greatest Rock 'N' Roll Band In The World*. It's fascinating to dip into, although some of Dalton's own writing is atrocious, for example: "'Satisfaction'… flashes the five flinty faces of these crystal quints at their most ferocious and feline. Released (unleashed?) in May, 'Satisfaction' was the 'sure-shot' heard around the world that propelled the Stones into myth-history and… megalomania".

THE ROLLING STONES – AN ILLUSTRATED RECORD

Roy Carr (1976)

Carr's *Illustrated Record* books for New English Library are truly a product of a bygone era: the title refers to the fact that the books were in the same 12-inch square format as a vinyl album, with the subject's album covers reproduced full-size alongside analysis of their contents. Also included were biographical details and discussion of all singles and B-sides. For this book, Carr secured an exclusive interview with Jagger and (though this isn't made explicitly clear) seems to be using previously unpublished Richards quotes. Carr seems overly sensitive about their criticism being levelled at the Stones for the latter-day product (and this was even before punk had hit) and belabours to the point of ranting Decca putting out sub-standard compilations post-1970. Nonetheless, the book is lavishly illustrated and well designed, and Carr's opinions and semi-conversational writing style are always highly readable. Recommended but beware: New English Library were a publisher notorious in the Seventies for using substandard glue in their books which caused the pages to start falling out within months of purchase, so second-hand copies in good condition will be very hard to find.

THE ROLLING STONES: OFF THE RECORD

Mark Paytress (2003)

The title is absurd: everything in this 450-page compendium of Stones quotes was, by definition, on the record. However, one suspects it was publishers Omnibus behind this title, them fearing that a book which is basically a massive cuttings job would put off the public. There's no reason why it should, it being an absorbing recounting of the Stones' career in their own contemporaneous words, quotes which crucially give viewpoints of events not filtered through revisionist hindsight and failing memories.

THE ROLLING STONES AN ORAL HISTORY

Alan Lysaght (2003)

This Canadian publication is not one of the more well-known Stones histories, but deserves to be. The result of a twenty-edition radio programme entitled *The Complete History Of The Rolling Stones*, Lysaght had access to endless hours of interviews for the project. That, and the fact that he is trusted and liked by the band, leads to relatively candid responses to his questions (none of which relate to their private lives). He elicits some hilarious comments from the ever-volatile Glyn Johns and from an irredeemably square Dick Rowe, apparently still smarting about the non-continuance of the Decca contract (Rowe: "If they were great

Stonesology

songwriters, by now it would show. Isn't there an expression – 'You can't fool all of the public all of the time'. As far as the Stones are concerned, you wanna bet?")

THE STONES

Philip Norman (1984)

Norman's Stones counterpart to his Beatles biography *Shout!* Unlike with that book, he was actually given some degree of access to the band during his research period, although this is not an official book by any means. In common with *Shout!*, though, Norman uses a slightly melodramatic tone throughout, as though artistic decline, Altamont or the mistreatment of Wyman necessarily makes the Stones' story a tragedy. However, he is not only a conscientious researcher but an elegant writer, his every sentence a pleasure to read.

THE TRUE ADVENTURES OF THE ROLLING STONES

Stanley Booth (1985)

Also known as *Dance With The Devil*, this book was originally intended to be the first substantial, authorized biography of the band, a sort of equivalent to the Beatles-blessed Hunter Davies book about the Fab Four. Booth followed the Stones on their 1969 American comeback tour and had access to all their personnel and some employees.

Unfortunately, due to problems in the author's private life, the project wasn't to be completed

for decades, which rendered a lot of the genuinely sensational/unknown material in it old hat by the time it saw print. The book alternates between chapters detailing band history and ones concerned with the '69 tour, the latter all moving with horrible inevitability toward the *denouement* of Altamont, whose own grisly climax he witnessed from a distance of mere yards. In point of fact, the '69 tour material is bitty and often boring, but the stuff on the early days fills in previously unplugged information gaps. The book overall is an interesting snapshot of the Stones when Jones' shadow still loomed large over them as they attempted to reinvent themselves with Taylor.

UP AND DOWN WITH THE ROLLING STONES

Tony Sanchez (1979)

Also published as *I Was Keith Richards' Drug Dealer*, this memoir (ghost-written by tabloid reporter John Blake) is of a Stones aide who moved in with Richards' family in the late Sixties as his gofer and was present at some of the most momentous moments in the life of the guitarist and the career of the Stones. Richards admitted to journalist Kurt Loder in 1981 that the book's events were essentially true (if melodramatically related). Which means that, for instance, Richards really did leave friend and head of Rolling Stones Records Marshall Chess for dead after the latter took some bad heroin and Richards – who had some of the same batch – didn't want to hear this inconvenient information. (Sanchez raced round to Chess' home and saved his life.) Although one takes the point of Keith Altham when he sardonically says of the author, "He was St Francis of Assisi," and although Sanchez understandably concentrates on the bad things the band members got up to – thoughtfulness and kindness don't make enthralling copy – it has to be said that many Stones fans will have any illusions they might have about their idols shattered by this grimly fascinating work.

THE MURDER OF BRIAN JONES

Anna Wohlin (2000)

WHO KILLED CHRISTOPHER ROBIN: THE MURDER OF A ROLLING STONE

Terry Rawlings (1994; revised 2005)

Brian Jones is one of the most interesting characters in rock history but what books there have been about him have been dominated by the admittedly fascinating mystery about his death. These two books (both of which inspired the 2005 Stephen Woolley movie *Stoned*, along with Geoffrey Giuliano's *Paint It Black*) are two of the best. Wohlin was Jones' last girlfriend, a live-in lover who was at Cotchford Farm on the night of the tragedy. Her contention is that Frank Thorogood, Jones' sinister builder, was the murderer of the title. Terry Rawlings also once held that view but, in the revised version of his book, is not so sure, pointing out that Thorogood's supposed deathbed confession to Jones' killing is unveri-

fied. He suggests that other parties might have had something to do with it, but his analysis of the bewildering and contradictory statements of witnesses, though intriguing, becomes confusing. However, he does put forward a very interesting theory elsewhere in the book that might explain the massive pay-off the band offered to Jones when they fired him: that Jones might have owned the rights to the name 'The Rolling Stones'.

MICK JAGGER/BRIAN JONES/ KEITH RICHARDS/CHARLIE WATTS

Alan Clayson (various years)

An interesting series of short books which each profile an individual Stone. It is admirable that Clayson chooses to give even supposedly minor Stones like Watts and (forthcoming) Wyman, Taylor and Wood their own books, even if a little padding is occasionally evident (as are some factual howlers). Though he has no access to band members, he has spoken to ex-girlfriends, friends and colleagues, so providing the occasional fresh insight. Clayson is also hoping to write books on Ian Stewart and Dick Taylor.

STONE ALONE (1990)
ROLLING WITH THE STONES (2002)

Bill Wyman

Stone Alone, Bill Wyman's memoir of the Stones in the Sixties, was eagerly anticipated by band fans who assumed that as the acknowledged archivist of the band and a man with an interesting story to tell, it could not fail to be a great read. How wrong those assumptions turned out to be. Wyman – assisted by his ghost-writer Ray Coleman, he of the 'Would You Let Your Sister Go With A Rolling Stone?' headline – tackles sex, drugs and rock 'n' roll with the finicky passionlessness of a librarian. As the reader waits in vain for Wyman to tell us what went on in the recording studio as classic songs were laid down, he finds his eyes glazing over as Wyman methodically details every teen riot that attended a Stones concert and every encounter with a groupie that followed it. His other motif – contrasting the glamour of the events he has just recounted with the paucity of his bank balance afterwards – is what Keith Richards says prevented him from finishing the book.

As if to compensate for the sheer tedium of *Stone Alone*, Wyman opted not to write Part Two of his Stones biography but to issue instead, in the shape of *Rolling With The Stones*, a coffee-table book telling the whole Stones story. Like all Dorling Kindersley products, the way it is laid out is utterly beautiful. However, there is more than just the lavish illustrations (often depicting Wyman's own memorabilia) to commend it. The text is endlessly fascinating, documenting all the recording session details and band intrigues which seemed to have been deliberately omitted from *Stone Alone*, all with helpful dates attached, courtesy of the diaries Wyman meticulously kept for decades.

STONED (2000)

2STONED (2002)

Andrew Loog Oldham

The first two volumes of the band's ex-manager's planned autobiographical quartet are the ones concerned with the Stones.

Both books employ a peculiar format whereby Oldham's written recollections are interspersed with the observations of people who knew Oldham, some famous, some not. To Oldham's credit, those observations are not always flattering (and his recounting of some "queer bashing" in book one drips with self-loathing). His own recollections cover aspects of the Stones story not usually addressed by the biographies, including the minutiae of his dealings with and falling out with Eric Easton and a bizarre meeting between Oldham and Jagger and ineffably bored movie man Nicholas Ray about the latter directing the Stones in a picture. Oldham corrects many myths and adds a few interesting in-hindsight possibilities (he suggests Jagger refused to mount the Palladium rostrum because he was still smarting over his being told by Oldham to sing "Let's spend some time together" on *The Ed Sullivan Show* the previous week.)

FILM & TELEVISION

CHARLIE IS MY DARLING

(Released 1966)

Shot on the Stones' Irish tour of September 1965 by Peter Whitehead (who would direct *The Trial of Oscar Wilde* style 'We Love You' promo), this hour-long documentary is actually quite advanced for its time and *milieu*. Dispensing with the (inane) commentary prevalent in documentaries of its era, it follows the Stones onstage and backstage to a quite mordant and almost pretentious soundtrack (including 'Heart of Stone' – both the Stones' and orchestral versions – and 'Play With Fire', as well as a classical version of 'Maybe It's Because I'm A Londoner', played only because the Stones are seen singing it on a train journey). The band are all interviewed and come across as thoughtful, especially Brian. The most arresting scene is also rail-related, seeing the group risking death by electrocution by scrambling across railway lines to avoid pursuing fans.

THE ROLLING STONES ROCK AND ROLL CIRCUS

(Filmed 1968; released 1996)

Getting the chance to finally see this legendary 1968 show after its quarter century in the vaults confirmed the rumour about this programme not being broadcast: The Who outshone the headliners. However, though the Stones did not match the incendiary performance by Townshend's mob of their mini-opera 'A Quick One, While He's Away', they were in no way terrible, even the disintegrating Jones entering full-heartedly and apparently competently into the spirit of things. Age, of course, has also improved the programme: the patina of legend makes everything more interesting, particularly the all-star group Dirty Mac made up of Lennon, Richards, Clapton and Mitch Mitchell.

GIMME SHELTER

(Released 1970)

Desiring a visual documentary of their come-back 1969 tour – or a revenue stream therefrom – the Stones reached an agreement with the Maysles Brothers to follow them on the road and in the studio. Neither the band or the film-makers had any way of knowing the dramatic nature of what they would capture. The onstage footage of the band therefore (which is in any case, like all stage recordings of that era, tinny by modern standards) is pared back so that the focus can settle on the absolute malevolence and chaos (a large dog even wanders across the stage at one point) of the Altamont festival. Offstage footage includes the band listening to playbacks of new recordings ('Brown Sugar' and 'Wild Horses' among them) and – in what was shortly to become a grotesque irony – the tortuous negotiations of their representatives to find a venue to play the free concert to climax the tour. Intercut with

Stonesology

this are the reactions of Jagger and Watts to the footage with which the Maysles emerged, which included the briefest flash of the incident that resulted in the death of Meredith Hunter.

LADIES AND GENTLEMEN THE ROLLING STONES (Released 1974)

COCKSUCKER BLUES (Not formally released)

Ladies And Gentlemen... is the official film of the 1972 Stones tour of America, and *Cocksucker Blues* the illicit (sort of) one. The former, directed by Hal Ashby, is somewhat bland, comprised of a mock concert – splicing songs from different gigs – and nothing else. In modern times, the quality of the music would compensate for this, but things were still relatively primitive back then, with the technology prohibiting, for instance, much use of acoustic guitars. It's also verging on the bizarre seeing the demonic 'Gimme Shelter' augmented by saxophone. Nonetheless, it's an important historical document of a band at the peak of their artistic powers and credibility (if not commercial success, which – almost unimaginably – they would achieve far more of). Whereas *Ladies And Gentlemen...* represents the tour as the audiences saw it, Robert Frank's *Cocksucker Blues* mainly shows the behind-the-scenes action, although onstage footage – shot by a different film crew – is interspersed. The film opens with a rendition of the obscene title song and descends from there. We see Keith throw a television set out of a hotel window, a couple of crew injecting each other with what is presumably heroin, Mick and Keith snorting what appears to be cocaine backstage, what looks like the preamble to a gang-bang onboard the Stones' jet (Jagger and Richards declining to take part but cheerleading with tambourine and bongos) and a costume change involving Mick's bare backside. It seems clear that some of this behaviour is staged or at least self-conscious, but at the same time it is a remarkably honest and graphic depiction of rock 'n' roll debauchery. There is also a lot of backstage boredom and hotel room hassle (Keith's – possibly drug-impeded – attempt to order fruit from room service is hilarious).

There has probably been worse behaviour captured on film since, but only by bands who – despite shifting millions of units – don't register on the public radar the way the Stones did. Due to a legal arrangement between Frank and the Stones, those wanting to see *Cocksucker Blues* can currently only do so at a screening at which Frank is in attendance.

LET'S SPEND THE NIGHT TOGETHER

(Released 1983)

Documentary of the Stones' 1981 American tour featuring a pseudo-concert (i.e. a full set, but spliced together from different venues) interspersed with some silent behind-the-scenes footage. It's visually much more interesting than *Ladies And Gentlemen, The Rolling Stones* chiefly because, unlike that film, it relies on a multitude of cameras, including some in the wings and backstage, rather than just a couple out front. The band play well and Jagger is a riveting frontman (although his singing is lazily full of shortcuts). The most noticeable aspect is the replacement of the menace of the 1969 tour and the sleaze of the 1972 tour with an actually quite touching benevolence and determination to give the audience a good time.

25x5

(Broadcast: 1990)

One critic once said that that this Nigel Finch-directed television documentary did in just over two hours what the Beatles *Anthology* took six hours to. It's a fair point, although the luxury afforded the producers of *Anthology* in being allowed to run songs to their full length created a sumptuous feel lacking in this more machine-gun like history. Nonetheless, despite this and the slightly bland results of it being an official history, it's an absorbing and enjoyable production. It's also well researched and diligently compiled, featuring such interesting archive film material as the *Dean Martin Show* on which they were so insulted by the host and the *Shindig* appearance with Howlin' Wolf.

BEING MICK

(Broadcast: 2001)

This TV documentary – broadcast to coincide with the release of Jagger's *Goddess In The Doorway* – posits Jagger as a loving fam-

ily man. Certainly, he is touchingly fond of his brood, who all appear (including – by telephone – Karis, his daughter with Marsha Hunt) in this fly-on-the-wall depiction of him at home and at work. Even the recently estranged Jerry Hall puts in an appearance. Though there is a grisly moment when Jagger tries to flirt with an uninterested female airport staff member – and one should be mindful of the fact that director Kevin MacDonald was afterwards embittered by the lack of creative control he says he was promised – this is an interesting film that suggests Beelzebub has reformed.

STONED

(Released 2005)

Stephen Woolley's movie focuses on the last few weeks of Brian Jones' life. Boasting sometimes uncanny casting, it falls down with the choice of Leo Gregory as Jones: he possesses little of Jones' beauty. Another black mark is the script's failure to convey Jones' multi-instrumental talents. However, *Stoned* is well-made and conscientiously researched. Though it unequivocally portrays Frank Thorogood as responsible for Jones' death, it also depicts him relatively sympathetically as a working man seduced by Jones' decadent lifestyle.

Stonesology

Stonesology

Websites

www.timeisonourside.com

The loving work of Ian McPherson, who has gathered quotes and facts on just about every Stones subject under the sun. Every Stones song is listed and – where quotes could be found – commented upon by band members. Gigs, support acts and band associates are also tackled. The Chronicle section is a fascinating, impartial year-by-year history. There's a pro-American bias when it comes to releases, and a puzzling absence of Mick Taylor in the Portraits section, but they are minor weak points in what is the best Rolling Stones site on the web.

www.beatzenith.com/the_rolling_stones /rs1main.htm

Like many sites, this one from Brian Darwin and AC Palacio is a discography of Stones releases. However, unlike many, it is accompanied by often fascinating scans of picture sleeves, labels, inserts and giveaways.

www.nzentgraf.de/books/tcw/works1.htm

The title of the site is pretty prosaic and so, some might think, are the contents. But Nico Zentgraf's catalogue of all Stones concerts, recording sessions and setlists is a mine of valuable information for the Stones scholar. He also has additional sections on Ron Wood and Mick Taylor, which – like the Stones data – are available to order as hard copy books.

www.angelfire.com/rock3/sixtiesfish/

Brian Jones tribute site run by Helen Hall features miscellany (magazine features, book scans, Public Office records) on Jones not often found on the web, though displays a strangely disproportionate antipathy toward Anita Pallenberg.

www.stonessessions.com

Website of the Martin Elliott book *Rolling Stones Complete Recording Sessions 1962–2002*. The website gives a flavour of an excellent (if badly sub-edited) book that provides the recording dates, locations and circumstances of every Stones track ever recorded, whether available legally or on bootleg or still in the vaults.

www.brianjonesfanclub.com

Very knowledgeable and enthusiastic site devoted to Jones, even if it seems more oriented toward the promotion of the club's AfterMath (sic) magazine than toward being a resource in and of itself.

mypage.bluewin.ch/aeppli/tug.htm#basic

Website of the *The Ultimate Guide To The First Forty Years* by Felix Aeppli, a CD-Rom of facts and figures that is another excellent Stones resource.

www.rollingstones.com

Depressingly corporate official site. In order to get access, one has to part with a $100 membership fee. What ones gets for adding to the mountains of cash that the Stones can already never spend in their lifetimes is pretty basic. There's a regular updated news section and an archive with a timeline which enable one to click on any day in Stones history and find out what events, tours or record releases were happening. However, in no sense is the site as sumptuous as what McPherson has produced with only the impetus of love.

www.keithrichards.com/

www.mickjagger.com/

Not only are both Glimmer Twins' official sites superior to the official band site but both are free. Interesting what the humility induced by the realization of your lesser individual pulling power can do. Richards' well-designed site has a good 'Ask Keith' section. Always less forthcoming, there's no such feature on Mick's site, although it does boast very good graphics, even if most of it is unwisely based on his execrable *Goddess In The Doorway* album.

SONGS ABOUT THE STONES

KEITH DON'T GO – NILS LOFGREN

At a time when Richards was being busted annually and for drugs far more dangerous than the rock star's normal diet of weed or cocaine, his (highly talented) wannabe wrote this quite moving and rather rockin' song pleading with his "main inspirer" not to "nail yourself to a cross".

BLAME IT ON THE STONES – KRIS KRISTOFFERSON

Kristofferson amazed many by opening his debut country album with this song about rock's ultimate idols. The bearded one uses the Stones as a metaphor for the way that some sections of society (Mr. Marvin Middle Class) select a bogeyman on which to project their misgivings about societal developments not to their approval, alluding to 'Mother's Little Helper' as he does so.

YOU'RE SO VAIN – CARLY SIMON

Technically, not about the Stones but about their frontman. Actually, technically almost certainly not about Jagger either. Though Simon has never disclosed the subject of this easy-rolling broadside against a preening male, Warren Beatty is generally considered its tar-get while Simon's ex-lover, James Taylor, has often been cited. However, the fact that Jagger fits that peacock description well and that he sang back-up vocals on the record has led the assumption that it is about him to linger in the culture.

GODSTAR – PSYCHIC TV

Psychic TV were hardly a pop band, but the normally avant garde group produced a highly melodic, anthemic single with this song whose subject was none other than Brian Jones. "They never even told your story", they – slightly mystifyingly – railed at Jones' "Laughing friends", although it's not clear whether this is the Stones or the people at the fatal pool party.

SHE'S IN LOVE WITH THE ROLLING STONES – THE TELEFONES

New wave song about a man who always loses out in the battle for his girlfriend's affections to the Stones.

10 STONES MYTHS

A band that has had as long and as colourful a career as the Stones will have accrued their fair share of stories, myths and legends. Here are ten of the erroneous (or are they?) stories surrounding the band.

1. THE MARS BAR INCIDENT

The 1967 drugs trial of Jagger and Richards gave the popular press a field day of scandal (supposed role models taking drugs) and sex (surrounded by men, a mystery woman was wearing only a rug). However, the most salacious gossip emanating from the trial did not see print, but instead was a true underground rumour, passed by word of mouth until virtually everyone in Britain had heard of it. This was that, when the police burst in that fateful night, they had found Jagger eating a Mars bar from the vagina of Marianne Faithfull (who was the woman in the rug but referred to only as 'Miss X' in press reports). Faithfull herself has denied it. Though Faithfull sometimes seems confused about details (in her autobiography she says *Let It Bleed* is her favourite Stones album and then proceeds to cite tracks from that and *Beggar's Banquet* and *Sticky Fingers*) she is hardly one to be anything less than candid about events. Even Tony Sanchez – whose book is a mine of dirt about the group – says it didn't happen. He wrote that, at the Jagger and Richards trial, "in a bar during a lunch break, two senior police officers gulped down bottles of beer with crime reporters and sniggeringly told "lewd and grossly exaggerated stories about Marianne's behaviour at the time of the raid... and a totally false and malicious rumour was begun which Marianne has never quite managed to live down."

2. THE KEITH RICHARDS BLOOD TRANSFUSION RUMOUR

Whereas Tony Sanchez did much to scotch the Mars Bar rumour, he was chiefly responsible for the legend that, in 1973, Richards – anxious to be 'clean' for an upcoming tour but unable to take the time to wean himself off smack – undertook a little-known rich addict's cure involving the wholesale replacement of his blood with that provided by a donor or donors. It's been repeated over and over in newspapers since whenever the Stones are touring and some juicy copy is required. Harry Shapiro of the charity Drugscope says, "It's rubbish. Drugs like heroin and coke wash out of the system in 24-48 hours. Detoxifying is not that much of a problem so long as you can deal with the withdrawals – it's staying off that is the issue – and that needs therapy, not a blood transfusion." Richards himself has also denied it. And yet... there is something convincing about the way Sanchez relates the story in his book, explaining that Marshall Chess – who had apparently taken the 'cure' before – told Richards of it, going into detail about the doctor who arranged it, the Swiss clinic at which it supposedly took place, the cost, the events surrounding it (including Richards' offer to pay for a cure for Sanchez, which he declined, fearing needles) and the way the cure gave Richards a cavalier attitude about getting hooked again, his reasoning being that it didn't matter because he now had a quick way of cleaning up any time he liked.

3. THE TWO MICKS RUMOUR

Again, mentioned in Sanchez's book. Sanchez said Taylor's partner, Rose, would have screaming arguments with the guitarist about his closeness to Jagger and that one day he found the two Micks asleep in bed together (Jagger said they'd taken too much coke and passed out – not the usual effect of coke.) The story was given credence by Taylor's by now ex-wife in a Nineties interview for a Christian magazine. Having found God, she unburdened herself of her alleged trauma at the affair her husband had openly had with the Stones frontman and said that the two had encouraged her to join in with them. For his part, Jagger (who is also rumoured to have had a sexual relationship with David Bowie) has said he tried bisexuality at school but not subsequently.

4. THE ALTAMONT RUMOUR

That the Stones had brought some bad karma on themselves – and others – with their dalliance with the dark stuff in life was confirmed for many with the reports immediately after Altamont that when Meredith Hunter was stabbed to death, the band were romping through 'Sympathy for The Devil'. It was too poetic a notion, for some, to bother checking their facts. *Rolling Stone* magazine was one of the guilty parties. As Stone staffer Greil Marcus noted, "We had a bad tape of the show — of course there was no announcement on the tape, 'The murder has taken place'." The magazine quickly attempted to make amends, not with a one-line correction but with a whole story. It had no effect – the myth prevailed, even though it was conclusively proven to be just that by the release of the *Gimme Shelter* movie that captured the incident forever on celluloid. "Every time Altamont was mentioned, so was the killing that had taken place during 'Sympathy For The Devil'..." says Marcus. "... this was an error that could not be corrected. 'Even if it didn't happen', the editor finally said, 'it did'."

5. THE HELL'S ANGELS RUMOUR

Though 'Sympathy for the Devil' consisting the soundtrack to Meredith Hunter's murder was a myth that did not have too much impact – even people who thought the Stones irresponsible in supposedly glamorizing devil worship didn't think they could be blamed for the killing – the belief that the Stones had hired the Hell's Angels as security at Altamont and were therefore indirectly responsible for what happened to Hunter did. The belief persists to this day and stands as a condemnation of the group's supposed naiveté in believing in a new social order that did not require the 'pigs' who would normally maintain order at such events. The assumption stems from the Stones' use of the Angels at Hyde Park five months before. In fact, it was the Grateful Dead who suggested the Angels – although of course it can be argued that the band did not have to take up their suggestion. Ironically, the Dead pulled out of the show after seeing the bad vibes at the venue.

6. MICK'S CROTCH

How deliciously daring it was in 1971 to buy an album whose cover consisted of a life-size (these were 12-inch sleeve days) bejeaned male loin region with a real zip that pulled down (or, in fact, went up – to prevent damage, the zip had to be down when shipped to the stores so that its weight when stacked would be on the record label, not the vinyl). The descended zipper revealed a man's occupied pair of underpants. Naturally, everybody assumed it was Mick Jagger – at that point the biggest male sex symbol in rock – that was bulging in their faces. In fact, it is believed to be one of Andy Warhol's cinematic 'Superstars' named Joe Dallesandro (immortalized as Little Joe in Lou Reed's '*Walk On The Wild Side*'). The model for the inner picture – who was noticeably less well endowed – is believed to be another Warhol acquaintance named Jed Johnson.

7. A CLOCKWORK ORANGE AND ONLY LOVERS LEFT ALIVE

The Stones never quite managed to make their own dramatic motion picture but were always rumoured to be planning one, even managing to wrest an extra £1.5m from Decca for the never-delivered soundtrack to the never-made adaptation of the novel *Only Lovers Left Alive*, a quite-good English *Blackboard Jungle*-variant novel by teacher Dave Wallis. The story that they were to appear in a film of the similarly themed *Clockwork Orange* was pure Oldham-inspired fiction. As he revealed in 2Stoned, he put the story about even though he had discovered the film rights weren't available.

8. OTIS REDDING WROTE SATISFACTION

Strip away the fuzztone guitar riff of 'Satisfaction' and take the edge off its snarled lyric and you have a stomping soul number the type of which proliferated on the Stax label in the mid-1960s. Perhaps it was this then that caused the *Toronto Telegram* to declare in February 1968, a couple of months after Stax artist Otis Redding's death in a plane crash, "It's High Time The Stones Acknowledged This Debt". The headline appeared over a story that alleged that the band had remained "stubbornly and disgustingly silent" about the 'fact' that they had bought the song off Redding for $10,000 when they had visited Memphis and heard him cut the track. The only shred of truth in the story was that Redding had recorded 'Satisfaction' – although as Steve Cropper (Redding's guitarist, who played on the track) pointed out, not until the Stones version had hit the store. "The story that Otis originally wrote 'Satisfaction' is completely false," Cropper said. The progress of the crusading journalist who wrote the story towards the Canadian equivalent of a Pulitzer Prize is not known.

9. MICK'S DEATH/MICK'S SEX CHANGE

Like Paul McCartney, Mick Jagger had his very own premature death rumour, although his one – not bolstered by apparently supporting messages on records and record sleeves – was fleeting. It happened in late 1966, due, from what can be gathered, to a LA radio station announcing its occurrence in London. Jagger put out a self-consciously bemused press statement through the band's PR man Leslie Perrin ("Mr. Jagger wishes to deny that he is dead and says the rumours have been grossly exaggerated"). Despite this – and despite having at times boasted of having a "very thick skin" about press comments – Jagger was not so amused when a dozen years later a rumour spread that he was having a sex change operation. The Stones PR man then was Keith Altham and it was he who was responsible for the story, having told a UK gossip columnist, when in a flippant mood, that Mick was having the snip done in a clinic in California and that this was much to the annoyance of his fellow Stones because they didn't want to tour with a girl singer. The columnist – William Hickey – did have the good sense to append to his piece, "I think Mr. Altham was pulling my leg", but that caveat was omitted from US press reports. The man who had cultivated the most androgynous image yet seen in rock had what

Altham called, a "humour failure" over the matter, due to the fact the he began receiving a considerable number of phone calls from the American media about it.

10. MARIANNE FAITHFULL'S 'SISTER MORPHINE' ROYALTIES

On later editions of *Sticky Fingers*, the original "Jagger/Richards" publishing credit attached to 'Sister Morphine' was changed to "Jagger/Richards/Faithfull". The assumption of many was that Faithfull had taken legal action against the Glimmer Twins over an arrogant refusal by the pair to acknowledge her creative input that was motivated either by greed or macho disinclination to admit needing to accept ideas from a woman. After all, by the time the amended credits appeared, it was a well-known fact that various ex-members/aides of the Stones were aggrieved at the way they felt they had been cheated on the credit/royalties front. On this one, though, Mick and Keith had clean hands. In fact, they had behaved admirably and chivalrously. In her autobiography, Faithfull revealed that Jagger and Richards wrote to Allen Klein before the album's release instructing him to make sure she got paid for her writing contribution but to not put her name on the label in case a former manager made a financial claim. A bizarre postscript to which is the fact that Faithfull admitted that her royalties from this addict's anthem is what funded her heroin junkiedom for a decade.

Index

Index

Index

Listen Up!

"You may be used to the Rough Guide series being comprehensive, but nothing will prepare you for the exhaustive Rough Guide to World Music . . . one of our books of the year."

Sunday Times, London

ROUGH GUIDE MUSIC TITLES

Bob Dylan • The Beatles • Classical Music • Elvis • Frank Sinatra • Heavy Metal • Hip-Hop
iPods, iTunes & music online • Jazz • Book of Playlists • Opera • Pink Floyd • Punk • Reggae
Rock • The Rolling Stones • Soul and R&B • World Music

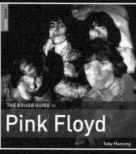

BROADEN YOUR HORIZONS